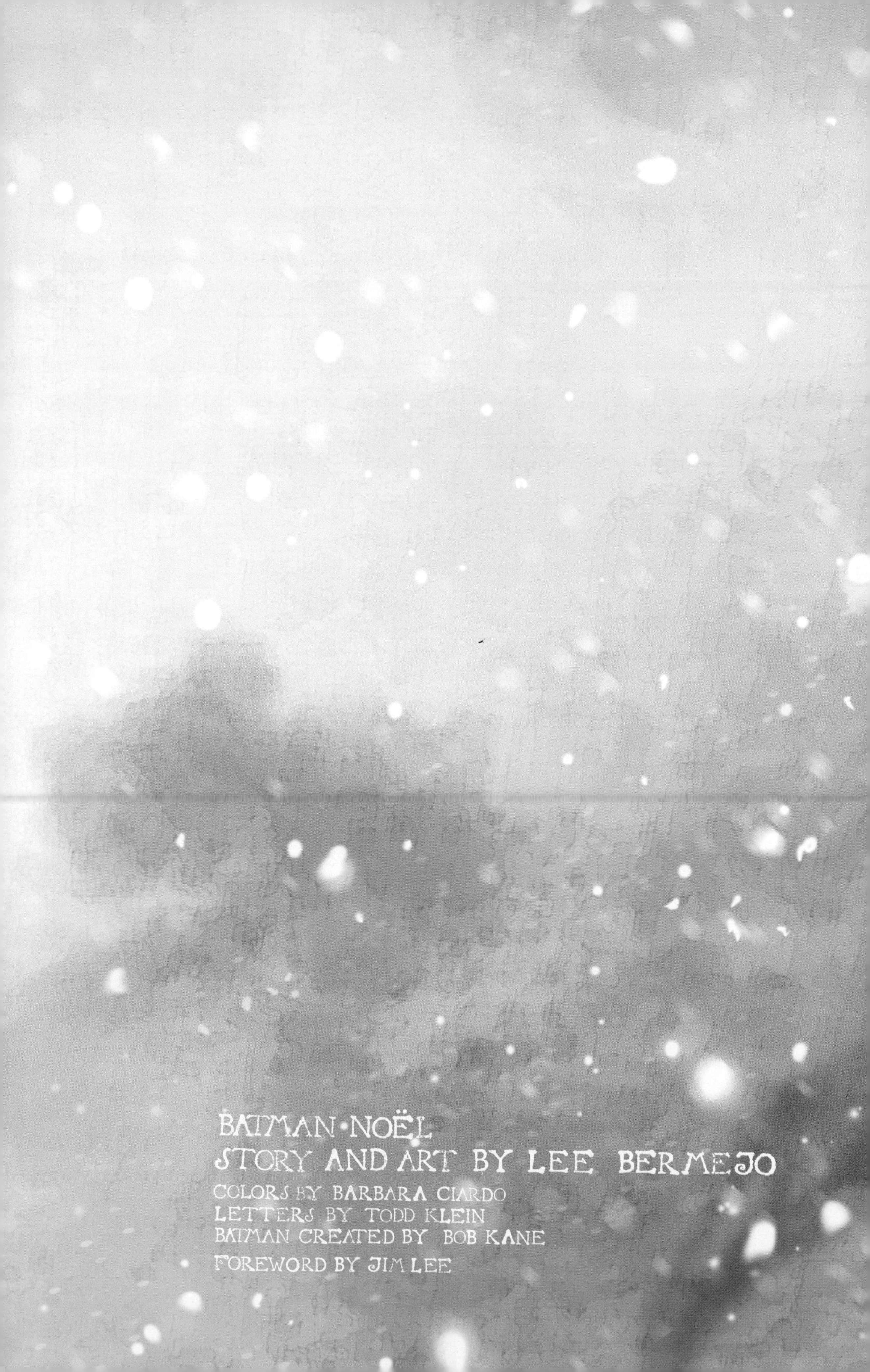

BATMAN·NOËL

STORY AND ART BY LEE BERMEJO

COLORS BY BARBARA CIARDO
LETTERS BY TODD KLEIN
BATMAN CREATED BY BOB KANE
FOREWORD BY JIM LEE

FOR MY GRANDMOTHER ALICE B. FLETCHER,
WHO GAVE ME MY FIRST DICKENS NOVEL,
AND MY WIFE, SARA, WHO GAVE ME EVERYTHING ELSE.

Mark Chiarello Editor
Camilla Zhang Assistant Editor
Robbin Brosterman Design Director – Books
Louis Prandi Publication Design

Bob Harras Senior VP – Editor-in-Chief, DC Comics

Diane Nelson President
Dan DiDio and Jim Lee Co-Publishers
Geoff Johns Chief Creative Officer
Amit Desai Senior VP – Marketing and Franchise Management
Amy Genkins Senior VP – Business and Legal Affairs
Nairi Gardiner Senior VP – Finance
Jeff Boison VP – Publishing Planning
Mark Chiarello VP – Art Direction and Design
John Cunningham VP – Marketing
Terri Cunningham VP – Editorial Administration
Larry Ganem VP – Talent Relations and Services
Alison Gill Senior VP – Manufacturing and Operations
Hank Kanalz Senior VP – Vertigo and Integrated Publishing
Jay Kogan VP – Business and Legal Affairs, Publishing
Jack Mahan VP – Business Affairs, Talent
Nick Napolitano VP – Manufacturing Administration
Sue Pohja VP – Book Sales
Fred Ruiz VP – Manufacturing Operations
Courtney Simmons Senior VP – Publicity
Bob Wayne Senior VP – Sales

BATMAN: NOËL

DC Comics, 1700 Broadway, New York, NY 10019
A Warner Bros. Entertainment Company
Printed by RR Donnelley, Salem, VA, USA. 2/12/15. Fourth Printing.
ISBN: 978-1-4012-3213-9

Library of Congress Cataloging-in-Publication Data

Bermejo, Lee.
Batman : noël / Lee Bermejo.
p. cm.
ISBN 978-1-4012-3213-9
1. Graphic novels. I. Title.
PN6728.B36B63 2012
741.5'973–dc23
2012037441

SUSTAINABLE FORESTRY INITIATIVE
Certified Chain of Custody
20% Certified Forest Content,
80% Certified Sourcing
www.sfiprogram.org
SFI-01042
APPLIES TO TEXT STOCK ONLY

For those of you lucky enough to be discovering Lee Bermejo's work for the first time and finding your jaws on the floor--you are not alone. Often times when a bright new talent like Lee comes onto the scene, it usually happens with a force and suddenness that many might misperceive or characterize as being an overnight success. The work may appear so complete that it seemingly arrives out of nowhere, fully formed without any gestation or development period. As with most "overnight successes" in general and Lee Bermejo in particular--nothing could be further from the truth.

One of the great joys of founding and running WildStorm Productions was nurturing new talent. I remembered how difficult it was breaking into the industry myself and how useful an art internship program would have been early in my career. I had also made it a point that WildStorm was not going to rely solely upon the same talent pool the rest of the industry was using, so to that end, we reviewed thousands of art samples and portfolios from all over North America, looking for the proverbial young guns. In the end, we only hired several dozen new in-house artists over a period of nearly twenty years.

Lee was in one of the last groups of art interns brought into WildStorm and to be honest--he was not a standout talent when he was first hired. Don't get me wrong--he was good, very good in fact, but nothing hinted at the truly dramatic style and atmospheric work he would develop later in his career. What set him apart, though, was his work ethic, his attitude and his intense love and passion for Art. He is one of the few talents I've met who has never taken any of his gifts for granted. Moreover, he took on every assignment no matter how big or small with the same zeal and relish: whether it was a trading card job or a backup Resident Evil short story--Lee viewed each assignment as nothing other than an opportunity to improve his craft. He was and is truly one of the hardest workers I have ever known. By pushing himself artistically, Lee came out of the Studio experience a force to be reckoned with. And that speaks to the magical power of Art. It transforms people. I truly wish I could claim some credit for this but as I said, it ALL came from within Lee.

Which brings us to Batman: Noel--the first project Lee has written and so masterfully illustrated. To say I am proud of his achievement would be an understatement. I am in sheer envy. It has been said that in the entertainment field you can either have commercial success or critical acclaim. Lee Bermejo is the rare bastard whose talent bridges both worlds and leaves us breathless with the majesty and beauty of his art. A true contradiction in styles, Lee's neo-Gothic work operates on the surface level to entice and please while painting a darker, more disturbing world just underneath that very same scintillating surface. His images are slick yet richly nuanced. Noir yet modern. Somber yet riveting. He creates a world so lushly layered and so crisply folded and starkly lit that color would seem superfluous. Luckily, his collaborator Barbara Ciardo knows how to best complement and build off the existing forms rather than overpower the scene with her exquisite colors. You can literally feel the divine warmth she brings to Superman's aura and the cool winter chill of her Gotham City. Added on top of this symphony of color and form is the work of comicdom's greatest letterer, Todd Klein, who brings a turn-of-the-century Victorian twist to the proceedings with his sharp, succinct chiseled fonts. The end result is not a good book; it's a GREAT one. There's another adage in our industry which states that when a talent starts out as an artist and then steps into the arena of writers, an extra level of scrutiny is applied to the work. Biases are hard to break down but lucky for us, Lee Bermejo is fearless and confident in both line and thought. Lucky for us, because the world would be far too clean and pristine without his singular, unique vision.

Jim Lee
La Jolla, CA

WITH RESPECT, TO CHARLES DICKENS.

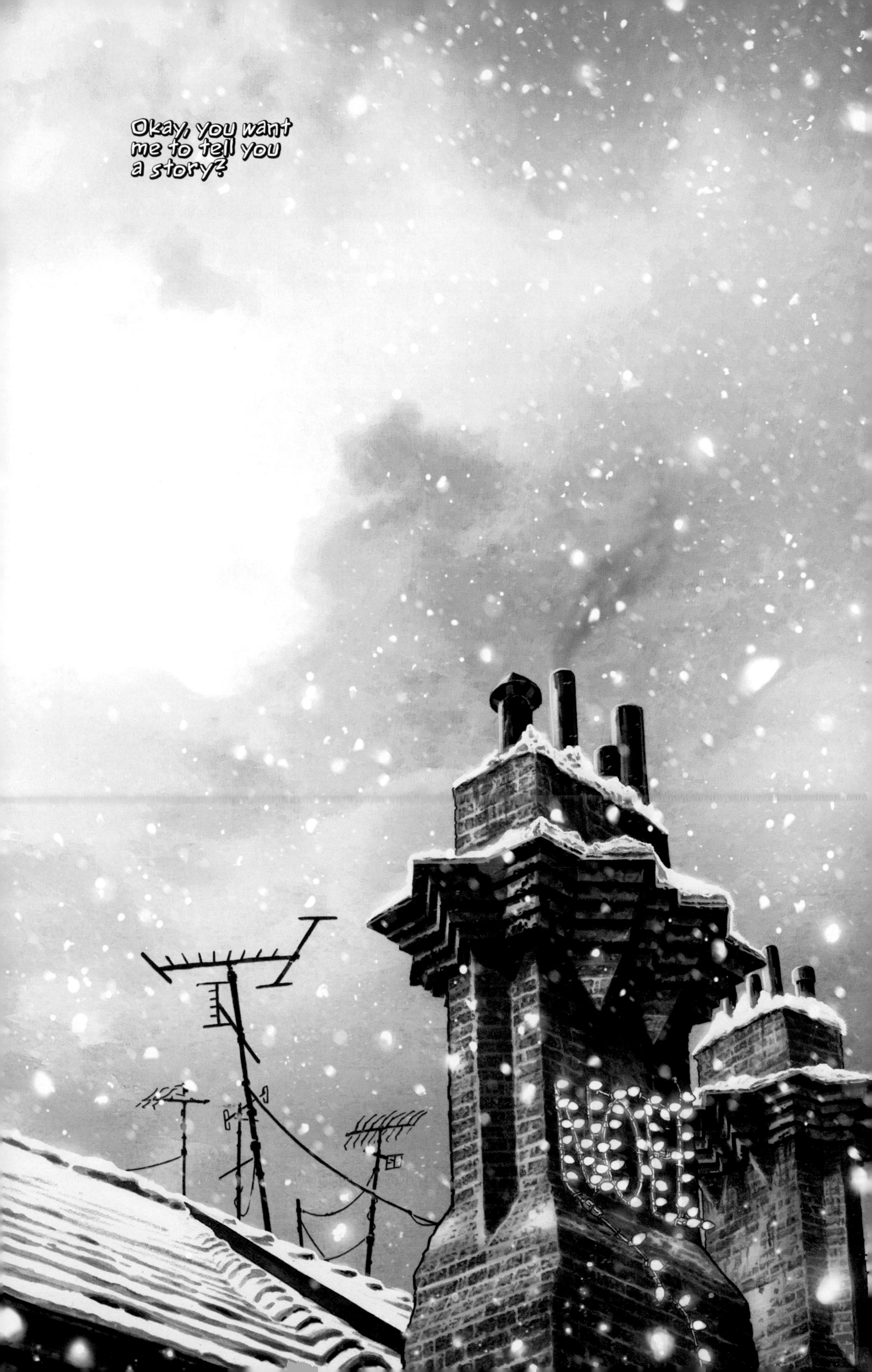
Okay, you want me to tell you a story?

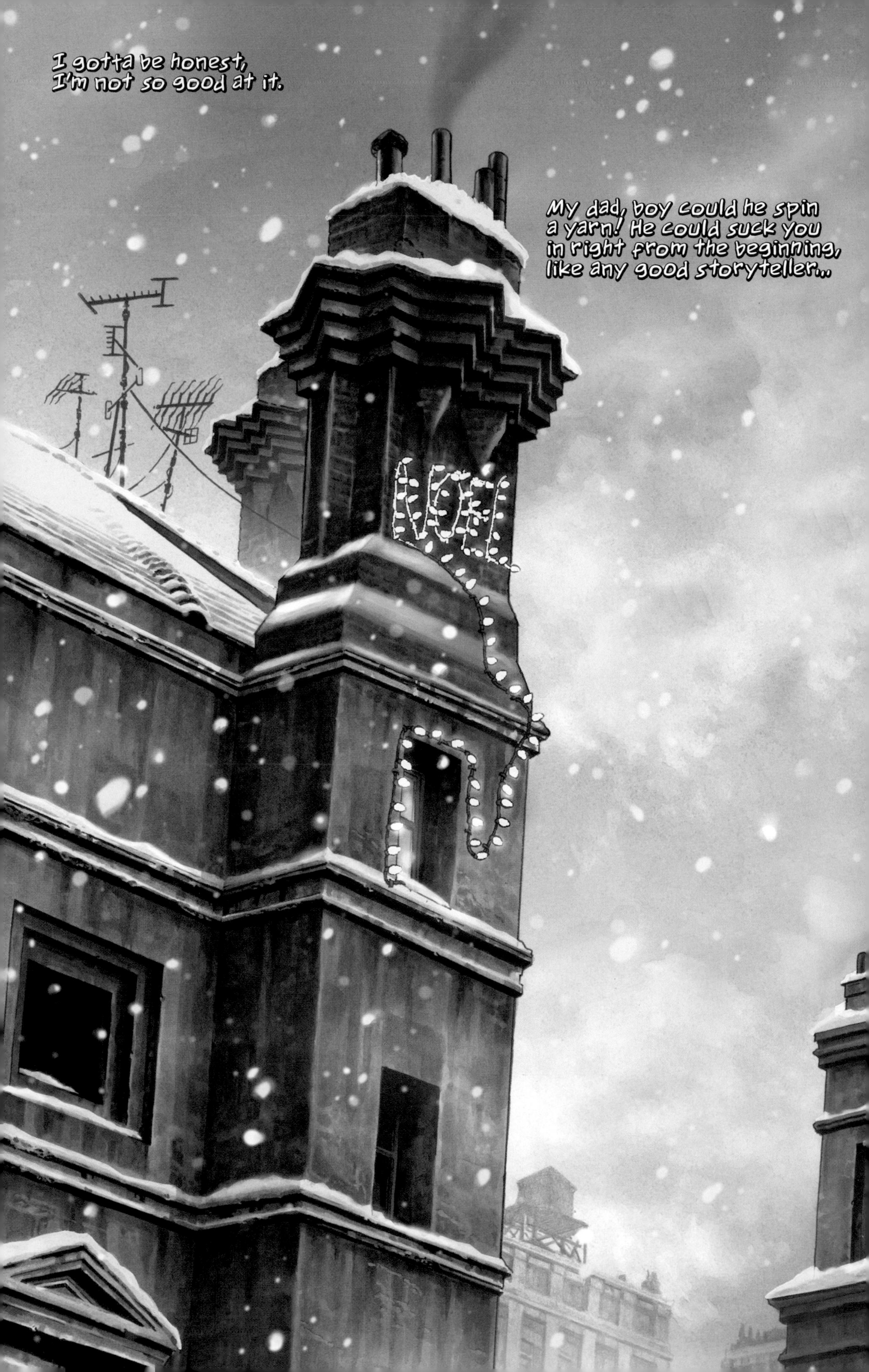
I gotta be honest,
I'm not so good at it.
My dad, boy could he spin
a yarn! He could suck you
in right from the beginning,
like any good storyteller...
NOEL

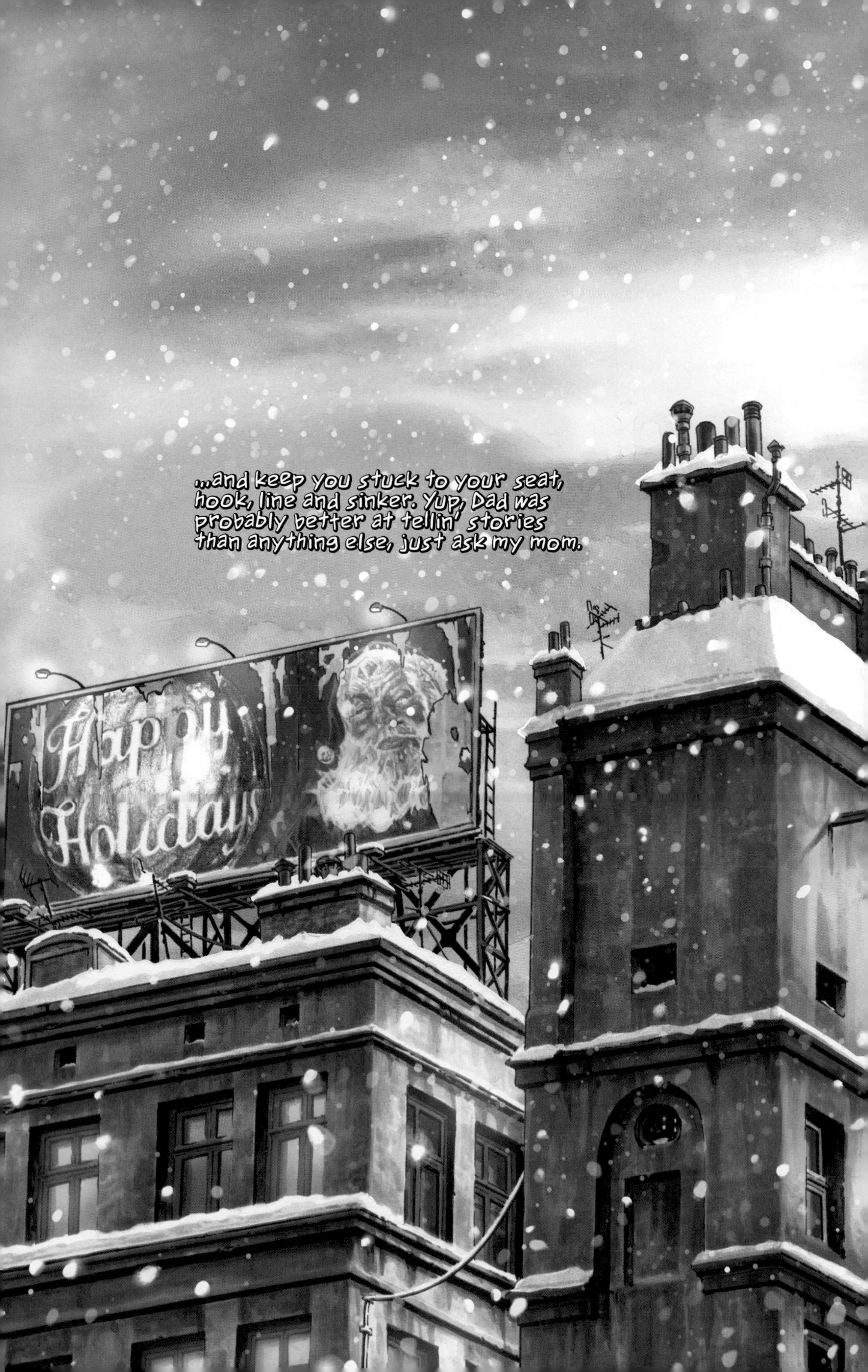
...and keep you stuck to your seat, hook, line and sinker. Yup, Dad was probably better at tellin' stories than anything else, just ask my mom.
Happy Holidays

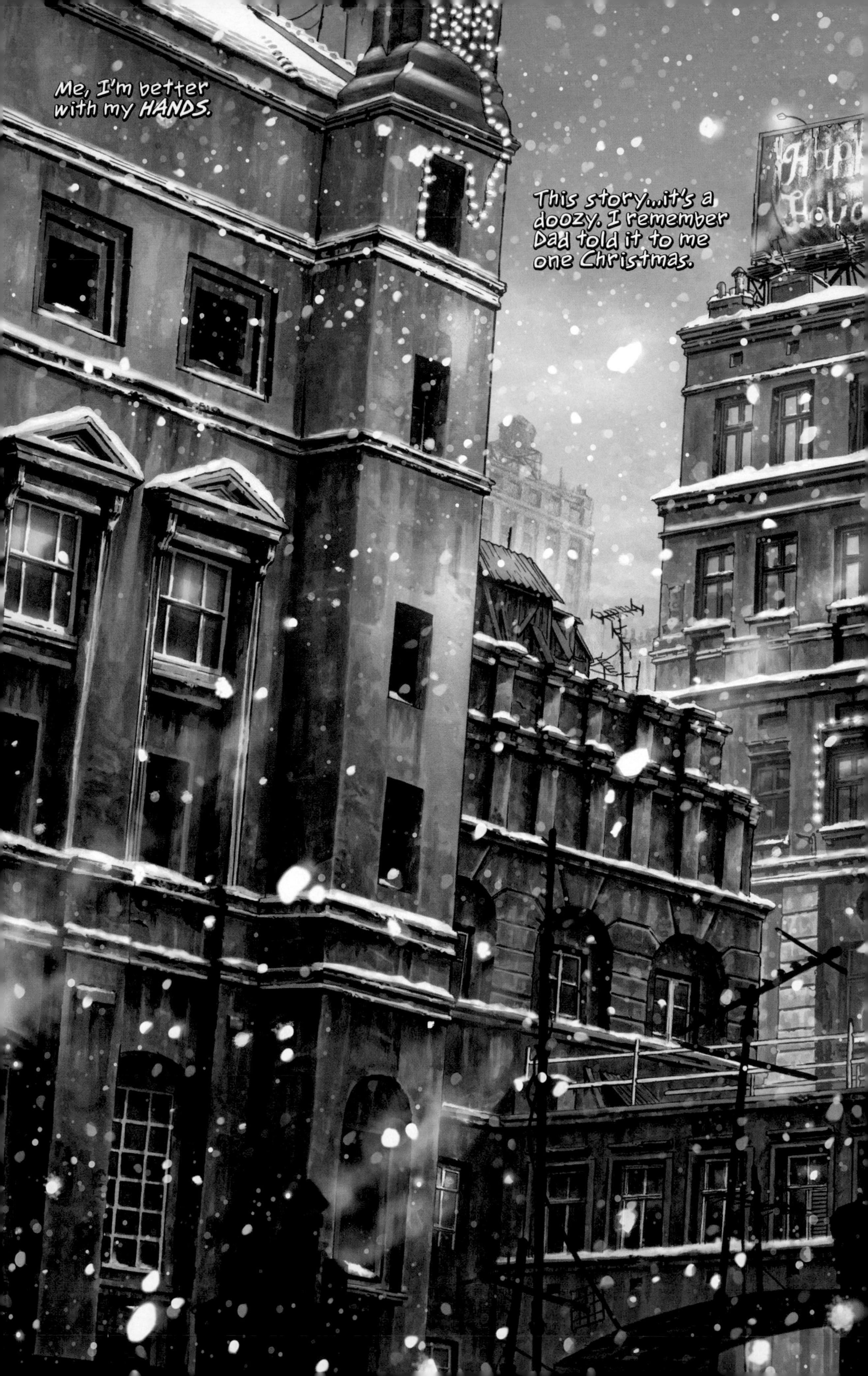
Me, I'm better with my HANDS.
This story...it's a doozy. I remember Dad told it to me one Christmas.

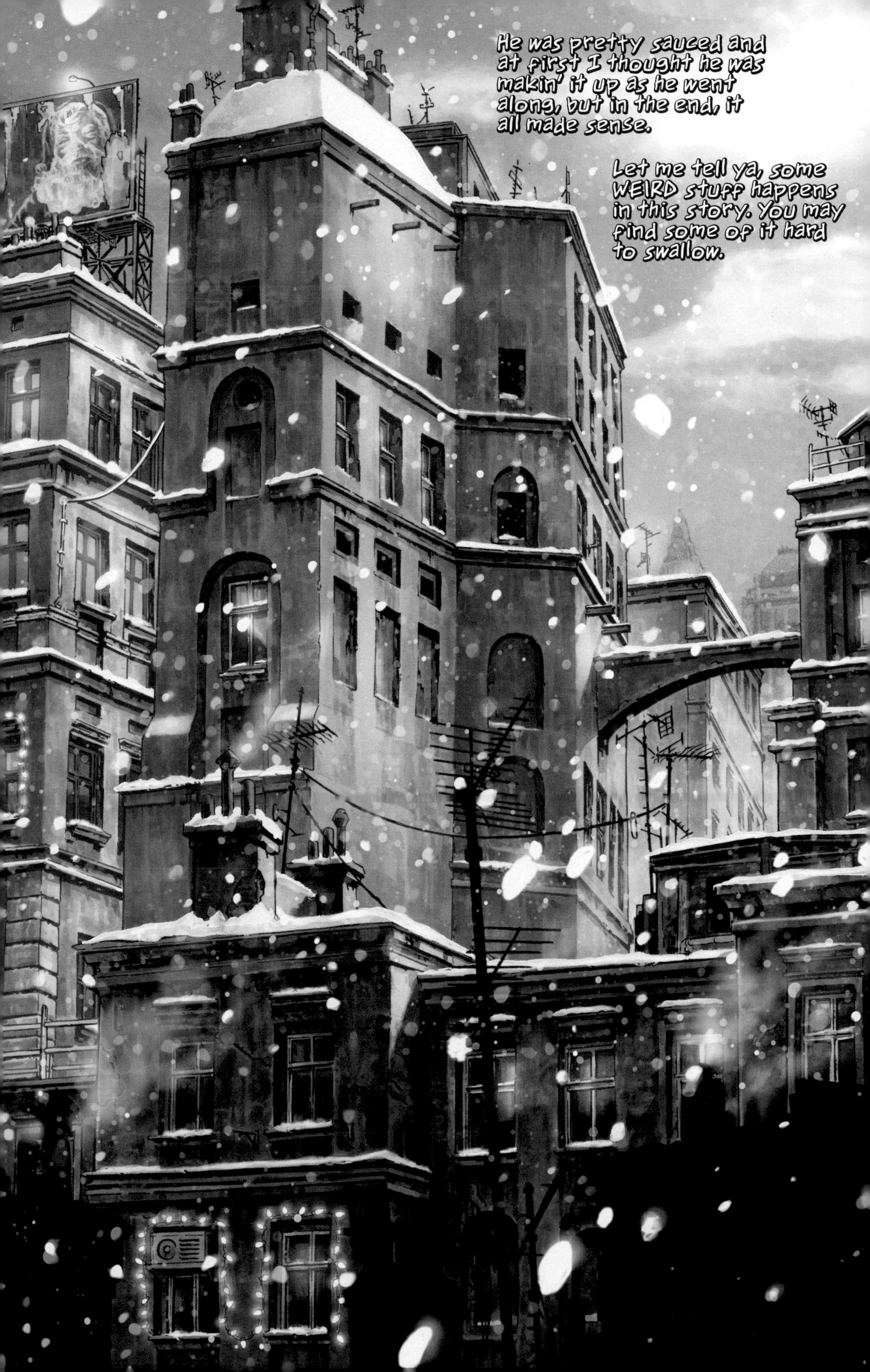
He was pretty sauced and at first I thought he was makin' it up as he went along, but in the end, it all made sense.
Let me tell ya, some WEIRD stuff happens in this story. You may find some of it hard to swallow.

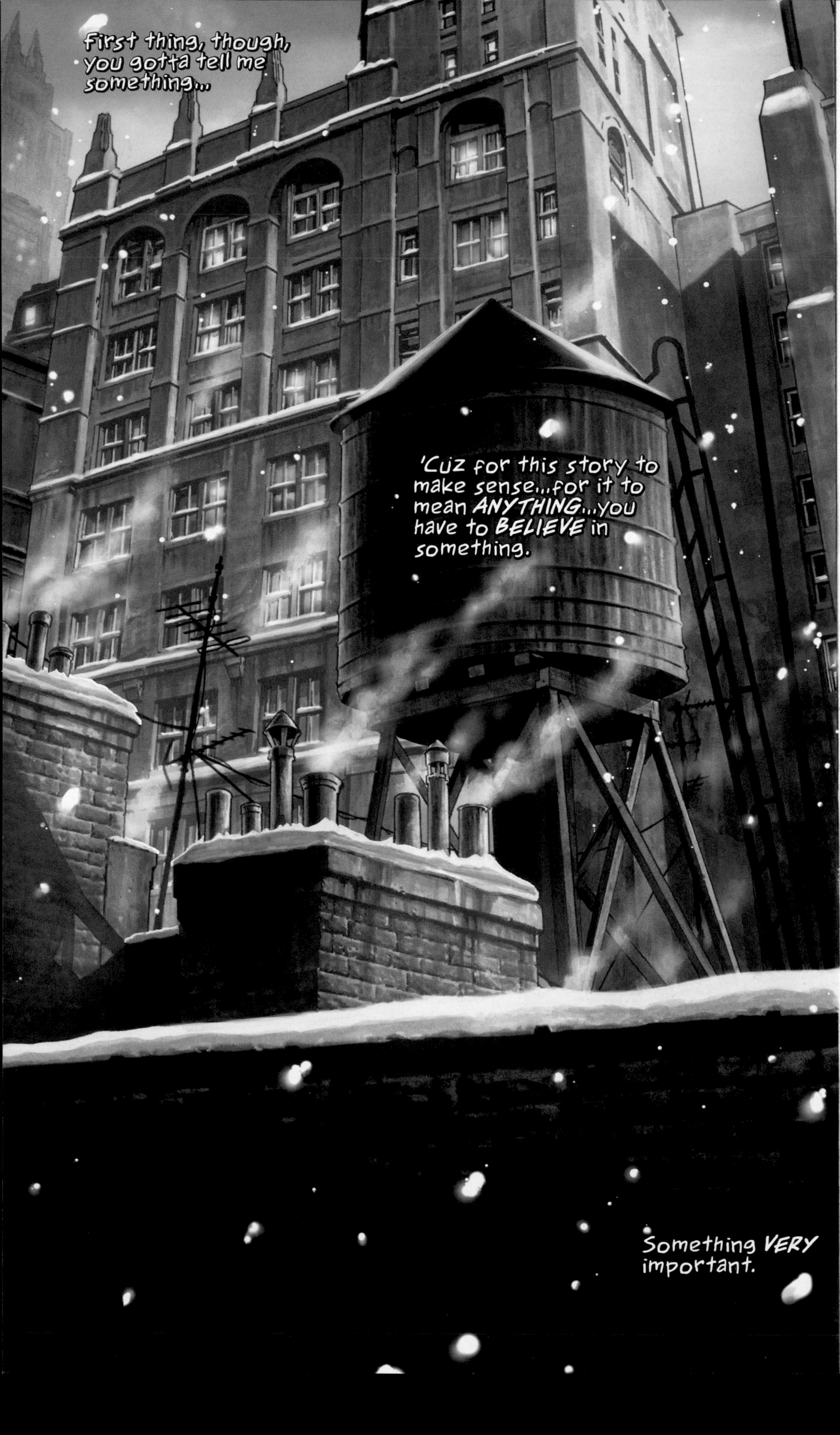
First thing, though, you gotta tell me something...
'Cuz for this story to make sense...for it to mean ANYTHING...you have to BELIEVE in something.
Something VERY important.

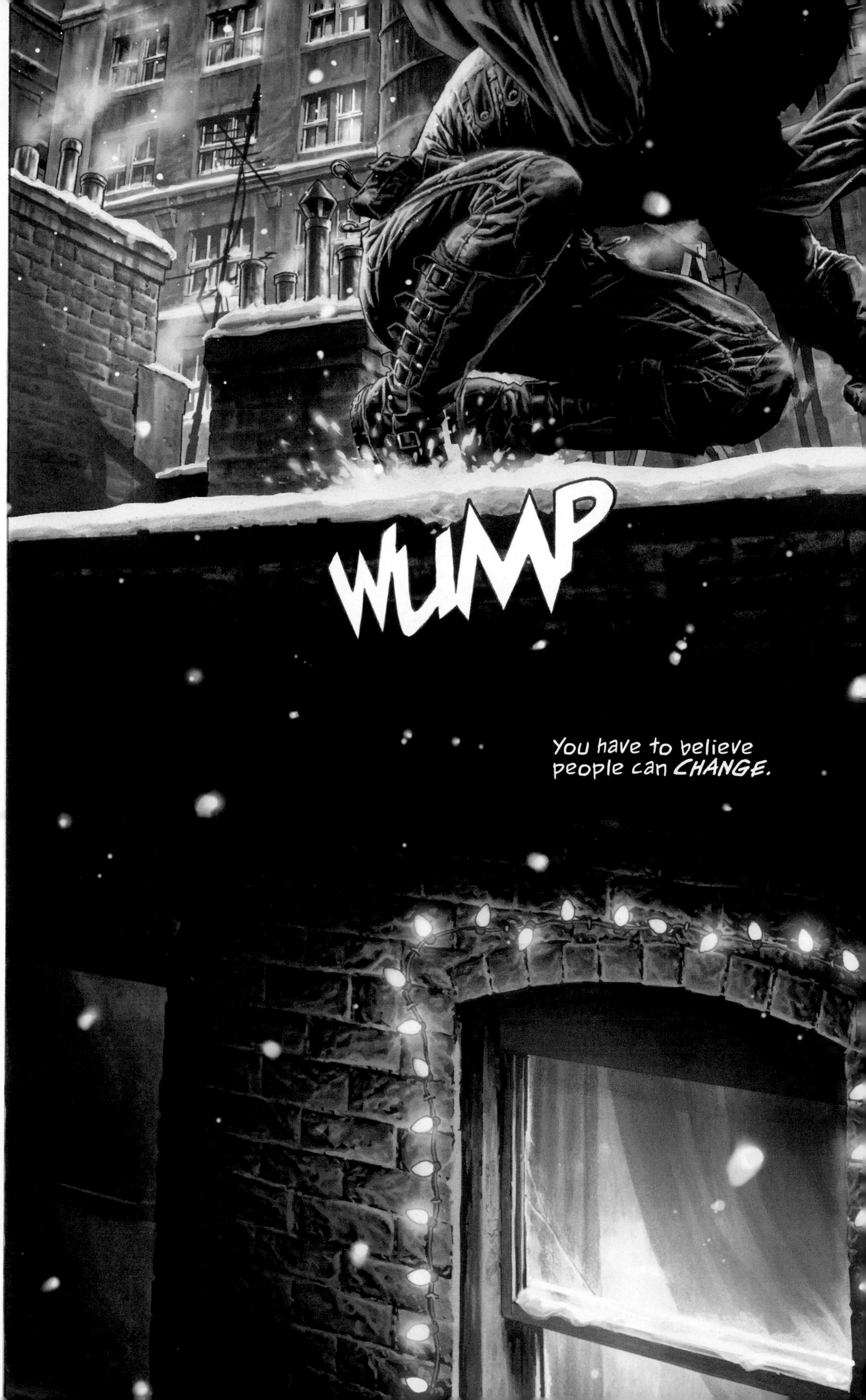
WUMP
You have to believe people can CHANGE.

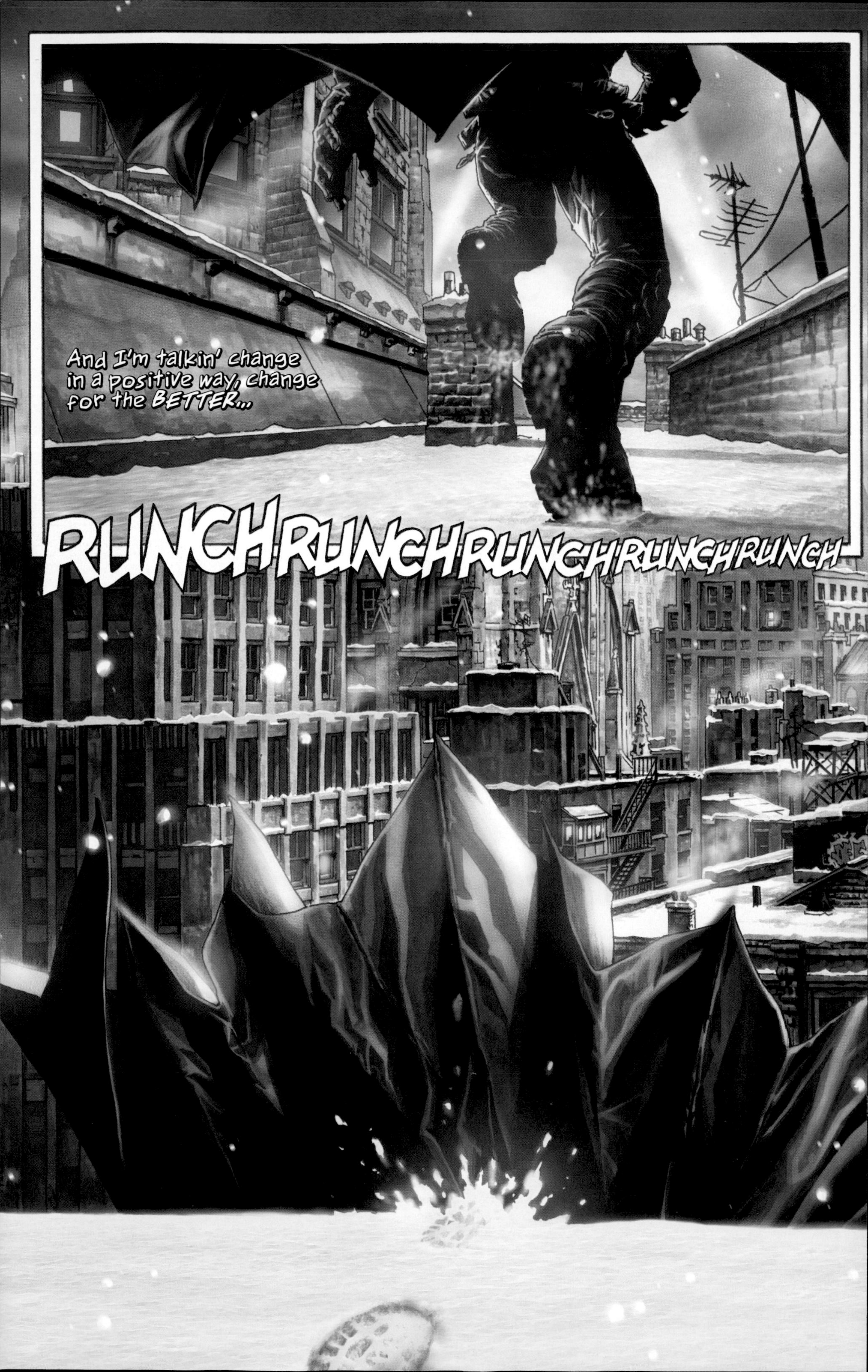
And I'm talkin' change in a positive way, change for the BETTER...
RUNCH RUNCH RUNCH RUNCH RUNCH

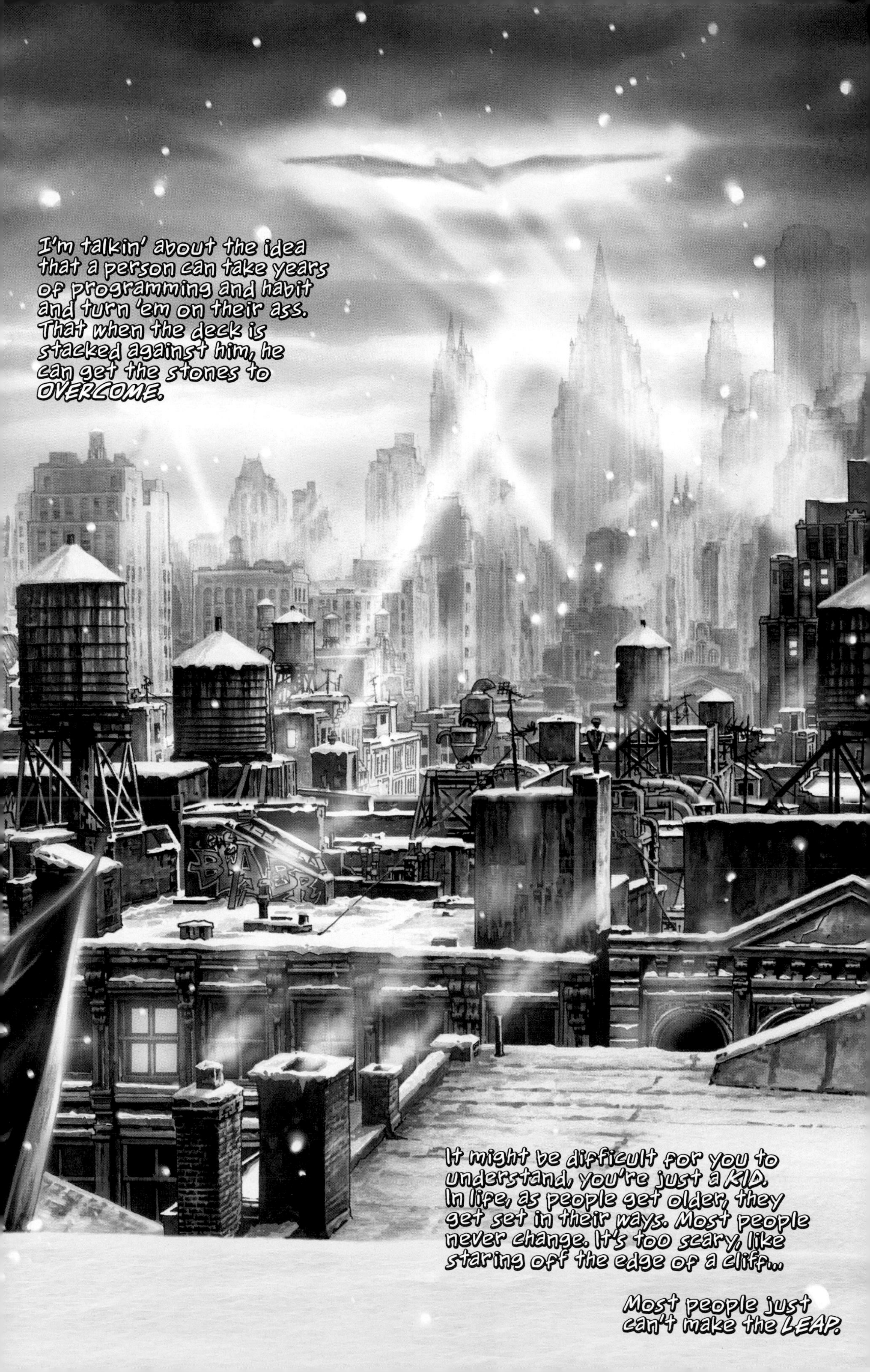
I'm talkin' about the idea that a person can take years of programming and habit and turn 'em on their ass. That when the deck is stacked against him, he can get the stones to OVERCOME.
It might be difficult for you to understand, you're just a KID. In life, as people get older, they get set in their ways. Most people never change. It's too scary, like staring off the edge of a cliff...
Most people just can't make the LEAP.

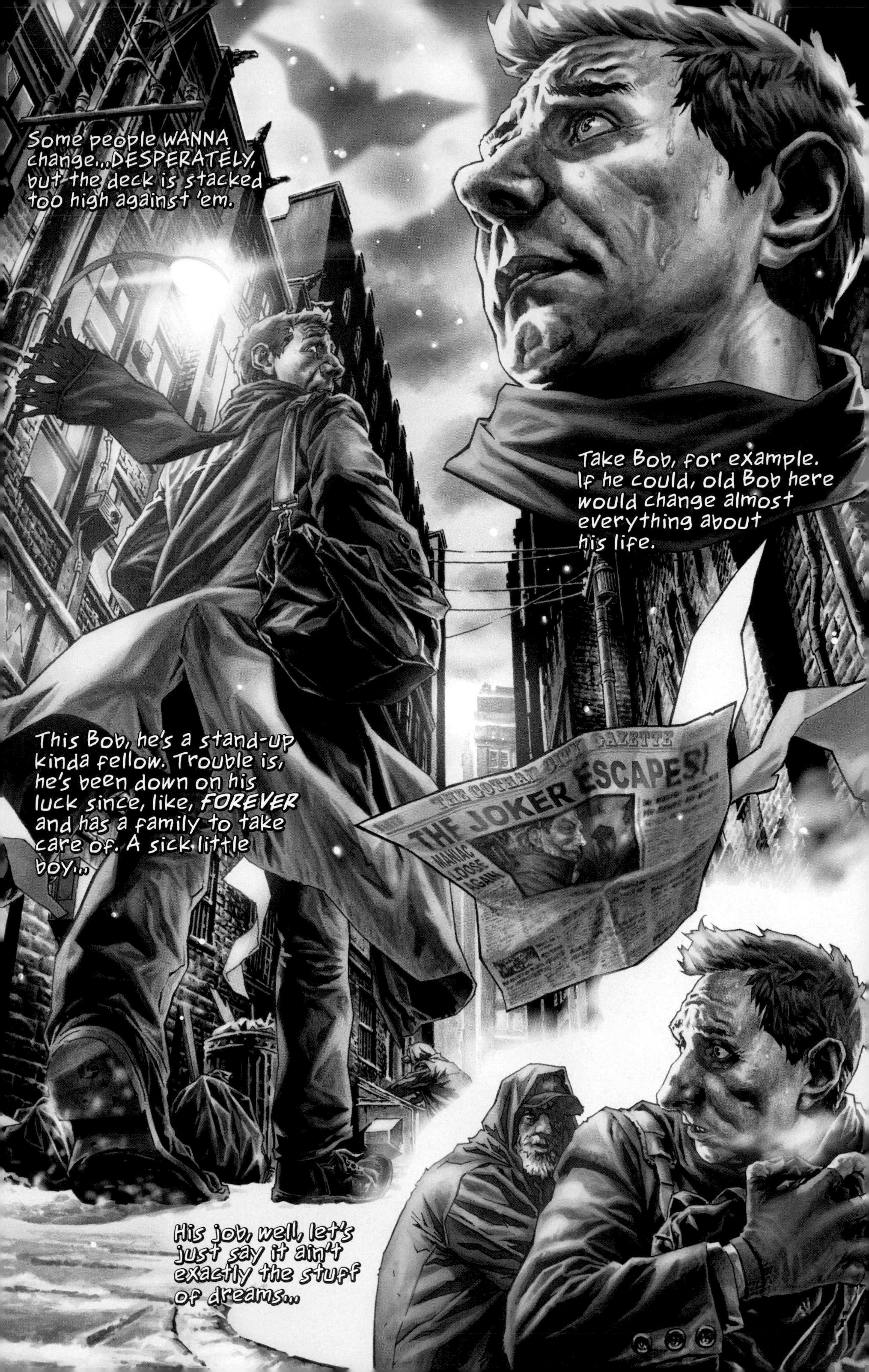
Some people WANNA change...DESPERATELY, but the deck is stacked too high against 'em.
Take Bob, for example. If he could, old Bob here would change almost everything about his life.
THE GOTHAM CITY GAZETTE
THE JOKER ESCAPES!
MANIAC LOOSE AGAIN
This Bob, he's a stand-up kinda fellow. Trouble is, he's been down on his luck since, like, FOREVER and has a family to take care of. A sick little boy...
His job, well, let's just say it ain't exactly the stuff of dreams...

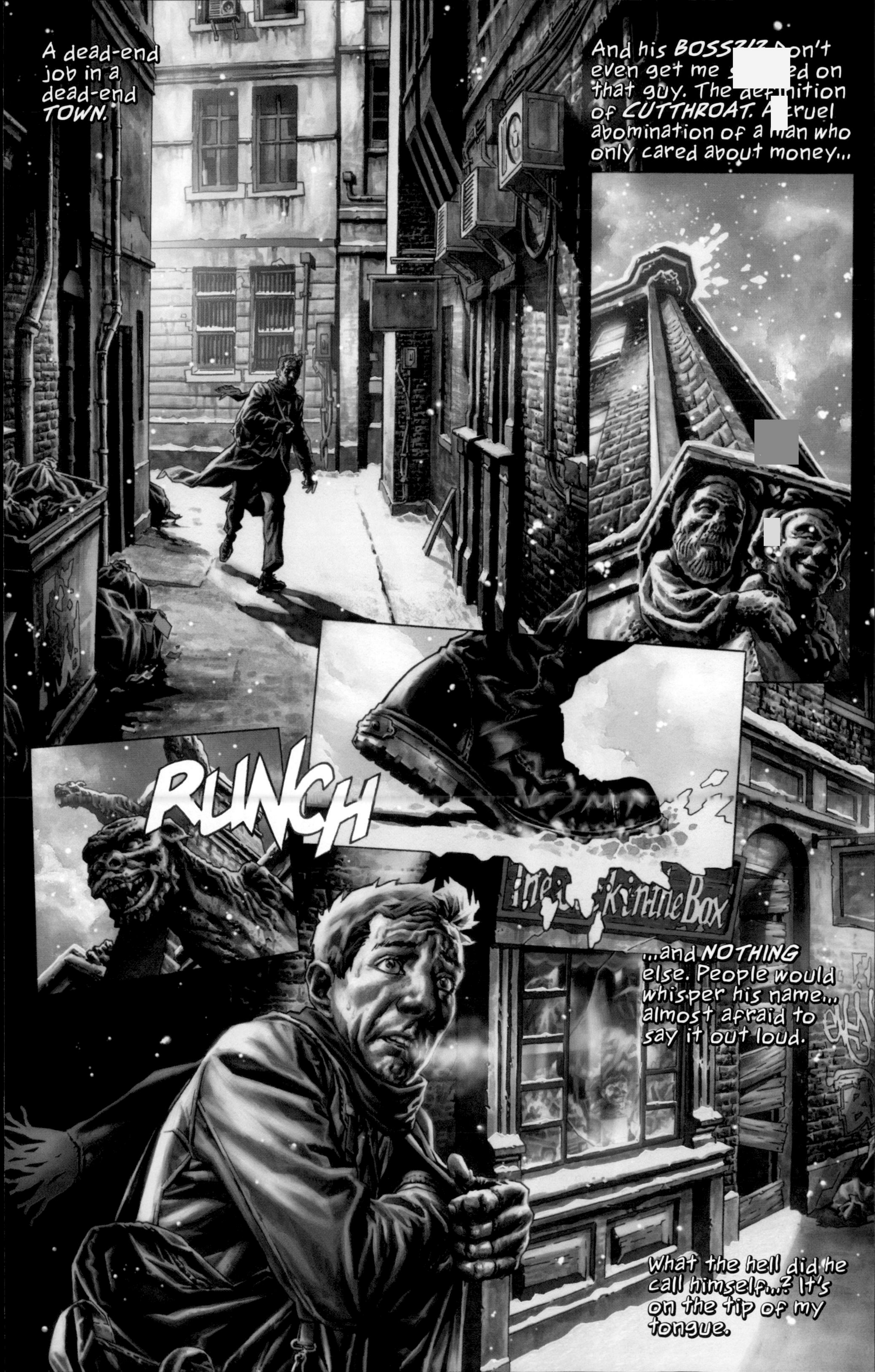
A dead-end job in a dead-end TOWN.
And his BOSS?!? Don't even get me s ed on that guy. The definition of CUTTHROAT. A cruel abomination of a man who only cared about money...
RUNCH
...and NOTHING else. People would whisper his name... almost afraid to say it out loud.
What the hell did he call himself...? It's on the tip of my tongue.

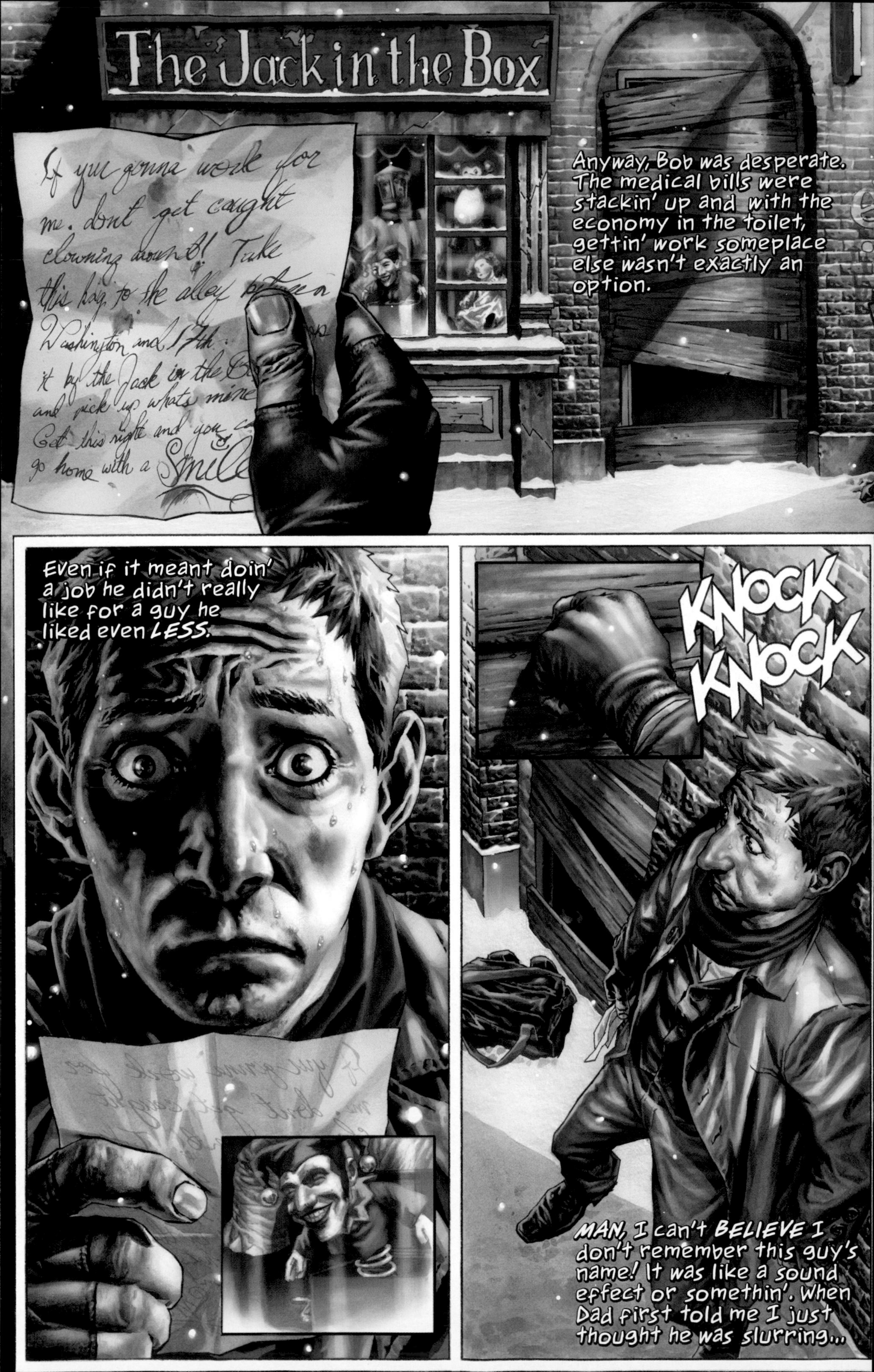
The Jack in the Box
If you gonna work for me. dont get caught clowning around! Take this bag to the alley
Washington and 17th
it by the Jack in the
and pick up whats mine
Get this right and you
go home with a
Anyway, Bob was desperate. The medical bills were stackin' up and with the economy in the toilet, gettin' work someplace else wasn't exactly an option.
Even if it meant doin' a job he didn't really like for a guy he liked even LESS.
KNOCK KNOCK
MAN, I can't BELIEVE I don't remember this guy's name! It was like a sound effect or somethin'. When Dad first told me I just thought he was slurring...

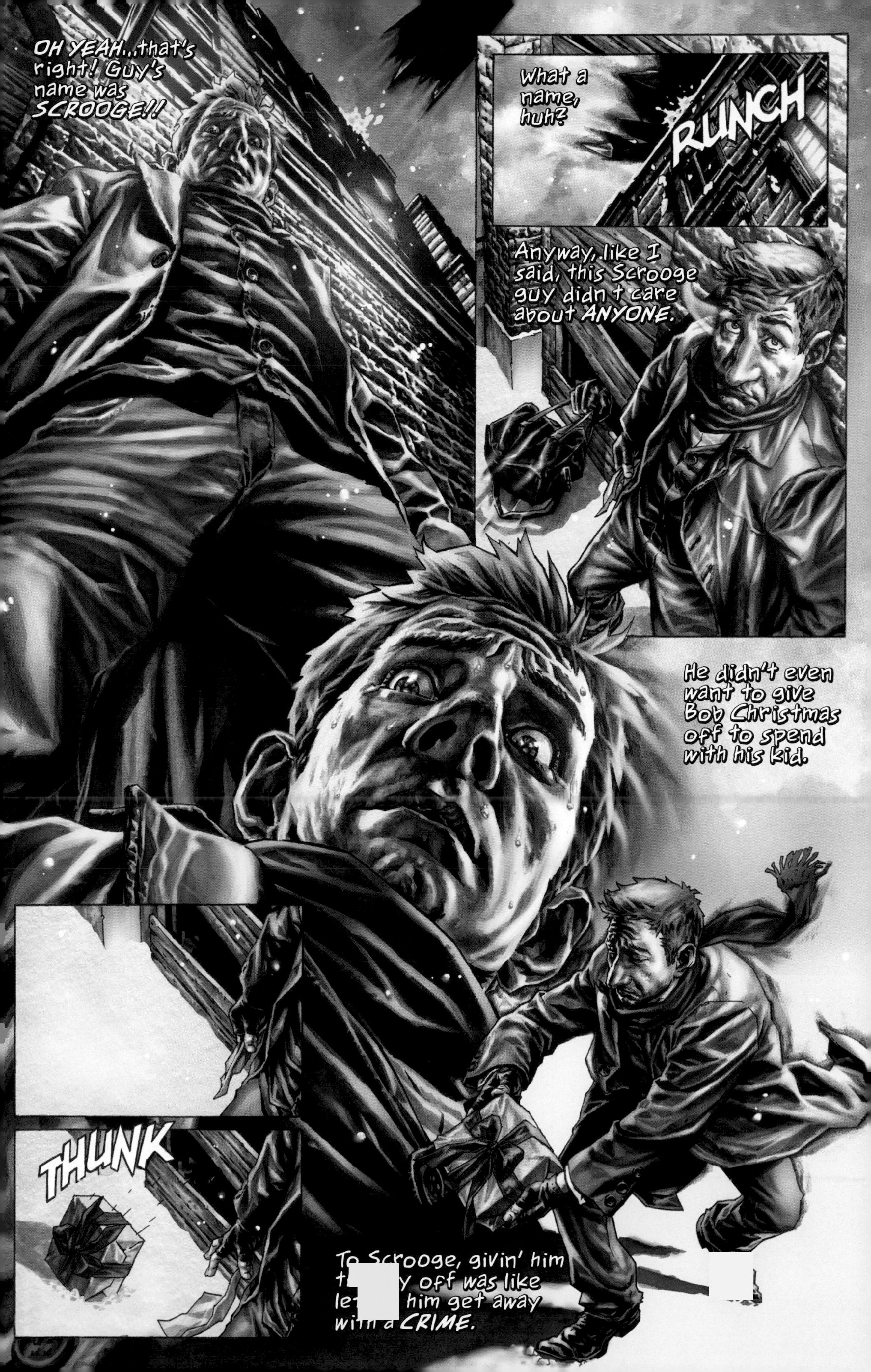
OH YEAH...that's right! Guy's name was SCROOGE!!
What a name, huh?
RUNCH
Anyway, like I said, this Scrooge guy didn't care about ANYONE.
He didn't even want to give Bob Christmas off to spend with his kid.
THUNK
To Scrooge, givin' him
y off was like
him get away
with a CRIME.

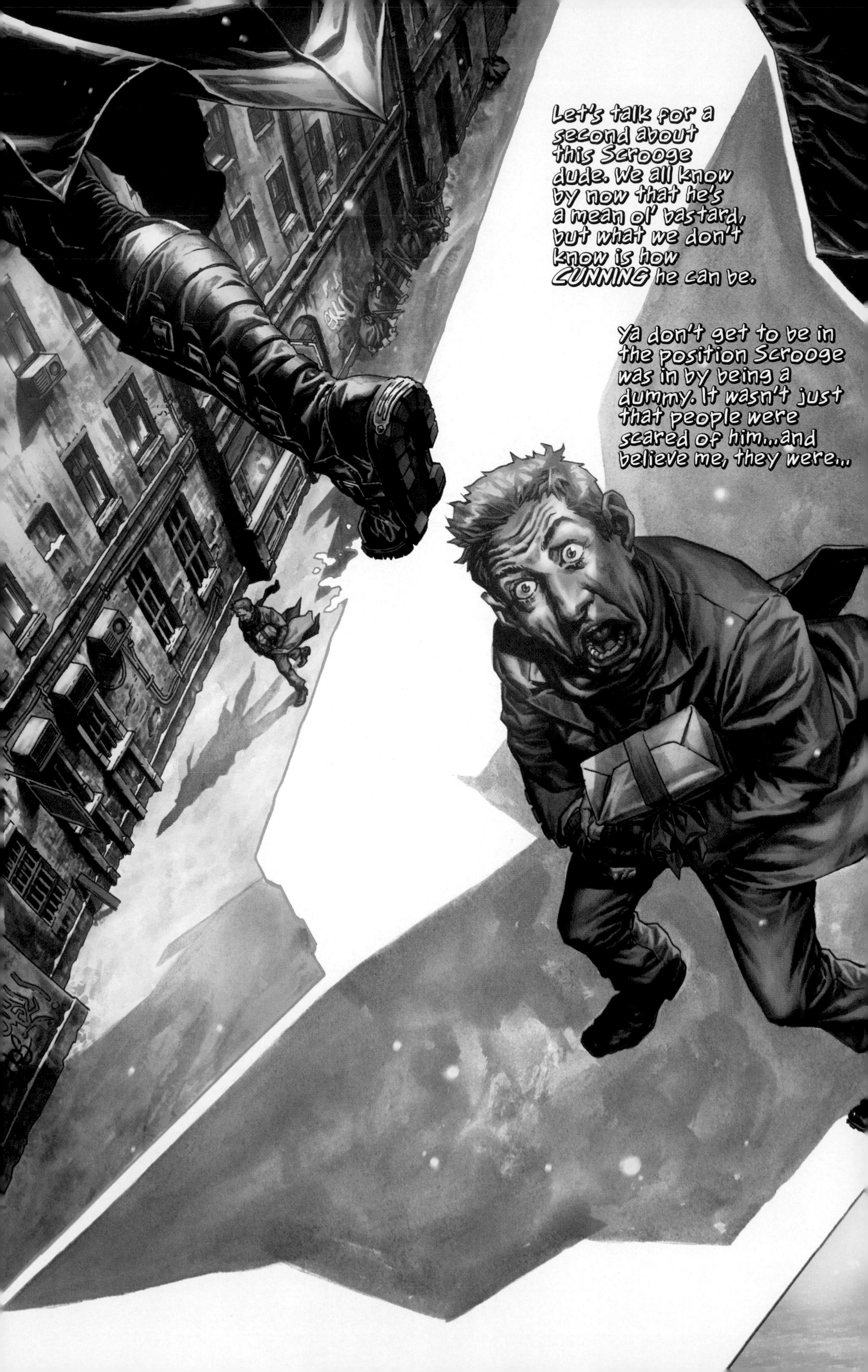

Let's talk for a second about this Scrooge dude. We all know by now that he's a mean ol' bastard, but what we don't know is how CUNNING he can be.
Ya don't get to be in the position Scrooge was in by being a dummy. It wasn't just that people were scared of him...and believe me, they were...

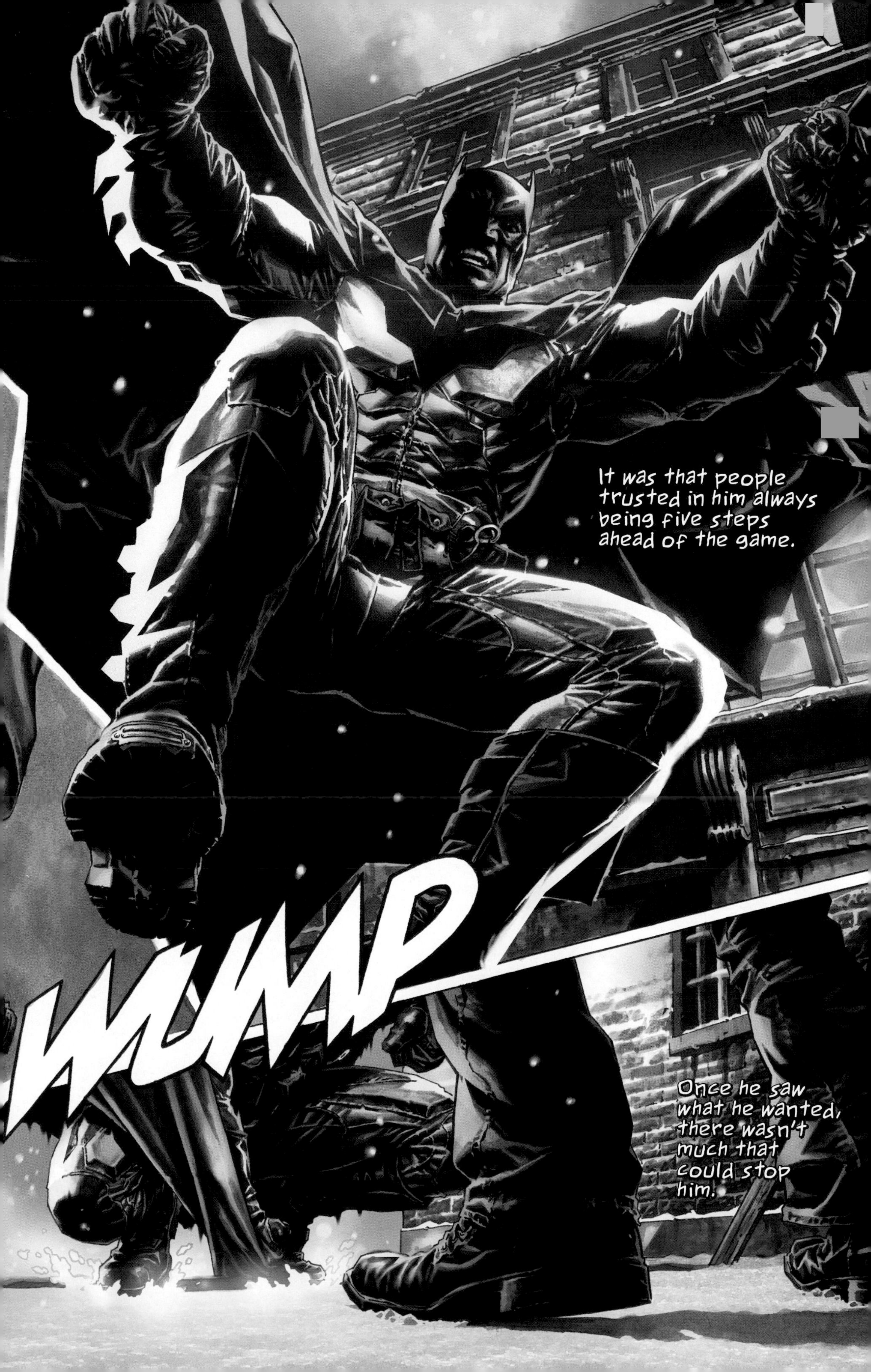
It was that people trusted in him always being five steps ahead of the game.
WUMP
Once he saw what he wanted, there wasn't much that could stop him.

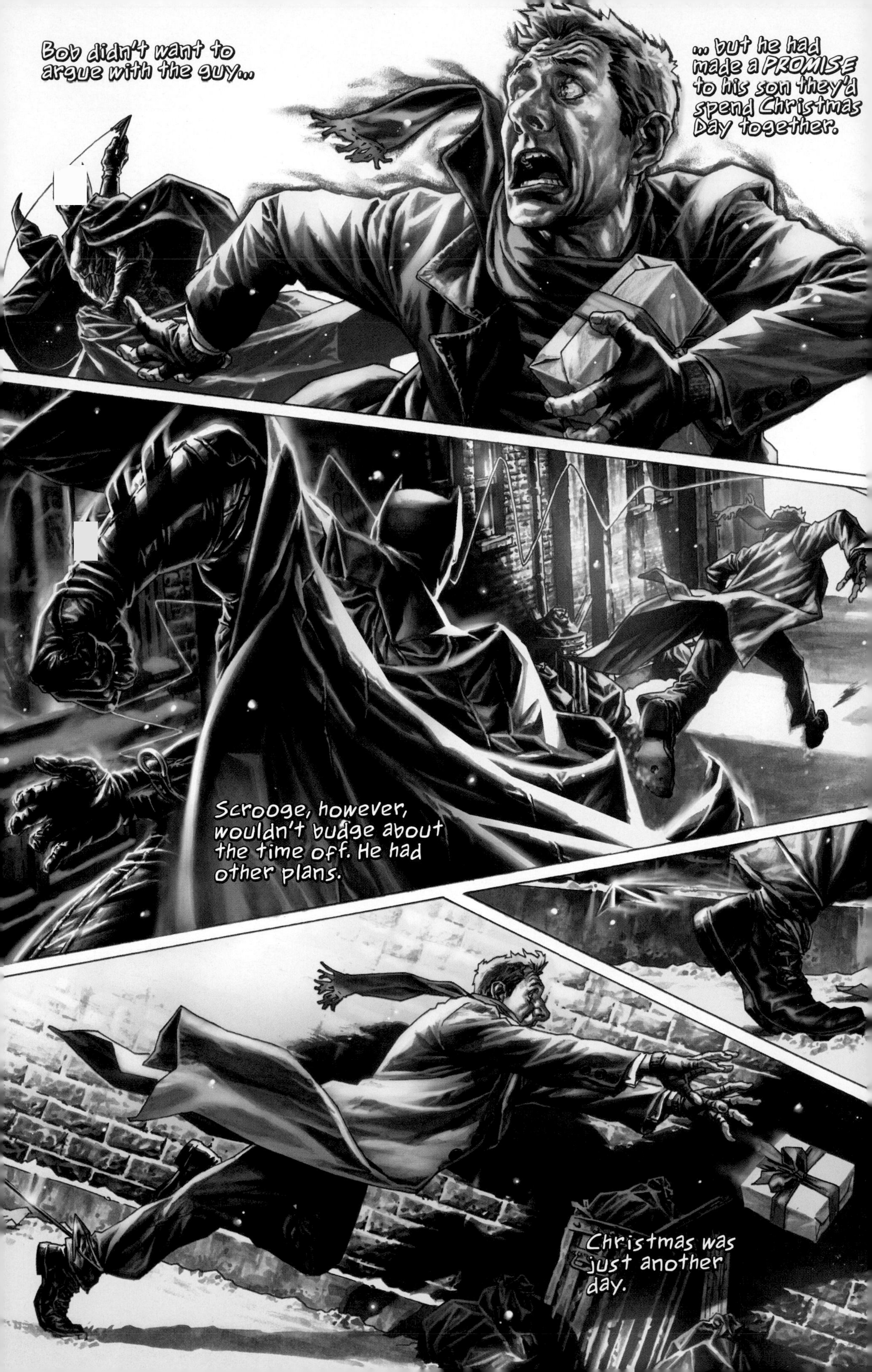
Bob didn't want to argue with the guy...
...but he had made a PROMISE to his son they'd spend Christmas Day together.
Scrooge, however, wouldn't budge about the time off. He had other plans.
Christmas was just another day.

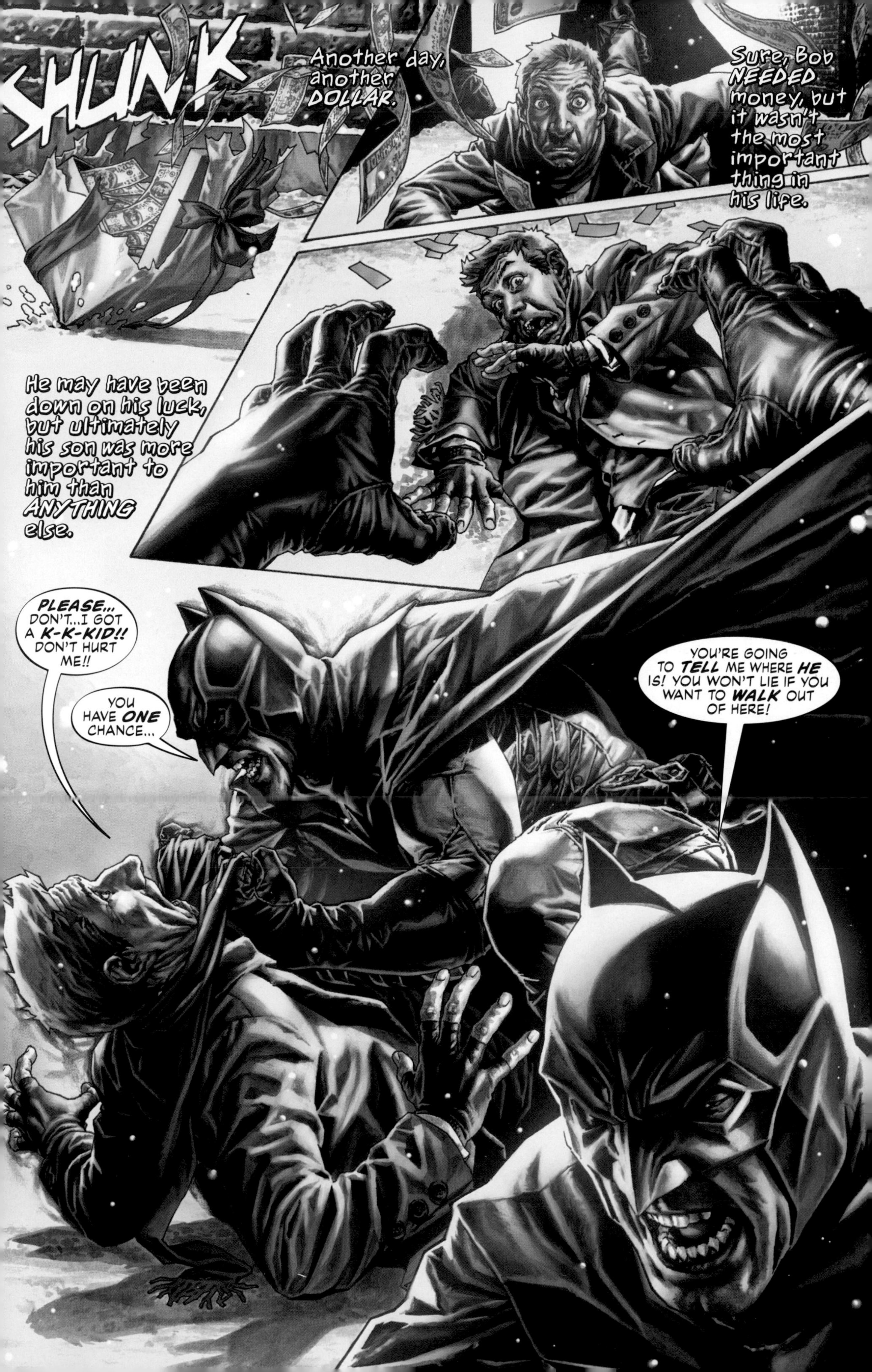
SHUNK
Another day, another DOLLAR.
Sure, Bob NEEDED money, but it wasn't the most important thing in his life.
He may have been down on his luck, but ultimately his son was more important to him than ANYTHING else.
PLEASE... DON'T...I GOT A K-K-KID!! DON'T HURT ME!!
YOU HAVE ONE CHANCE...
YOU'RE GOING TO TELL ME WHERE HE IS! YOU WON'T LIE IF YOU WANT TO WALK OUT OF HERE!

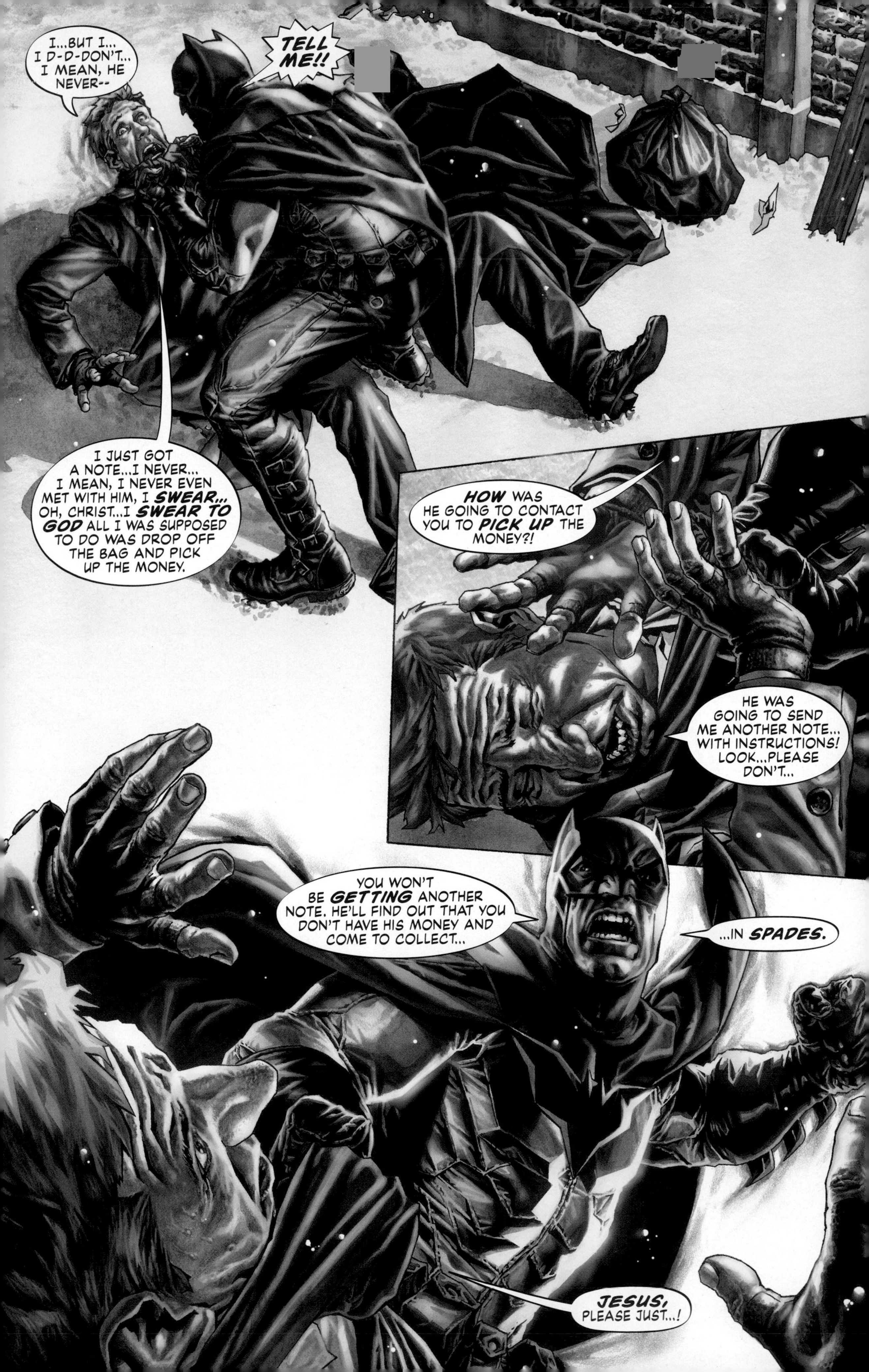
I...BUT I... I D-D-DON'T... I MEAN, HE NEVER--
TELL ME!!
I JUST GOT A NOTE...I NEVER... I MEAN, I NEVER EVEN MET WITH HIM, I SWEAR... OH, CHRIST...I SWEAR TO GOD ALL I WAS SUPPOSED TO DO WAS DROP OFF THE BAG AND PICK UP THE MONEY.
HOW WAS HE GOING TO CONTACT YOU TO PICK UP THE MONEY?!
HE WAS GOING TO SEND ME ANOTHER NOTE... WITH INSTRUCTIONS! LOOK...PLEASE DON'T...
YOU WON'T BE GETTING ANOTHER NOTE. HE'LL FIND OUT THAT YOU DON'T HAVE HIS MONEY AND COME TO COLLECT...
...IN SPADES.
JESUS, PLEASE JUST...!

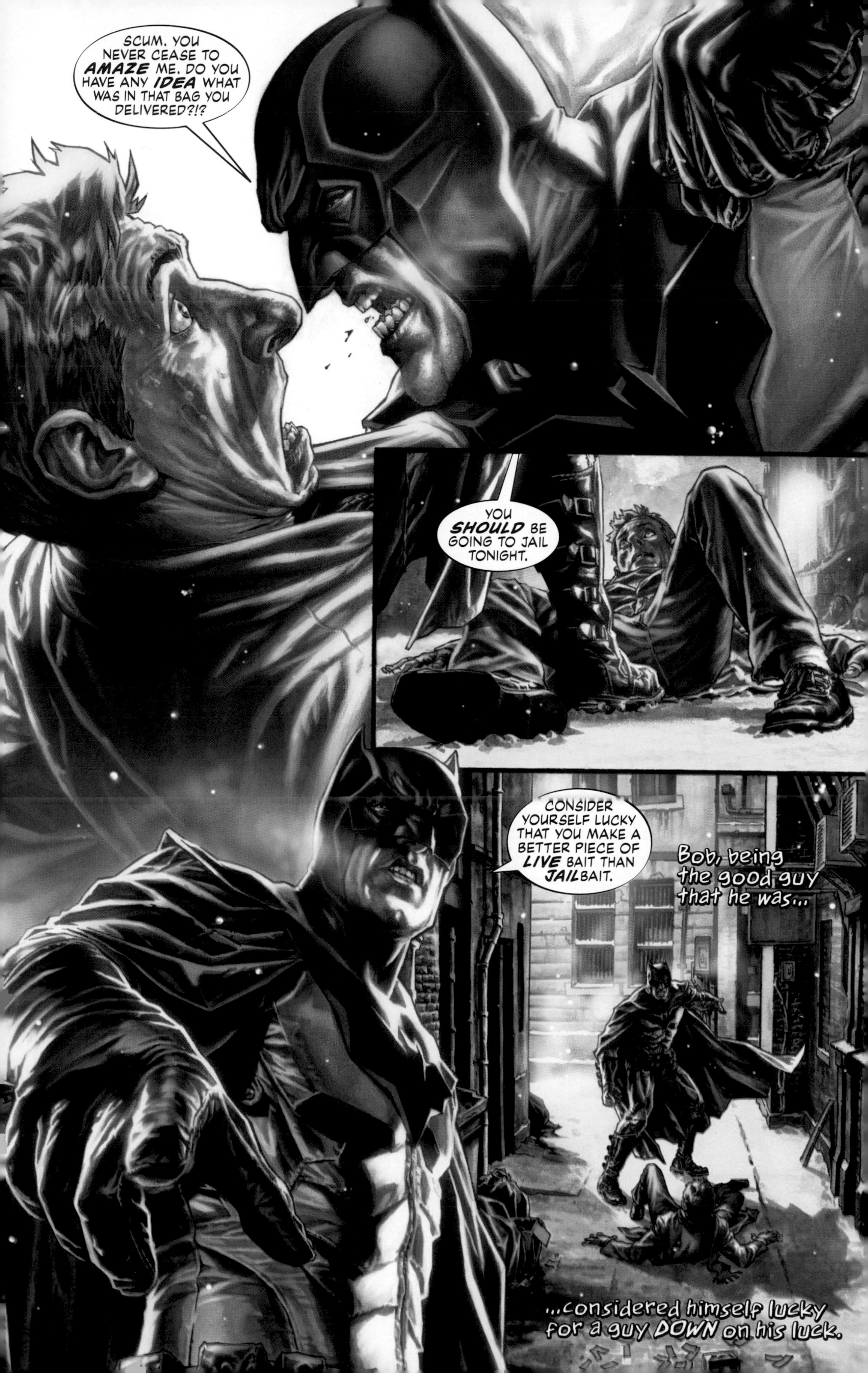
SCUM. YOU NEVER CEASE TO AMAZE ME. DO YOU HAVE ANY IDEA WHAT WAS IN THAT BAG YOU DELIVERED?!?
YOU SHOULD BE GOING TO JAIL TONIGHT.
CONSIDER YOURSELF LUCKY THAT YOU MAKE A BETTER PIECE OF LIVE BAIT THAN JAILBAIT.
Bob, being the good guy that he was...
...considered himself lucky for a guy DOWN on his luck.

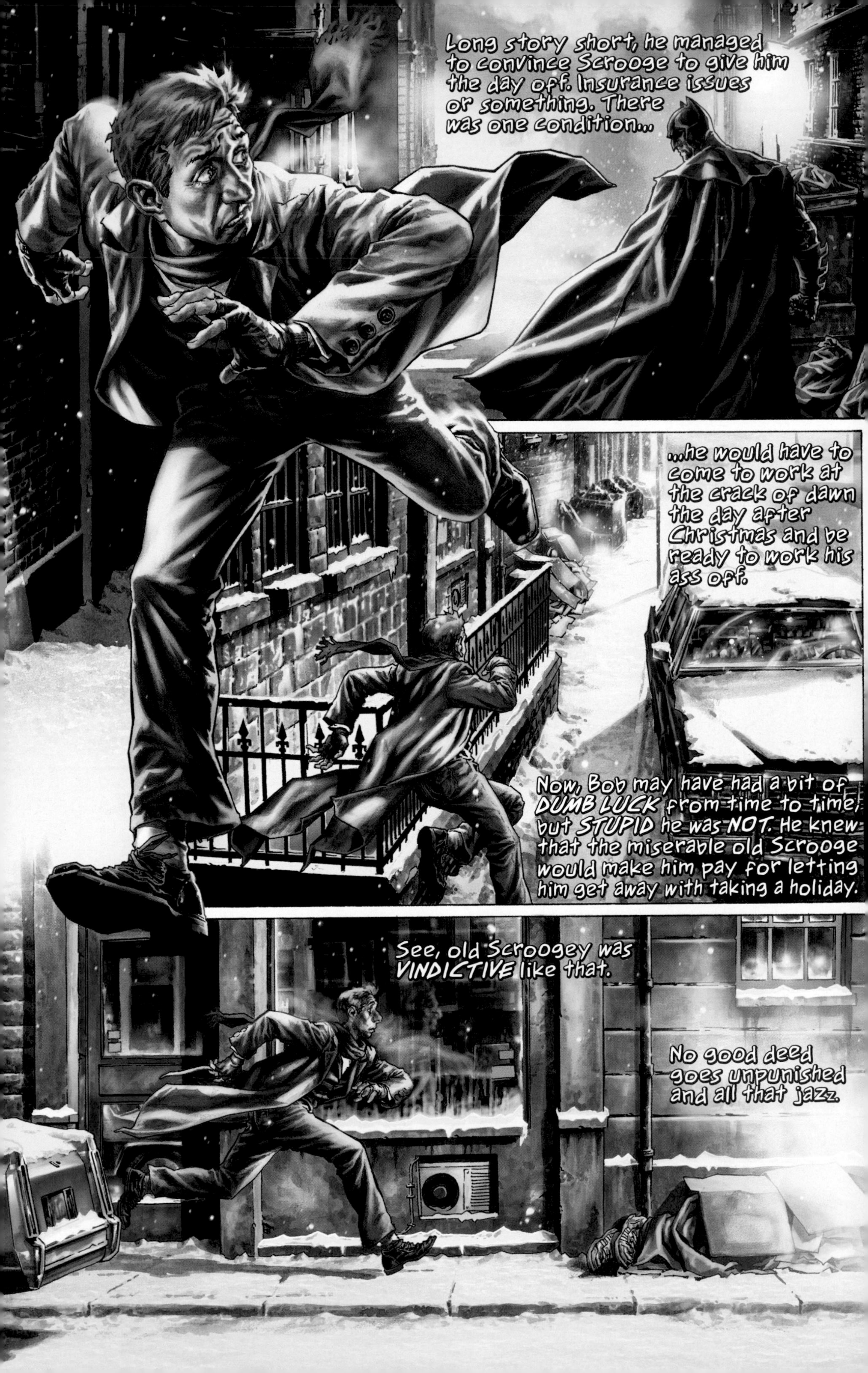
Long story short, he managed to convince Scrooge to give him the day off. Insurance issues or something. There was one condition...
...he would have to come to work at the crack of dawn the day after Christmas and be ready to work his ass off.
Now, Bob may have had a bit of DUMB LUCK from time to time, but STUPID he was NOT. He knew that the miserable old Scrooge would make him pay for letting him get away with taking a holiday.
See, old Scroogey was VINDICTIVE like that.
No good deed goes unpunished and all that jazz.

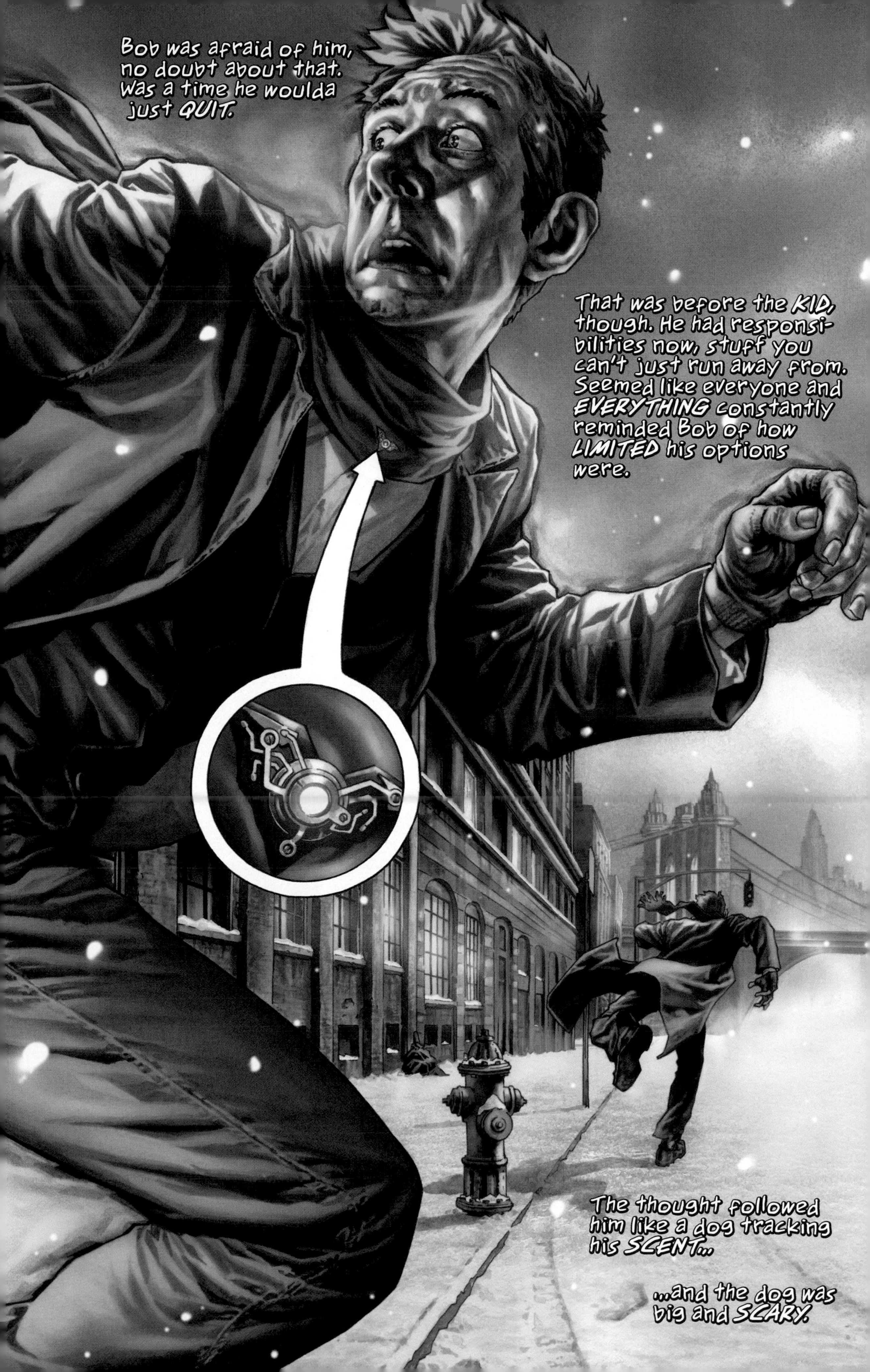
Bob was afraid of him, no doubt about that. Was a time he woulda just QUIT.
That was before the KID, though. He had responsi-bilities now, stuff you can't just run away from. Seemed like everyone and EVERYTHING constantly reminded Bob of how LIMITED his options were.
The thought followed him like a dog tracking his SCENT...
...and the dog was big and SCARY.

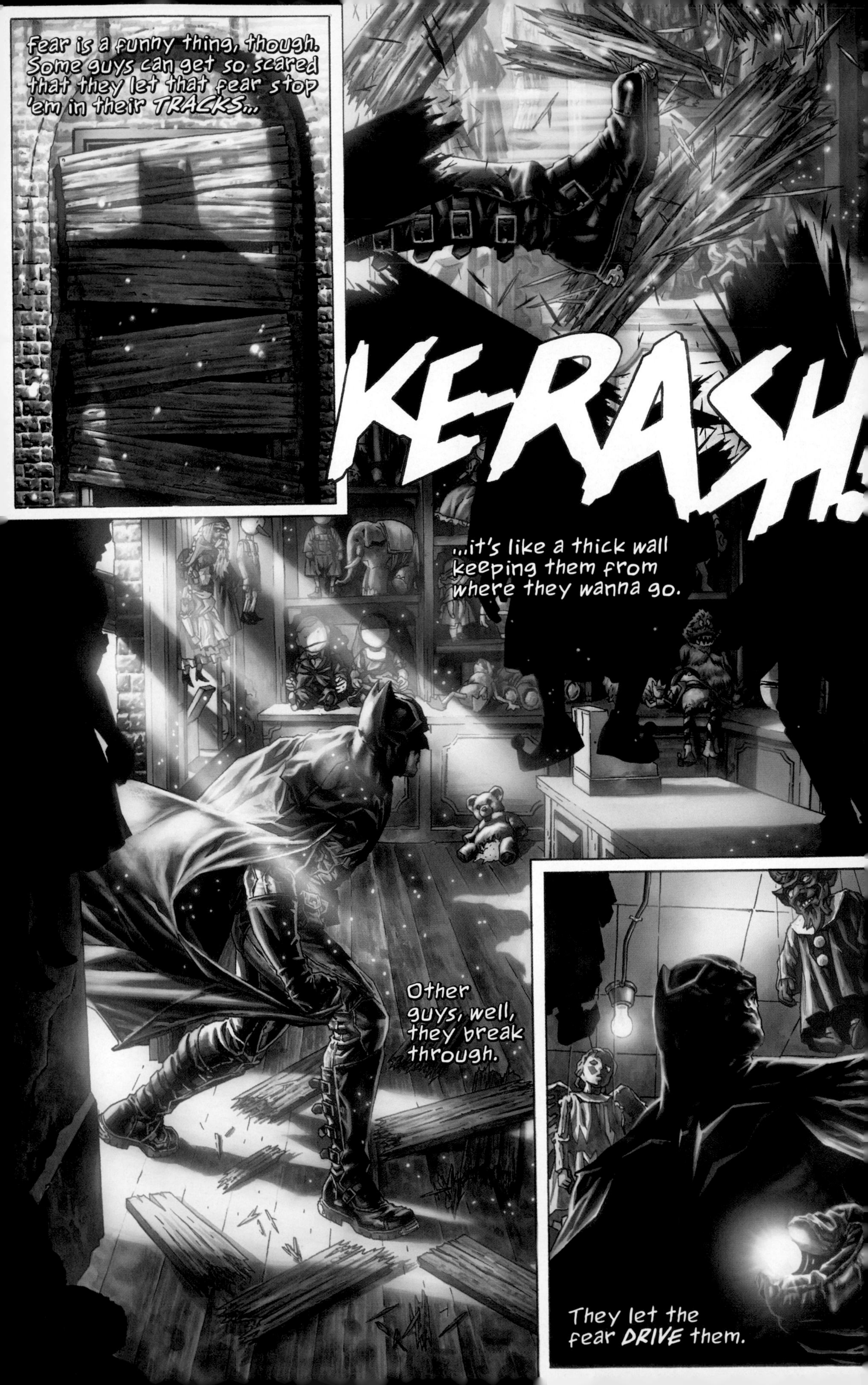
Fear is a funny thing, though. Some guys can get so scared that they let that fear stop 'em in their TRACKS...
KERASH!
...it's like a thick wall keeping them from where they wanna go.
Other guys, well, they break through.
They let the fear DRIVE them.

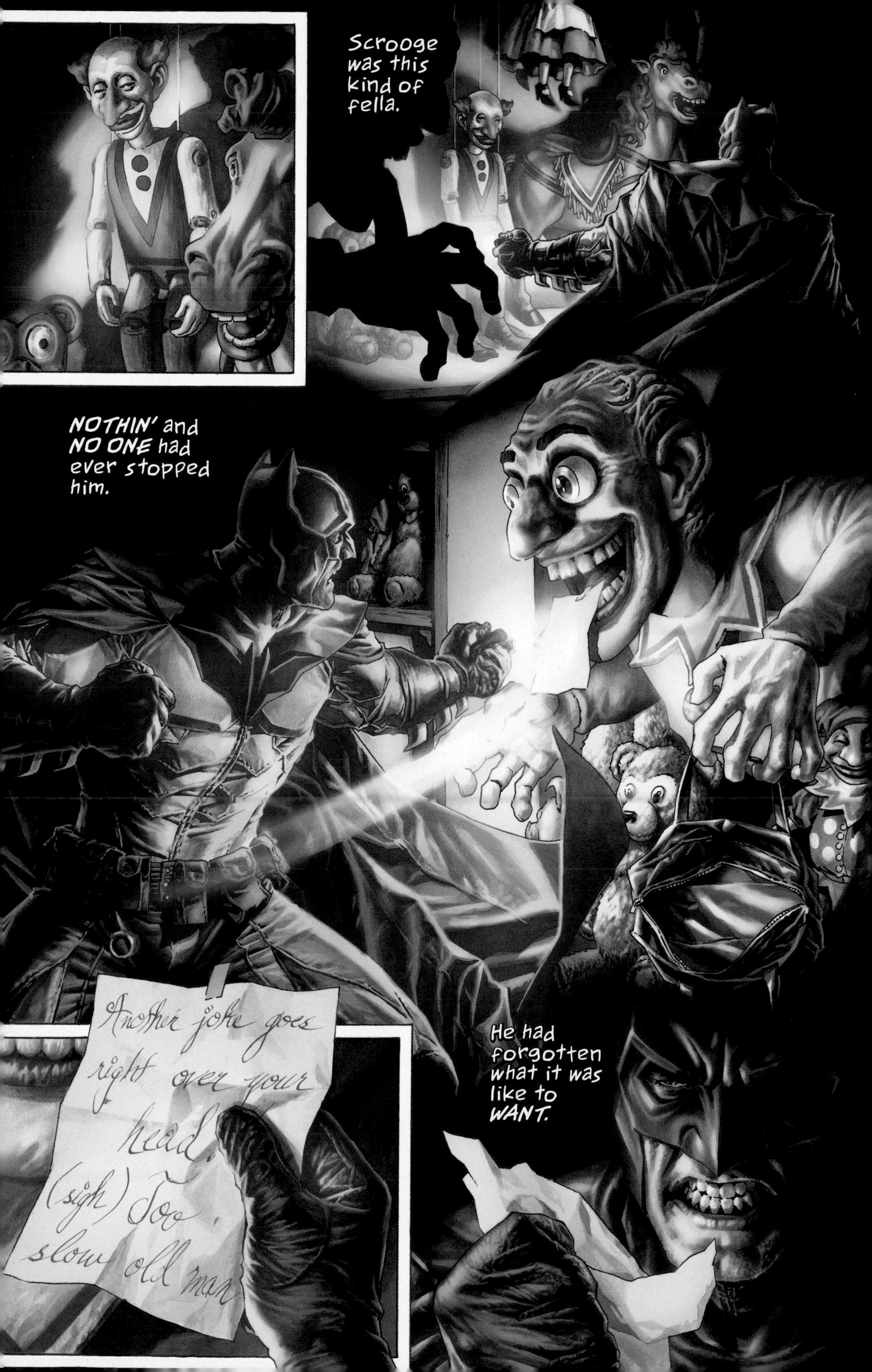
Scrooge was this kind of fella.
NOTHIN' and NO ONE had ever stopped him.
Another joke goes right over your head. (sigh) Too slow old man
He had forgotten what it was like to WANT.

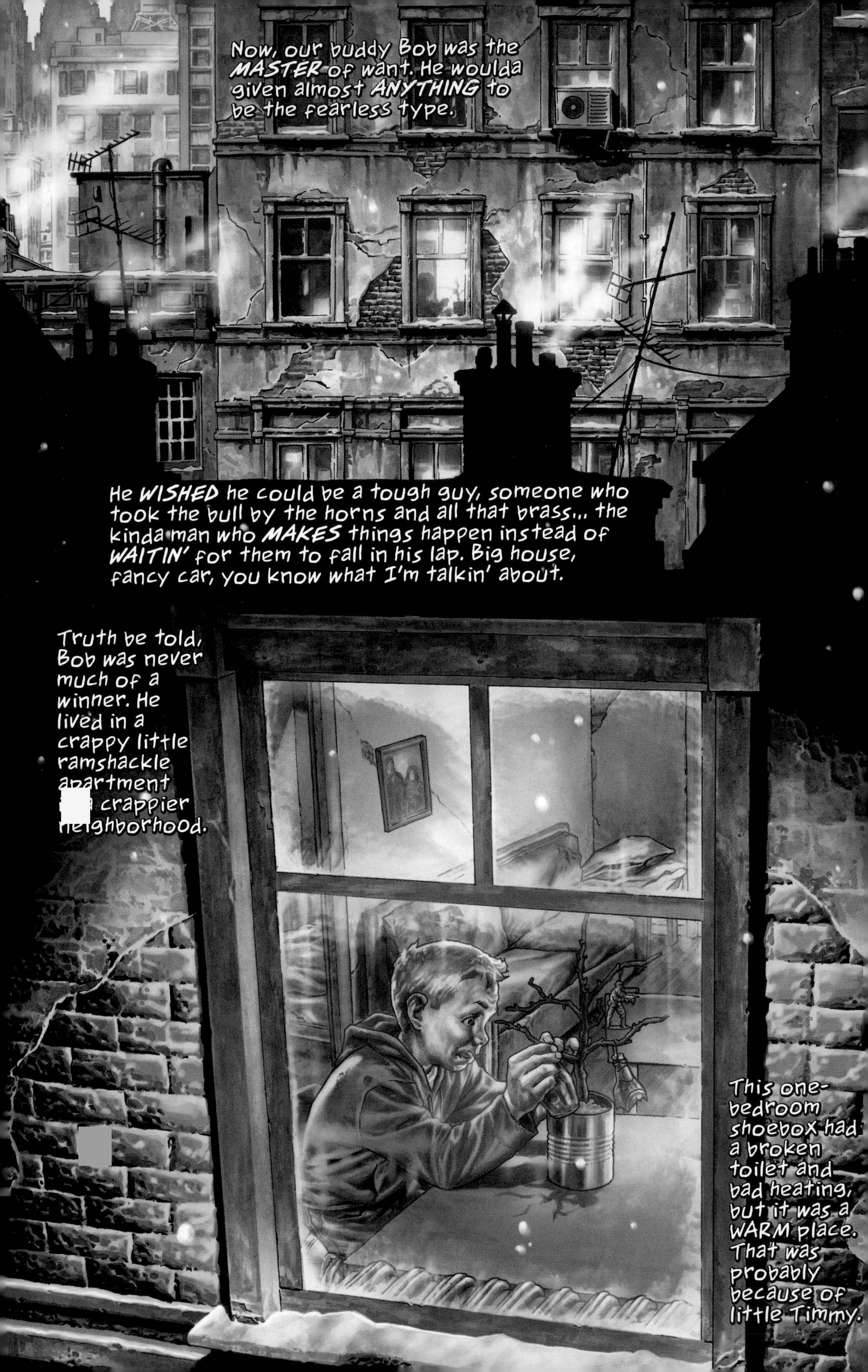
Now, our buddy Bob was the MASTER of want. He woulda given almost ANYTHING to be the fearless type.
He WISHED he could be a tough guy, someone who took the bull by the horns and all that brass... the kinda man who MAKES things happen instead of WAITIN' for them to fall in his lap. Big house, fancy car, you know what I'm talkin' about.
Truth be told, Bob was never much of a winner. He lived in a crappy little ramshackle apartment a crappier neighborhood.
This one-bedroom shoebox had a broken toilet and bad heating, but it was a WARM place. That was probably because of little Timmy.

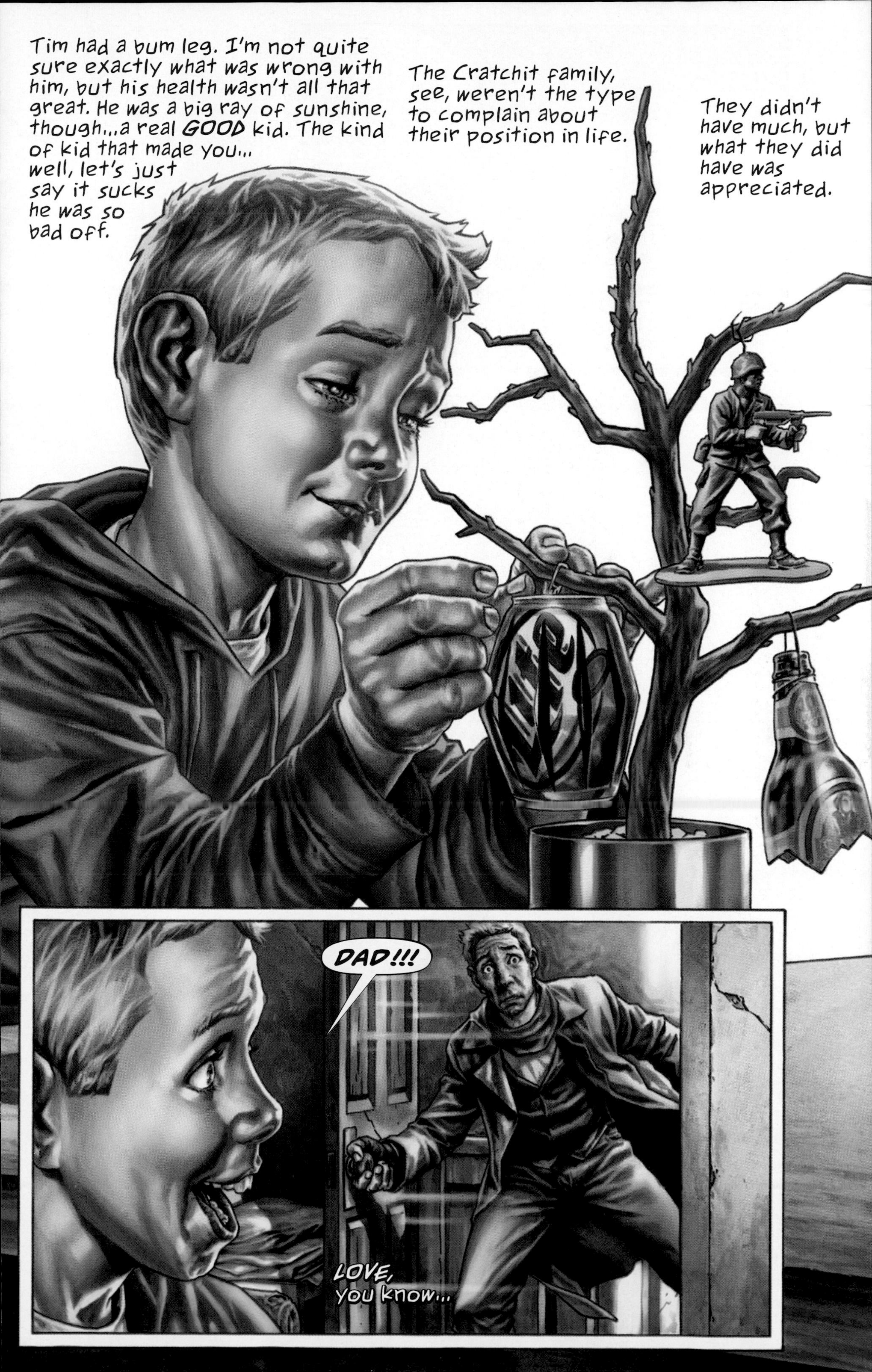
Tim had a bum leg. I'm not quite sure exactly what was wrong with him, but his health wasn't all that great. He was a big ray of sunshine, though...a real GOOD kid. The kind of kid that made you... well, let's just say it sucks he was so bad off.
The Cratchit family, see, weren't the type to complain about their position in life.
They didn't have much, but what they did have was appreciated.
DAD!!!
LOVE, you know...

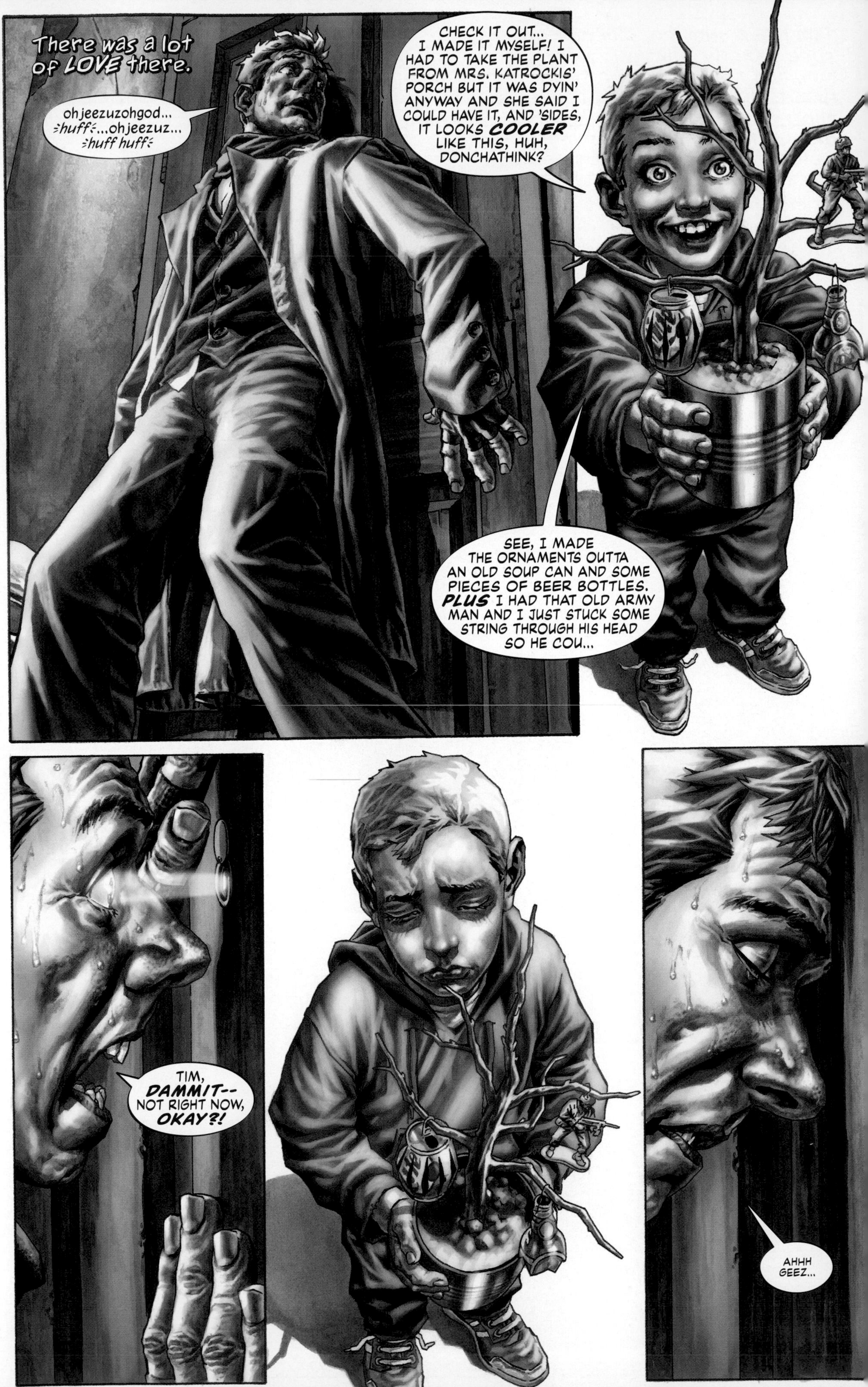
There was a lot of LOVE there.
ohjeezuzohgod... huff ...ohjeezuz... huff huff
CHECK IT OUT... I MADE IT MYSELF! I HAD TO TAKE THE PLANT FROM MRS. KATROCKIS' PORCH BUT IT WAS DYIN' ANYWAY AND SHE SAID I COULD HAVE IT, AND 'SIDES, IT LOOKS COOLER LIKE THIS, HUH, DONCHATHINK?
SEE, I MADE THE ORNAMENTS OUTTA AN OLD SOUP CAN AND SOME PIECES OF BEER BOTTLES. PLUS I HAD THAT OLD ARMY MAN AND I JUST STUCK SOME STRING THROUGH HIS HEAD SO HE COU...
TIM, DAMMIT-- NOT RIGHT NOW, OKAY?!
AHHH GEEZ...

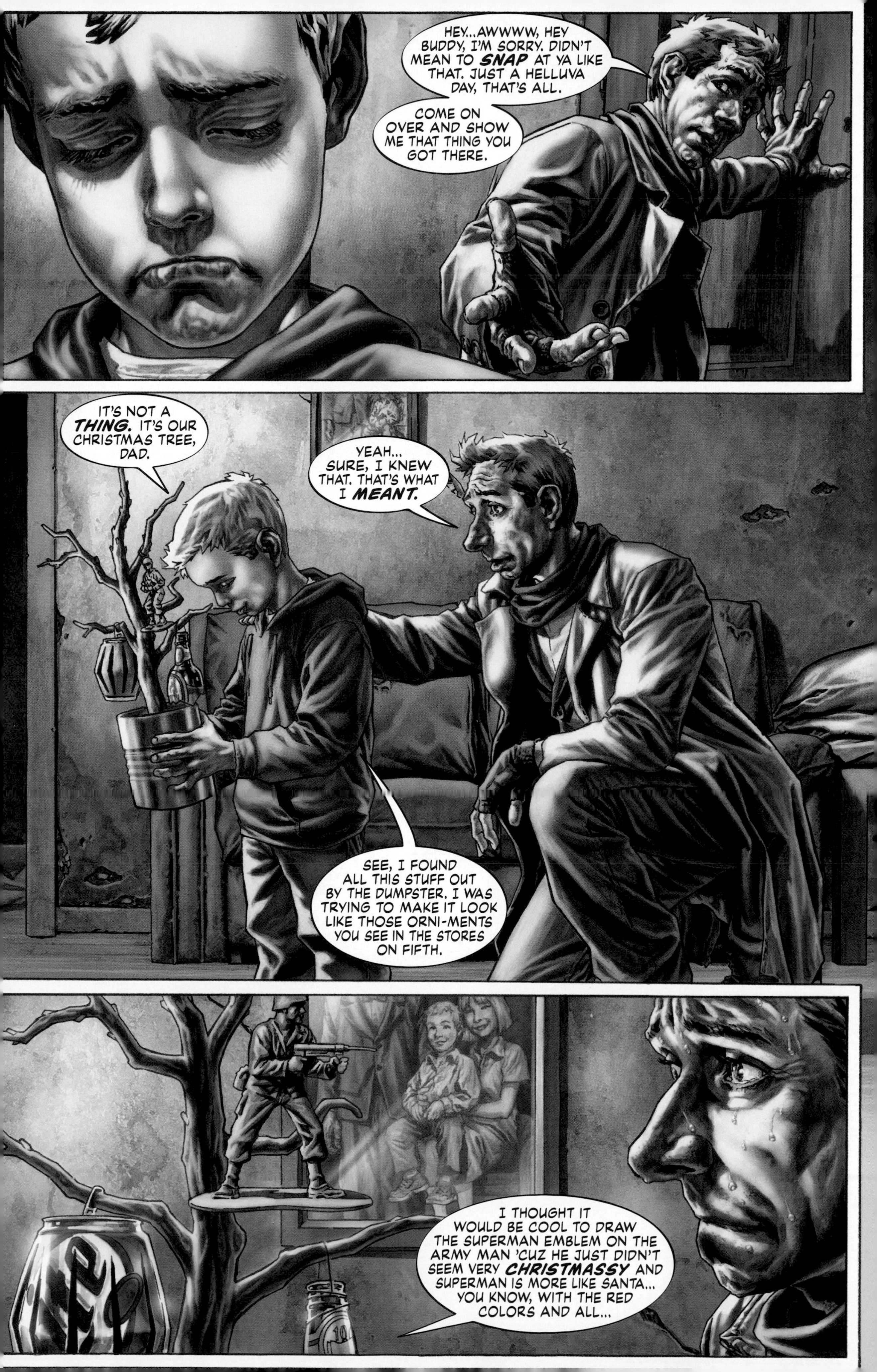
HEY...AWWWW, HEY BUDDY, I'M SORRY. DIDN'T MEAN TO SNAP AT YA LIKE THAT. JUST A HELLUVA DAY, THAT'S ALL.
COME ON OVER AND SHOW ME THAT THING YOU GOT THERE.
IT'S NOT A THING. IT'S OUR CHRISTMAS TREE, DAD.
YEAH... SURE, I KNEW THAT. THAT'S WHAT I MEANT.
SEE, I FOUND ALL THIS STUFF OUT BY THE DUMPSTER. I WAS TRYING TO MAKE IT LOOK LIKE THOSE ORNI-MENTS YOU SEE IN THE STORES ON FIFTH.
I THOUGHT IT WOULD BE COOL TO DRAW THE SUPERMAN EMBLEM ON THE ARMY MAN 'CUZ HE JUST DIDN'T SEEM VERY CHRISTMASSY AND SUPERMAN IS MORE LIKE SANTA... YOU KNOW, WITH THE RED COLORS AND ALL...

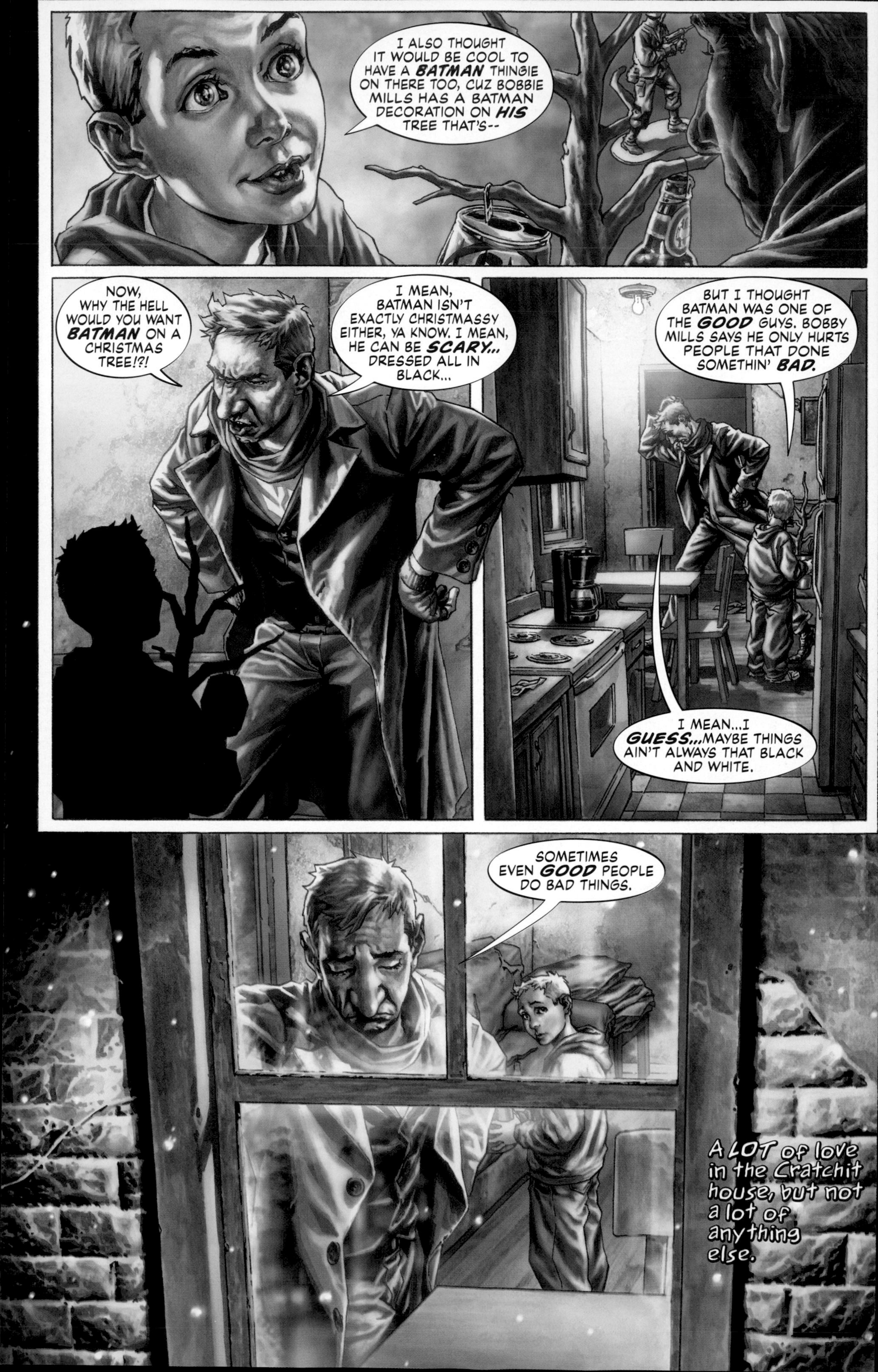
I ALSO THOUGHT IT WOULD BE COOL TO HAVE A BATMAN THINGIE ON THERE TOO, CUZ BOBBIE MILLS HAS A BATMAN DECORATION ON HIS TREE THAT'S--
NOW, WHY THE HELL WOULD YOU WANT BATMAN ON A CHRISTMAS TREE!?!
I MEAN, BATMAN ISN'T EXACTLY CHRISTMASSY EITHER, YA KNOW. I MEAN, HE CAN BE SCARY... DRESSED ALL IN BLACK...
BUT I THOUGHT BATMAN WAS ONE OF THE GOOD GUYS. BOBBY MILLS SAYS HE ONLY HURTS PEOPLE THAT DONE SOMETHIN' BAD.
I MEAN...I GUESS...MAYBE THINGS AIN'T ALWAYS THAT BLACK AND WHITE.
SOMETIMES EVEN GOOD PEOPLE DO BAD THINGS.
A LOT of love in the Cratchit house, but not a lot of anything else.

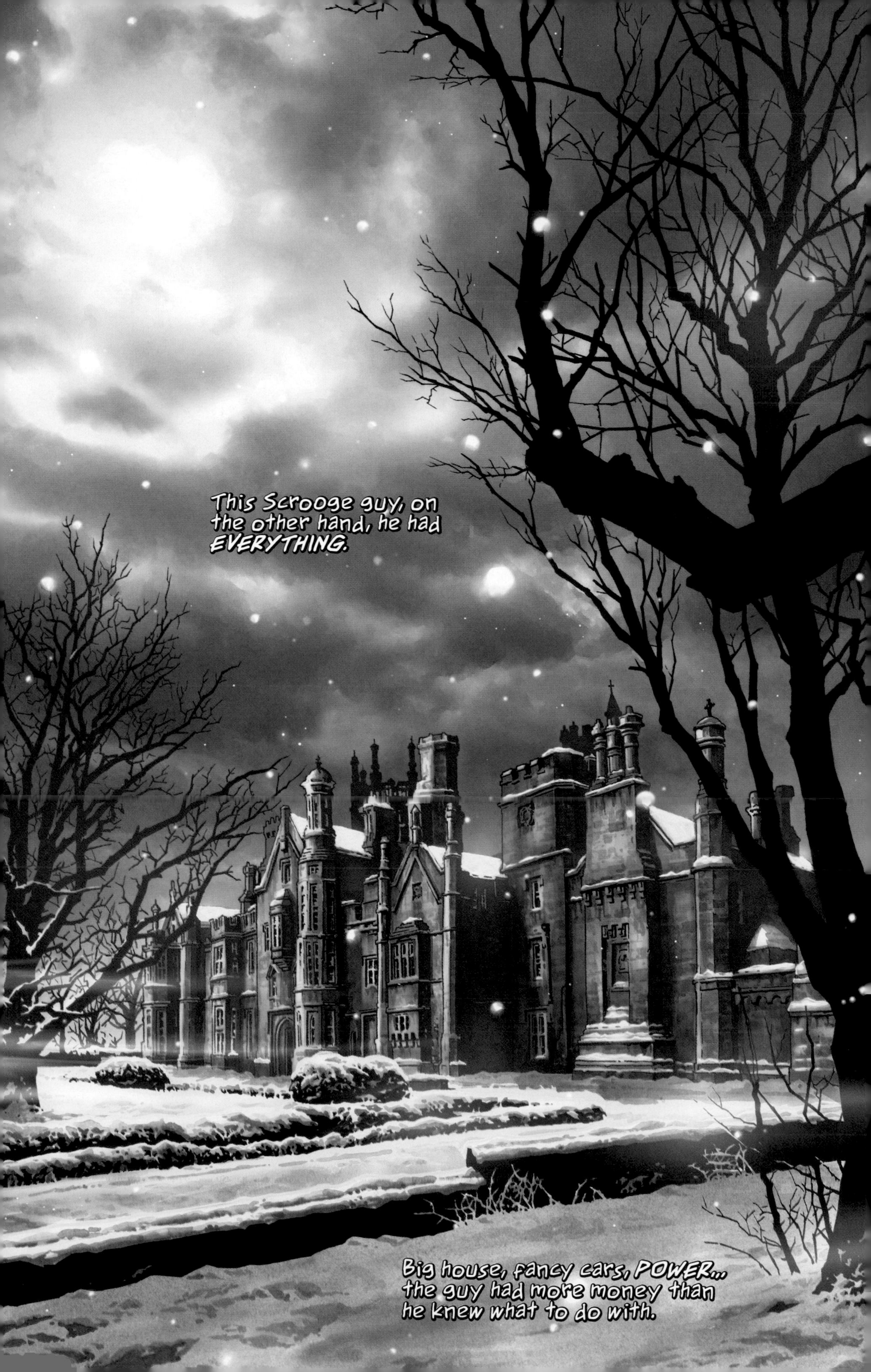
This Scrooge guy, on the other hand, he had EVERYTHING.
Big house, fancy cars, POWER... the guy had more money than he knew what to do with.

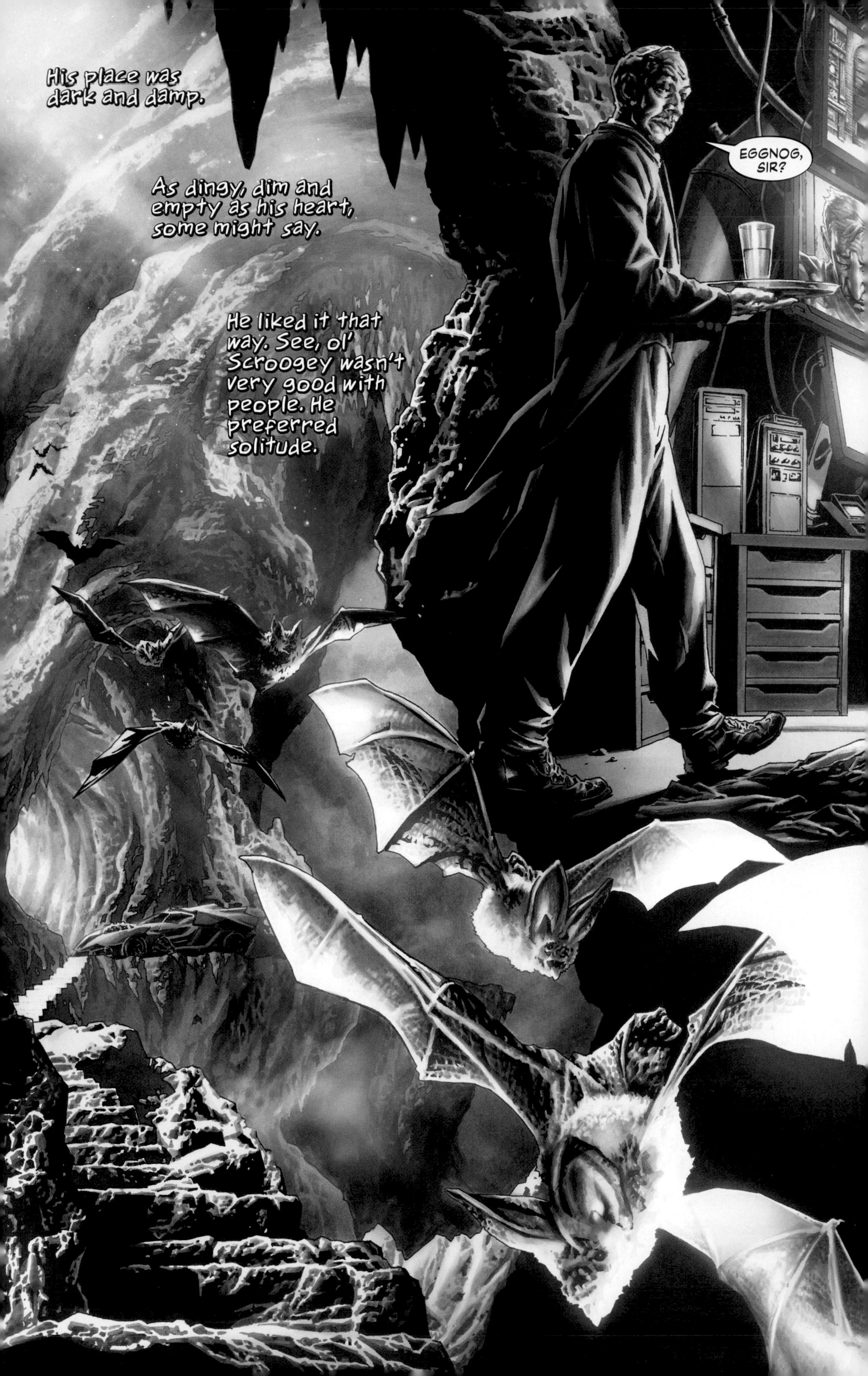
His place was dark and damp.
As dingy, dim and empty as his heart, some might say.
EGGNOG, SIR?
He liked it that way. See, ol' Scroogey wasn't very good with people. He preferred solitude.

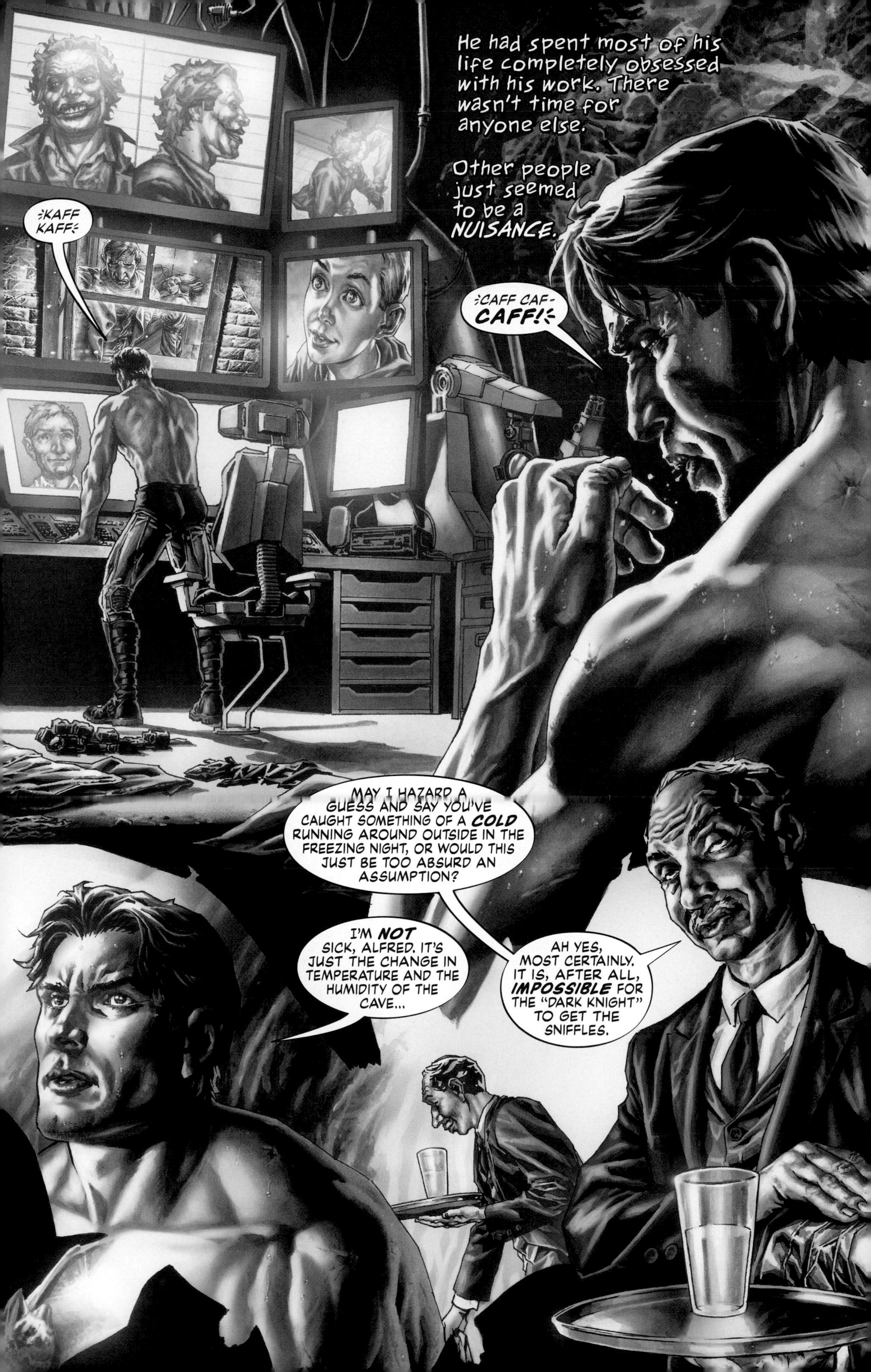
He had spent most of his life completely obsessed with his work. There wasn't time for anyone else.
Other people just seemed to be a NUISANCE.
KAFF KAFF
CAFF CAF- CAFF!
MAY I HAZARD A GUESS AND SAY YOU'VE CAUGHT SOMETHING OF A COLD RUNNING AROUND OUTSIDE IN THE FREEZING NIGHT, OR WOULD THIS JUST BE TOO ABSURD AN ASSUMPTION?
I'M NOT SICK, ALFRED. IT'S JUST THE CHANGE IN TEMPERATURE AND THE HUMIDITY OF THE CAVE...
AH YES, MOST CERTAINLY. IT IS, AFTER ALL, IMPOSSIBLE FOR THE "DARK KNIGHT" TO GET THE SNIFFLES.

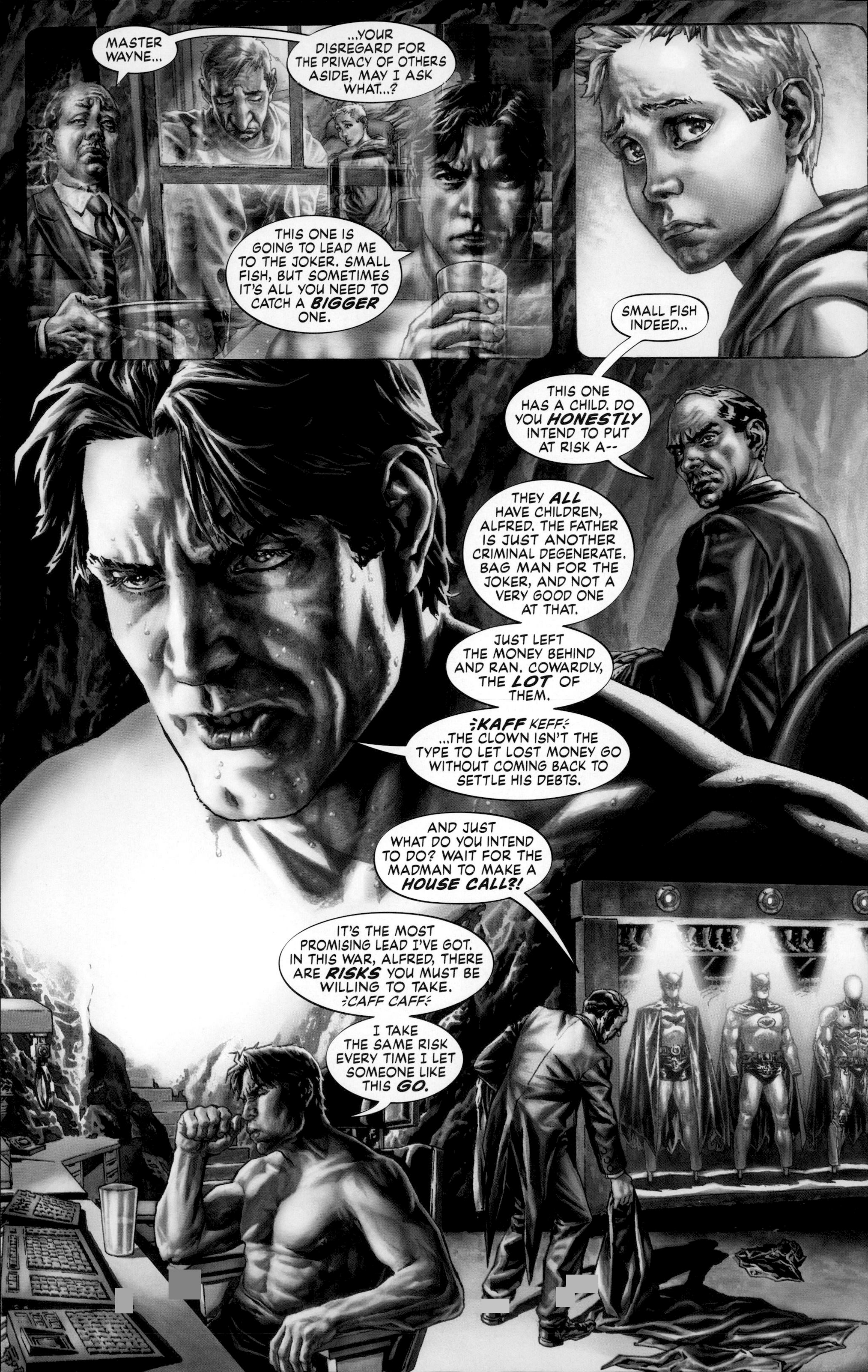
MASTER WAYNE...
...YOUR DISREGARD FOR THE PRIVACY OF OTHERS ASIDE, MAY I ASK WHAT...?
THIS ONE IS GOING TO LEAD ME TO THE JOKER. SMALL FISH, BUT SOMETIMES IT'S ALL YOU NEED TO CATCH A BIGGER ONE.
SMALL FISH INDEED...
THIS ONE HAS A CHILD. DO YOU HONESTLY INTEND TO PUT AT RISK A--
THEY ALL HAVE CHILDREN, ALFRED. THE FATHER IS JUST ANOTHER CRIMINAL DEGENERATE. BAG MAN FOR THE JOKER, AND NOT A VERY GOOD ONE AT THAT.
JUST LEFT THE MONEY BEHIND AND RAN. COWARDLY, THE LOT OF THEM.
KAFF KEFF
...THE CLOWN ISN'T THE TYPE TO LET LOST MONEY GO WITHOUT COMING BACK TO SETTLE HIS DEBTS.
AND JUST WHAT DO YOU INTEND TO DO? WAIT FOR THE MADMAN TO MAKE A HOUSE CALL?!
IT'S THE MOST PROMISING LEAD I'VE GOT. IN THIS WAR, ALFRED, THERE ARE RISKS YOU MUST BE WILLING TO TAKE.
CAFF CAFF
I TAKE THE SAME RISK EVERY TIME I LET SOMEONE LIKE THIS GO.

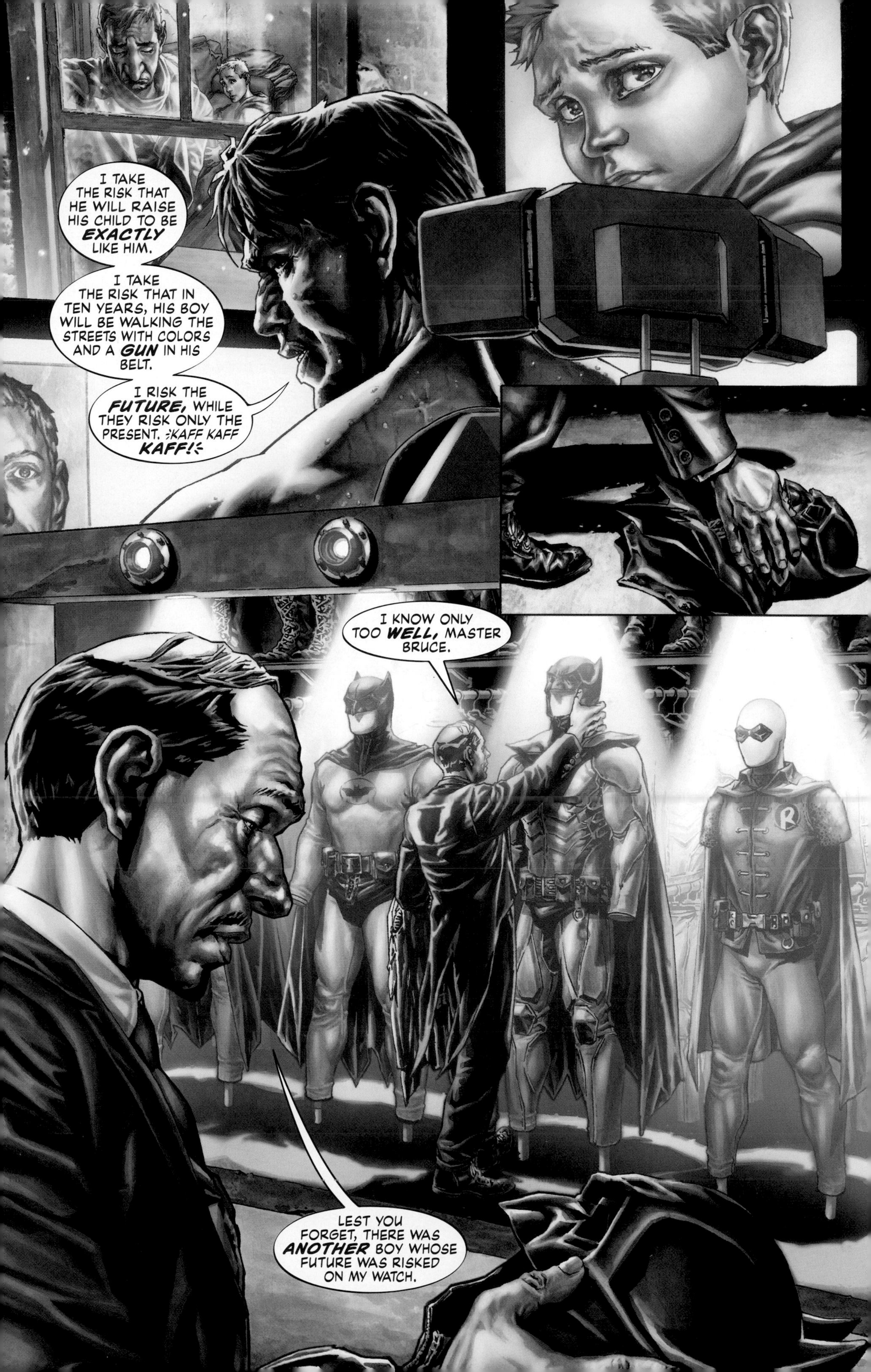
I TAKE THE RISK THAT HE WILL RAISE HIS CHILD TO BE EXACTLY LIKE HIM.
I TAKE THE RISK THAT IN TEN YEARS, HIS BOY WILL BE WALKING THE STREETS WITH COLORS AND A GUN IN HIS BELT.
I RISK THE FUTURE, WHILE THEY RISK ONLY THE PRESENT. KAFF KAFF KAFF!
I KNOW ONLY TOO WELL, MASTER BRUCE.
LEST YOU FORGET, THERE WAS ANOTHER BOY WHOSE FUTURE WAS RISKED ON MY WATCH.

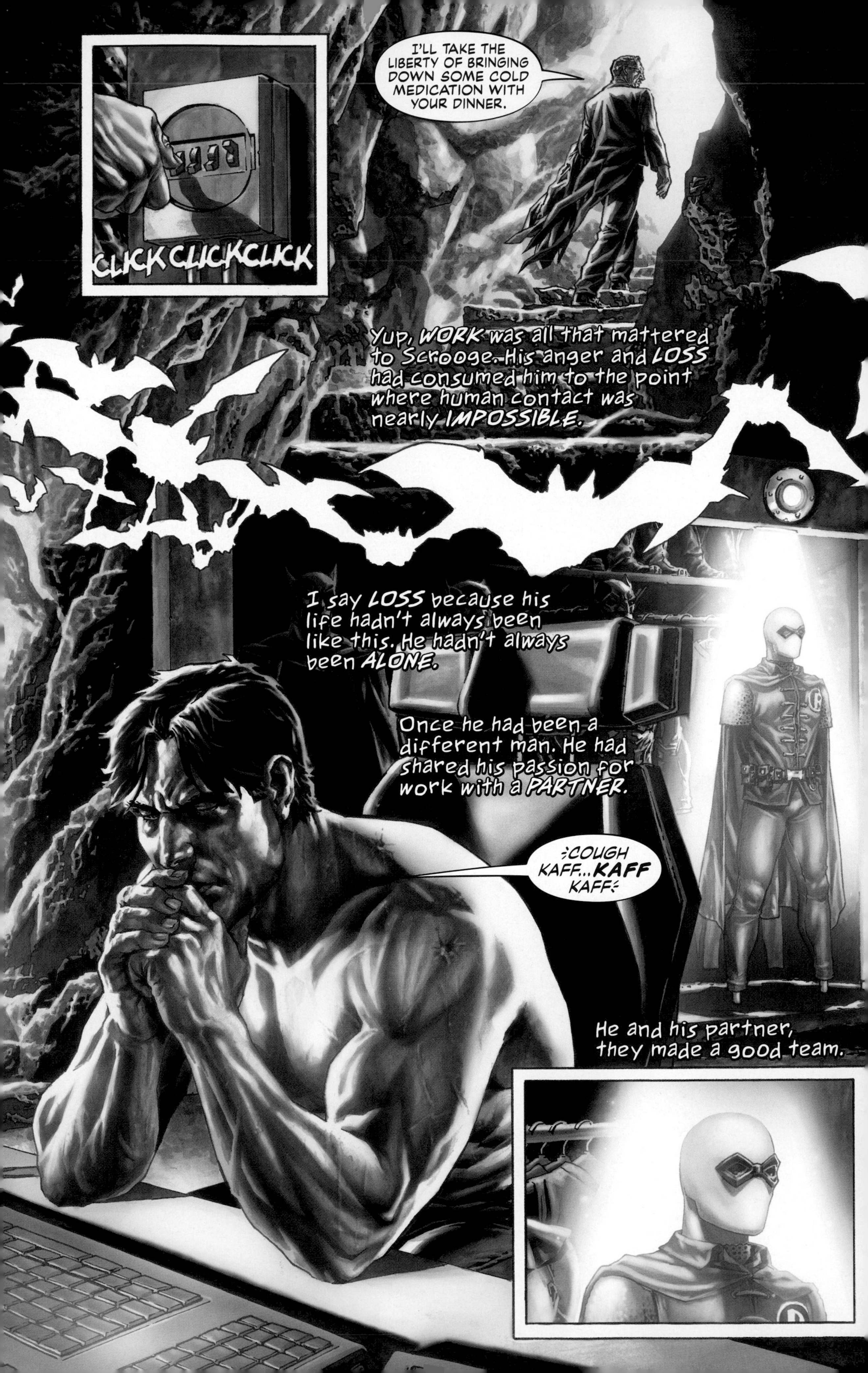
CLICK CLICK CLICK
I'LL TAKE THE LIBERTY OF BRINGING DOWN SOME COLD MEDICATION WITH YOUR DINNER.
Yup, WORK was all that mattered to Scrooge. His anger and LOSS had consumed him to the point where human contact was nearly IMPOSSIBLE.
I say LOSS because his life hadn't always been like this. He hadn't always been ALONE.
Once he had been a different man. He had shared his passion for work with a PARTNER.
COUGH KAFF...KAFF KAFF
He and his partner, they made a good team.

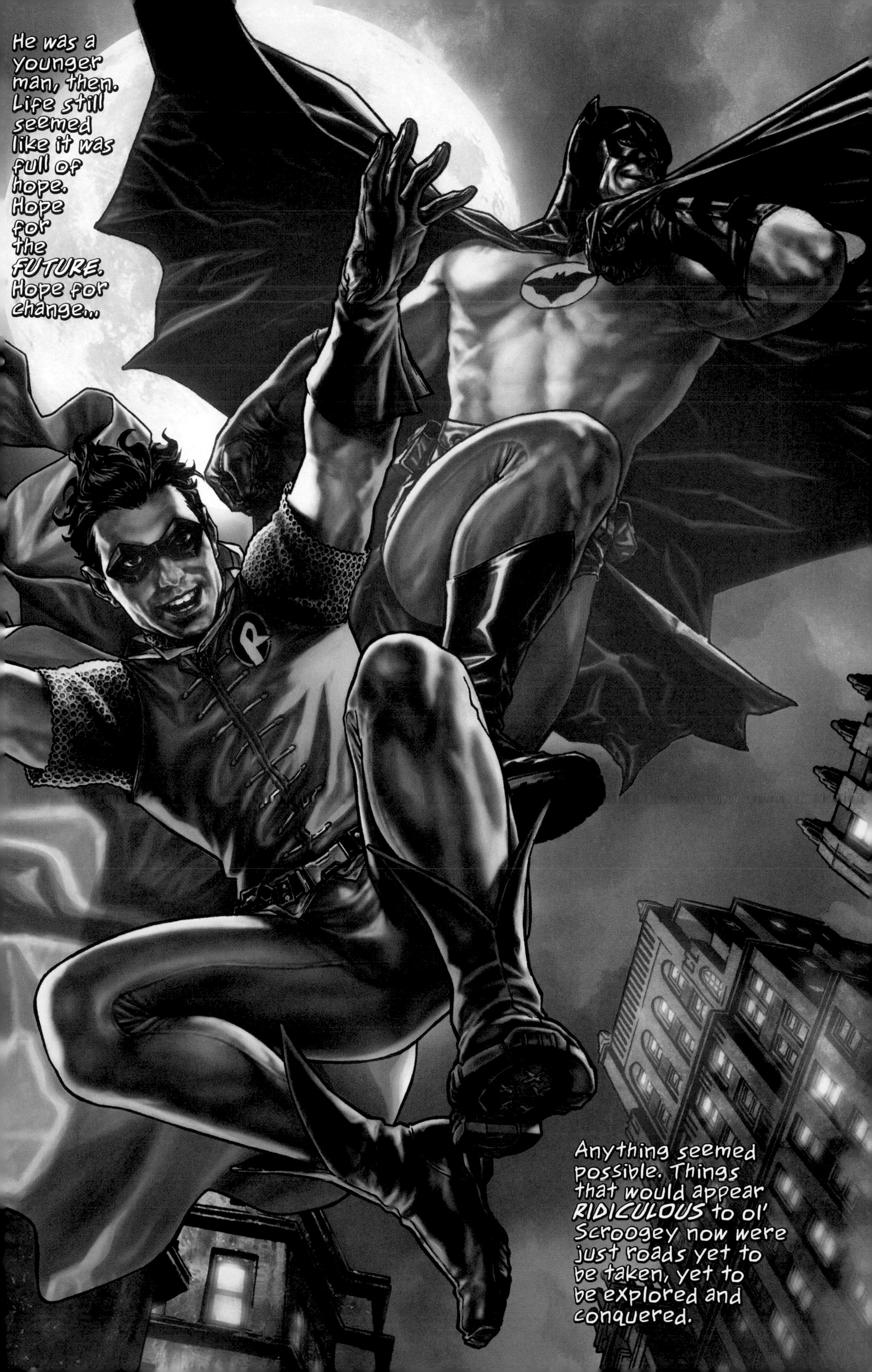
He was a younger man, then. Life still seemed like it was full of hope. Hope for the FUTURE. Hope for change...
Anything seemed possible. Things that would appear RIDICULOUS to ol' Scroogey now were just roads yet to be taken, yet to be explored and conquered.

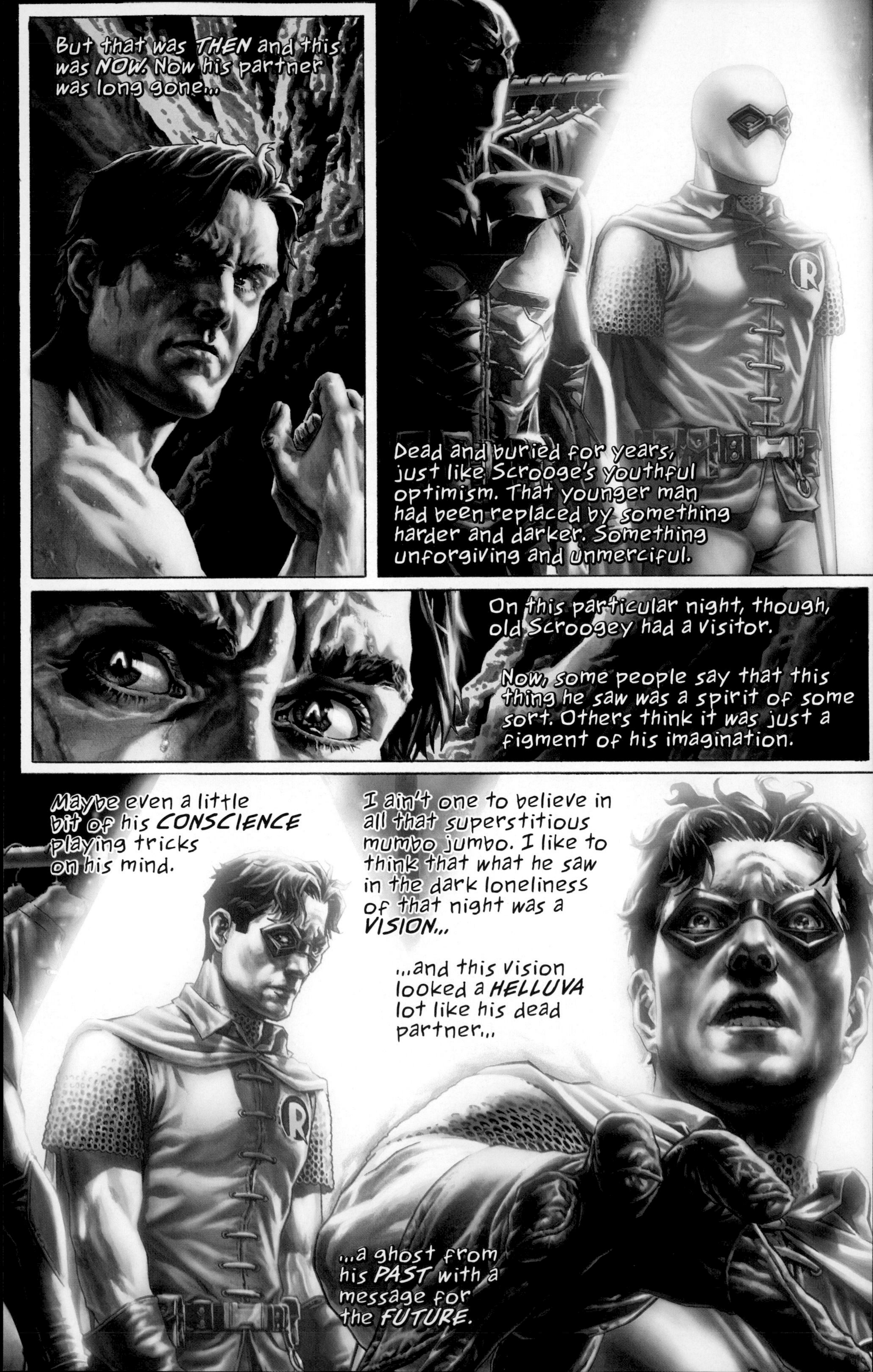
But that was THEN and this was NOW. Now his partner was long gone...
Dead and buried for years, just like Scrooge's youthful optimism. That younger man had been replaced by something harder and darker. Something unforgiving and unmerciful.
On this particular night, though, old Scroogey had a visitor.
Now, some people say that this thing he saw was a spirit of some sort. Others think it was just a figment of his imagination.
Maybe even a little bit of his CONSCIENCE playing tricks on his mind.
I ain't one to believe in all that superstitious mumbo jumbo. I like to think that what he saw in the dark loneliness of that night was a VISION...
...and this vision looked a HELLUVA lot like his dead partner...
...a ghost from his PAST with a message for the FUTURE.

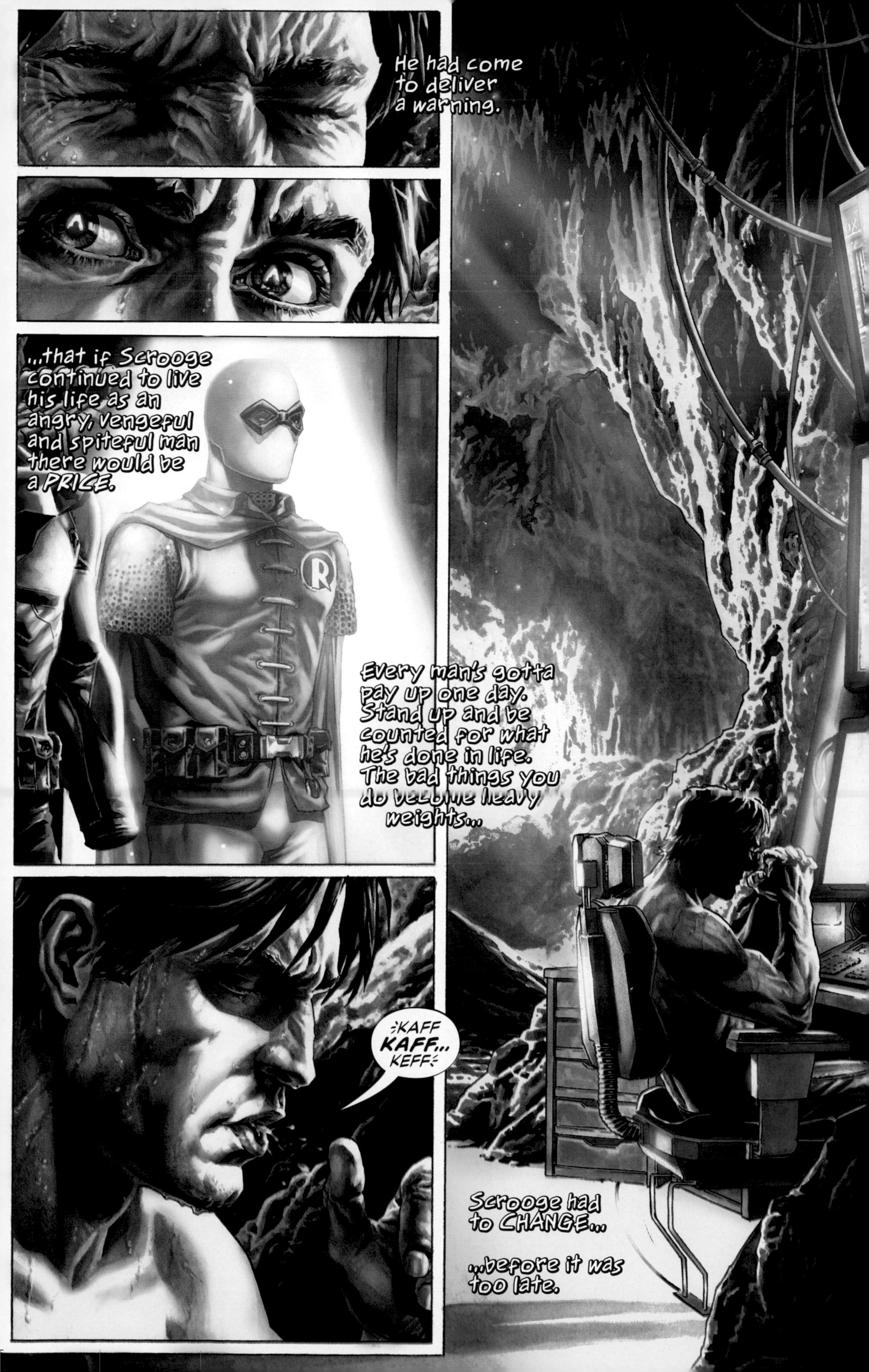
He had come to deliver a warning.
...that if Scrooge continued to live his life as an angry, vengeful and spiteful man there would be a PRICE.
Every man's gotta pay up one day. Stand up and be counted for what he's done in life. The bad things you do become heavy weights...
KAFF KAFF... KEFF
Scrooge had to CHANGE...
...before it was too late.

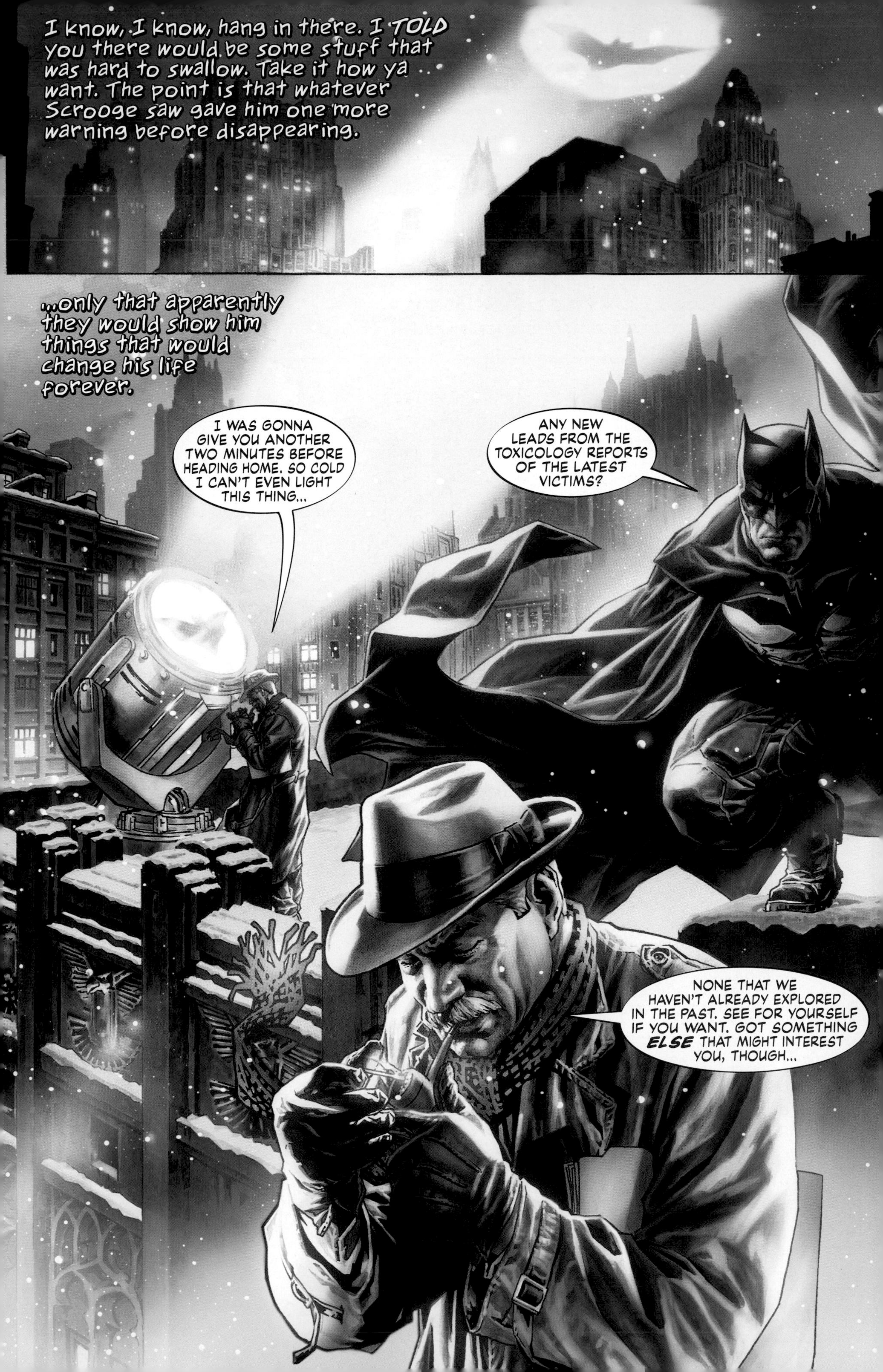

I know, I know, hang in there. I TOLD you there would be some stuff that was hard to swallow. Take it how ya want. The point is that whatever Scrooge saw gave him one more warning before disappearing.
...only that apparently they would show him things that would change his life forever.
I WAS GONNA GIVE YOU ANOTHER TWO MINUTES BEFORE HEADING HOME. SO COLD I CAN'T EVEN LIGHT THIS THING...
ANY NEW LEADS FROM THE TOXICOLOGY REPORTS OF THE LATEST VICTIMS?
NONE THAT WE HAVEN'T ALREADY EXPLORED IN THE PAST. SEE FOR YOURSELF IF YOU WANT. GOT SOMETHING ELSE THAT MIGHT INTEREST YOU, THOUGH...

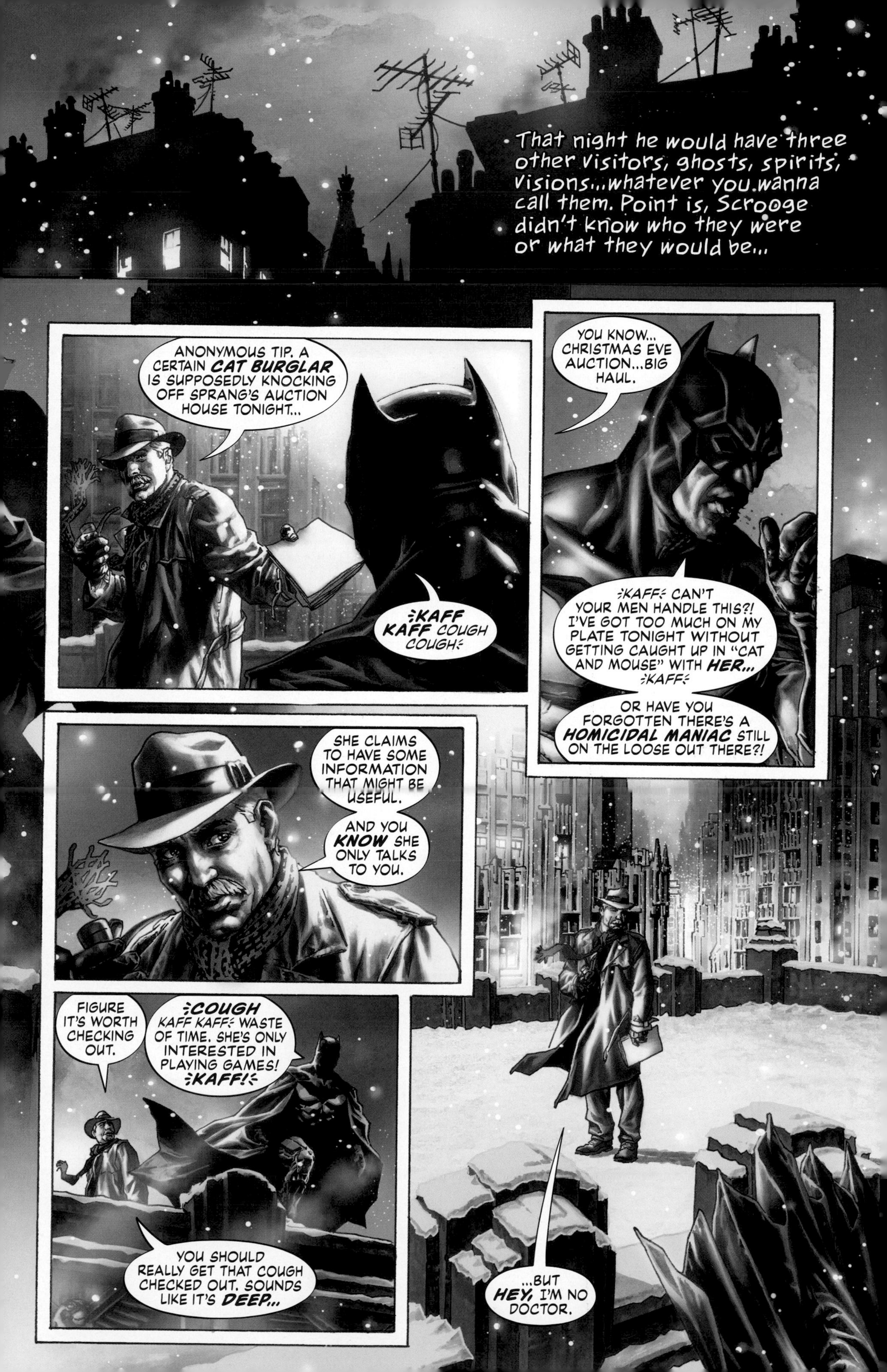
That night he would have three other visitors, ghosts, spirits, visions...whatever you wanna call them. Point is, Scrooge didn't know who they were or what they would be...
ANONYMOUS TIP. A CERTAIN CAT BURGLAR IS SUPPOSEDLY KNOCKING OFF SPRANG'S AUCTION HOUSE TONIGHT...
KAFF KAFF COUGH COUGH
YOU KNOW... CHRISTMAS EVE AUCTION...BIG HAUL.
KAFF CAN'T YOUR MEN HANDLE THIS?! I'VE GOT TOO MUCH ON MY PLATE TONIGHT WITHOUT GETTING CAUGHT UP IN "CAT AND MOUSE" WITH HER... KAFF
OR HAVE YOU FORGOTTEN THERE'S A HOMICIDAL MANIAC STILL ON THE LOOSE OUT THERE?!
SHE CLAIMS TO HAVE SOME INFORMATION THAT MIGHT BE USEFUL.
AND YOU KNOW SHE ONLY TALKS TO YOU.
FIGURE IT'S WORTH CHECKING OUT.
COUGH KAFF KAFF WASTE OF TIME. SHE'S ONLY INTERESTED IN PLAYING GAMES! KAFF!
YOU SHOULD REALLY GET THAT COUGH CHECKED OUT. SOUNDS LIKE IT'S DEEP...
...BUT HEY, I'M NO DOCTOR.

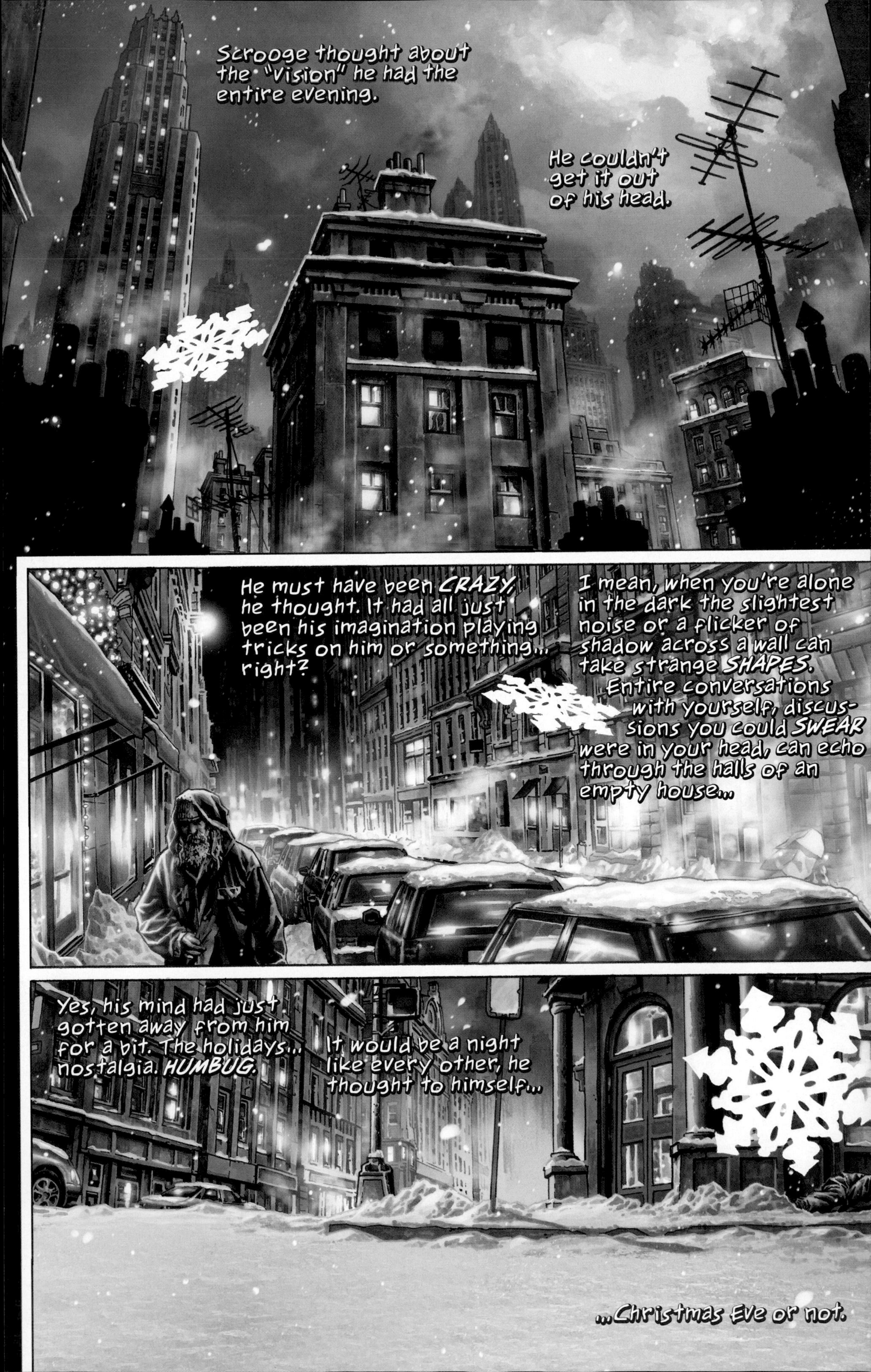
Scrooge thought about the "vision" he had the entire evening.
He couldn't get it out of his head.
He must have been CRAZY, he thought. It had all just been his imagination playing tricks on him or something... right?
I mean, when you're alone in the dark the slightest noise or a flicker of shadow across a wall can take strange SHAPES.
Entire conversations with yourself, discussions you could SWEAR were in your head, can echo through the halls of an empty house...
Yes, his mind had just gotten away from him for a bit. The holidays... nostalgia. HUMBUG.
It would be a night like every other, he thought to himself...
...Christmas Eve or not.

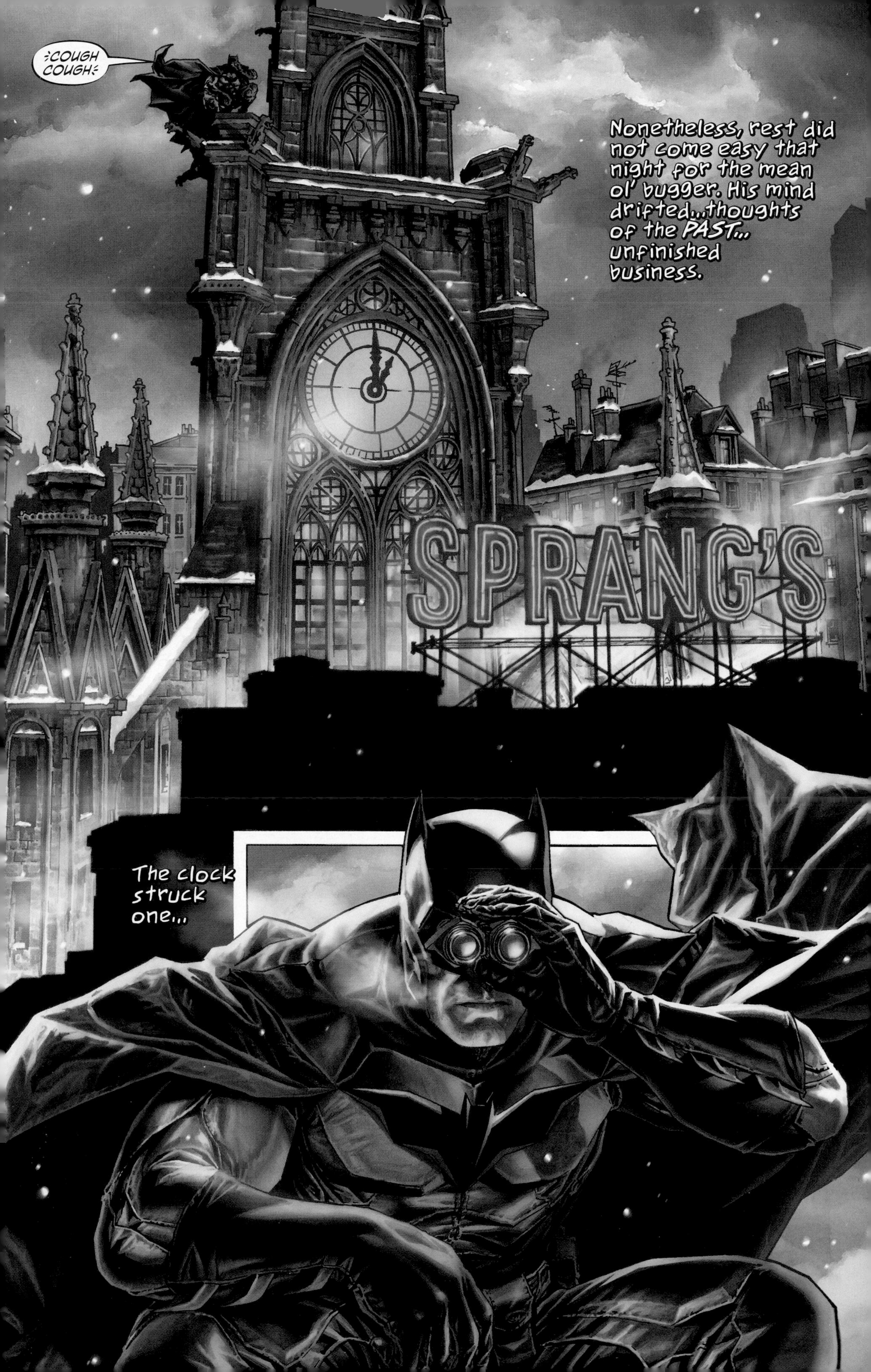
:COUGH COUGH:
Nonetheless, rest did not come easy that night for the mean ol' bugger. His mind drifted...thoughts of the PAST... unfinished business.
SPRANG'S
The clock struck one...

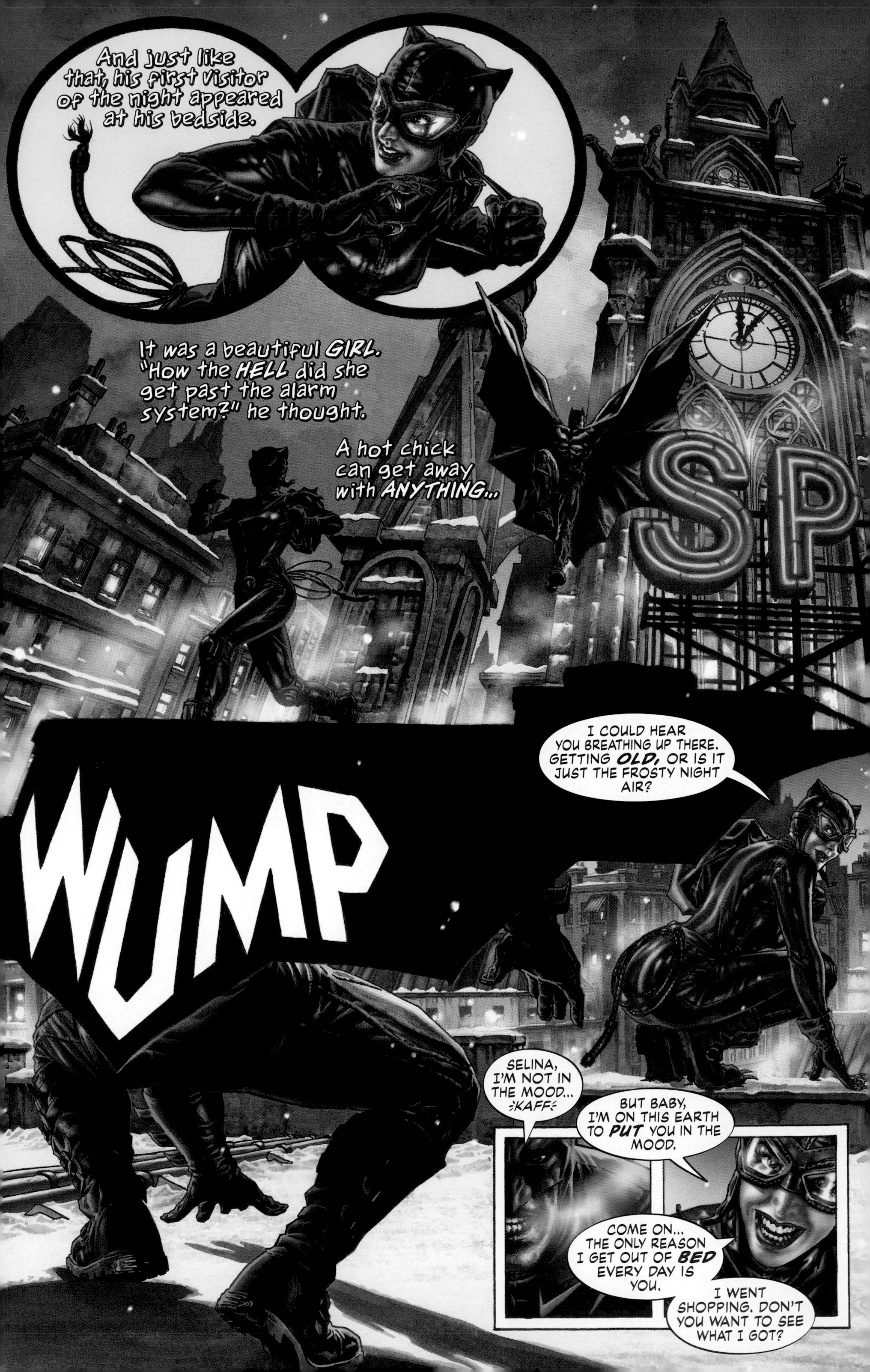
And just like that, his first visitor of the night appeared at his bedside.
It was a beautiful GIRL. "How the HELL did she get past the alarm system?" he thought.
A hot chick can get away with ANYTHING...
SP
WUMP
I COULD HEAR YOU BREATHING UP THERE. GETTING OLD, OR IS IT JUST THE FROSTY NIGHT AIR?
SELINA, I'M NOT IN THE MOOD... KAFF
BUT BABY, I'M ON THIS EARTH TO PUT YOU IN THE MOOD.
COME ON... THE ONLY REASON I GET OUT OF BED EVERY DAY IS YOU.
I WENT SHOPPING. DON'T YOU WANT TO SEE WHAT I GOT?

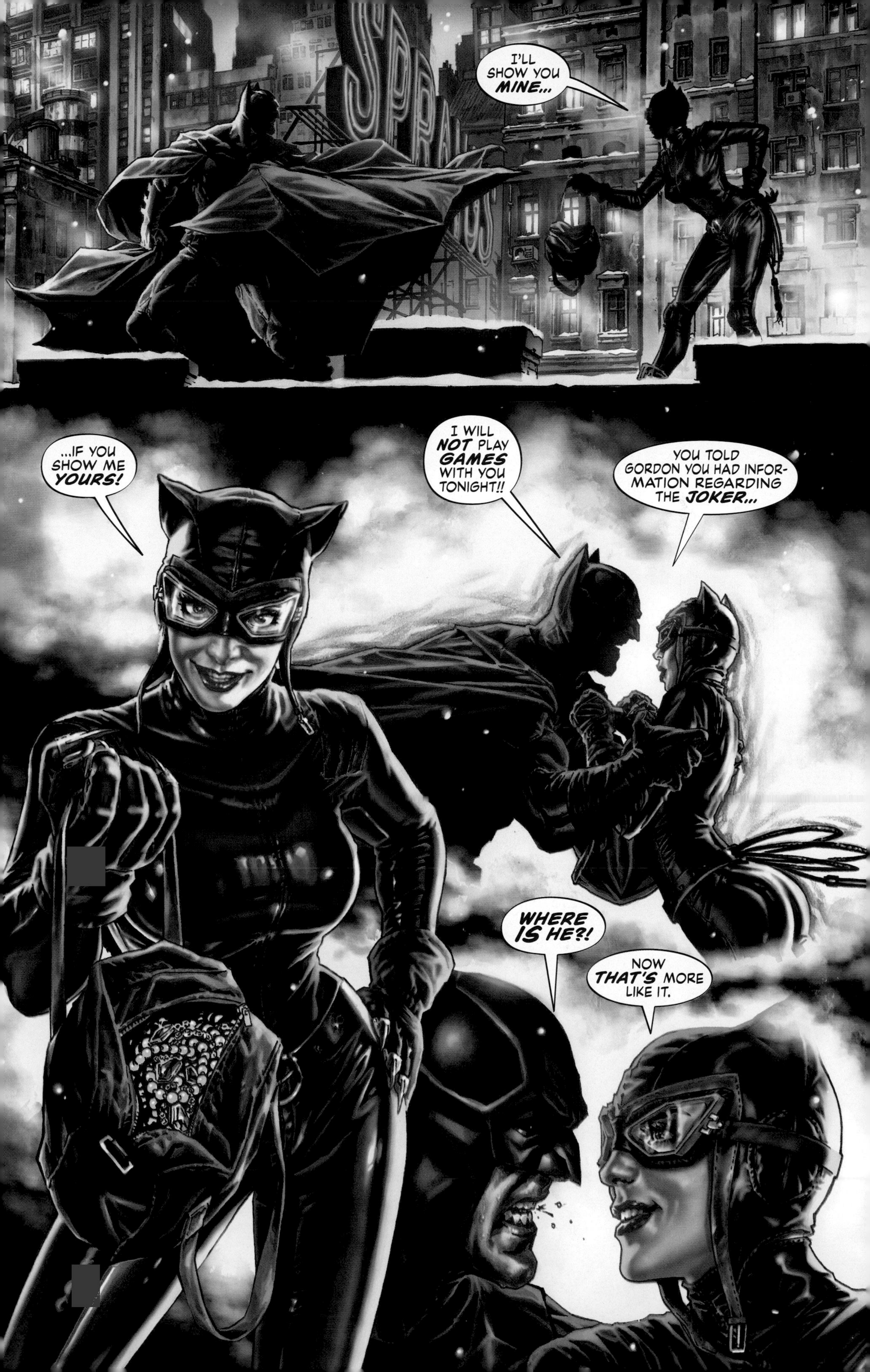
I'LL SHOW YOU MINE...
...IF YOU SHOW ME YOURS!
I WILL NOT PLAY GAMES WITH YOU TONIGHT!!
YOU TOLD GORDON YOU HAD INFORMATION REGARDING THE JOKER...
WHERE IS HE?!
NOW THAT'S MORE LIKE IT.

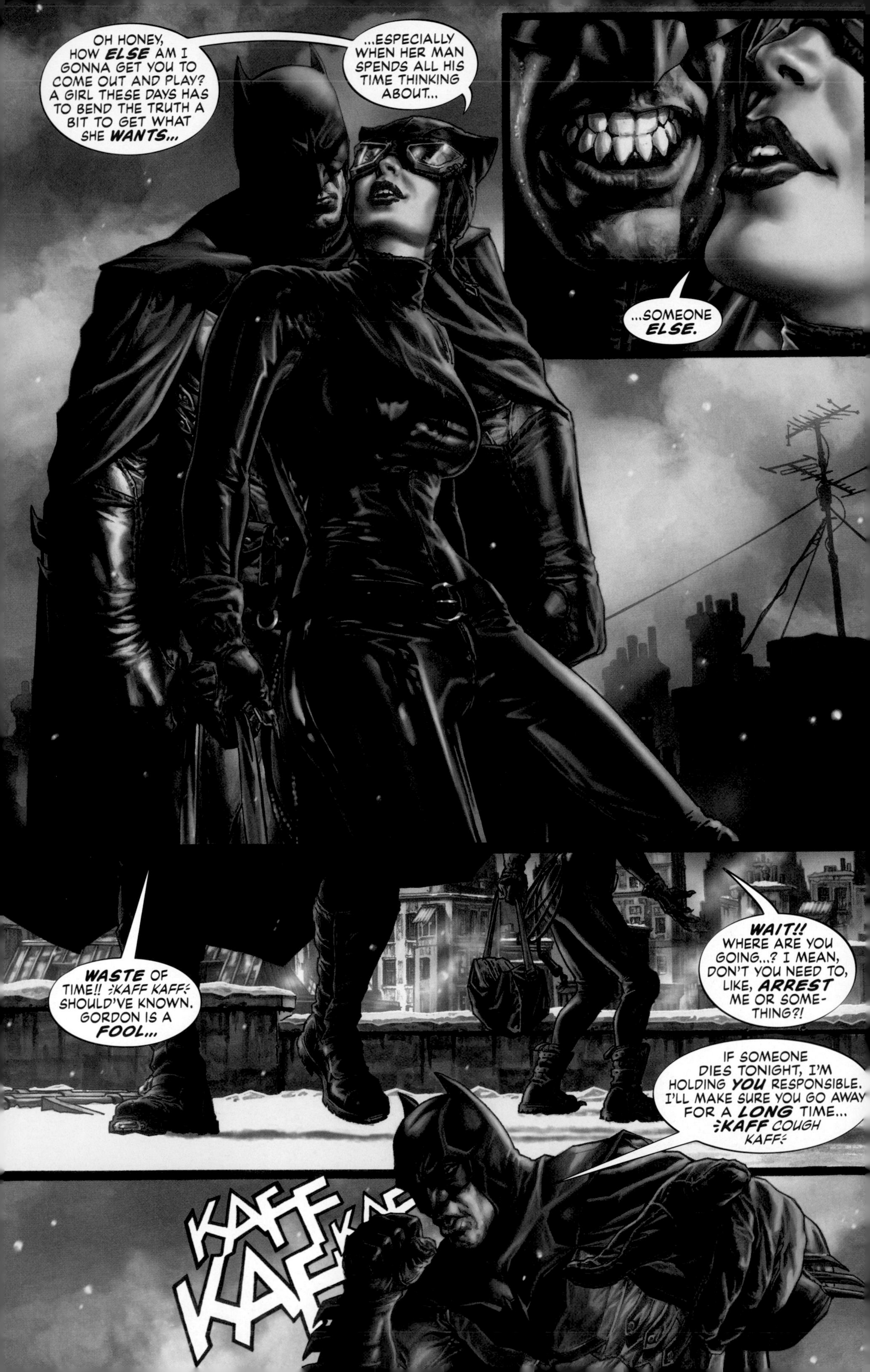
OH HONEY, HOW ELSE AM I GONNA GET YOU TO COME OUT AND PLAY? A GIRL THESE DAYS HAS TO BEND THE TRUTH A BIT TO GET WHAT SHE WANTS...
...ESPECIALLY WHEN HER MAN SPENDS ALL HIS TIME THINKING ABOUT...
...SOMEONE ELSE.
WASTE OF TIME!! KAFF KAFF SHOULD'VE KNOWN. GORDON IS A FOOL...
WAIT!! WHERE ARE YOU GOING...? I MEAN, DON'T YOU NEED TO, LIKE, ARREST ME OR SOME-THING?!
IF SOMEONE DIES TONIGHT, I'M HOLDING YOU RESPONSIBLE. I'LL MAKE SURE YOU GO AWAY FOR A LONG TIME... KAFF COUGH KAFF
KAFF
KAFF

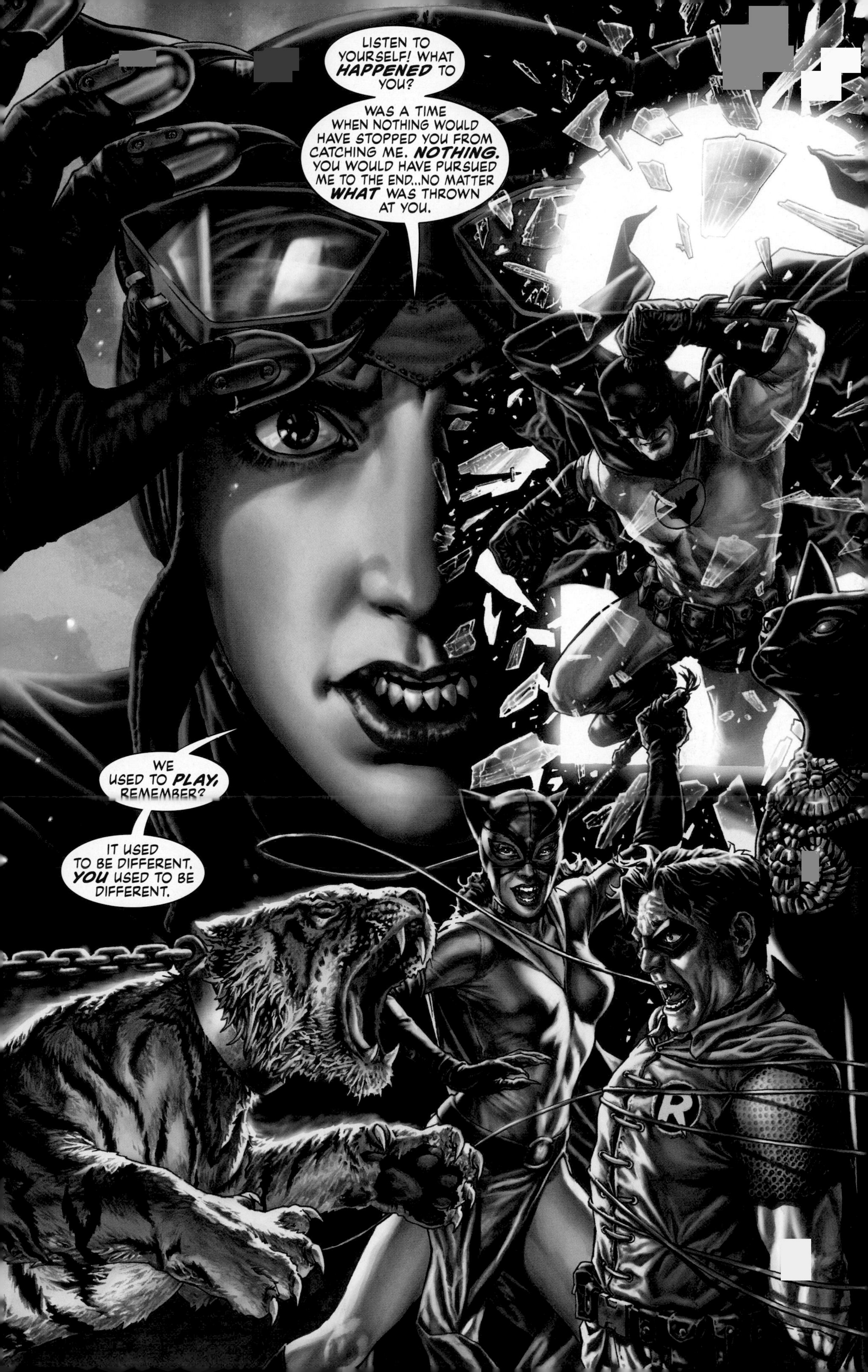
LISTEN TO YOURSELF! WHAT HAPPENED TO YOU?
WAS A TIME WHEN NOTHING WOULD HAVE STOPPED YOU FROM CATCHING ME. NOTHING. YOU WOULD HAVE PURSUED ME TO THE END...NO MATTER WHAT WAS THROWN AT YOU.
WE USED TO PLAY, REMEMBER?
IT USED TO BE DIFFERENT. YOU USED TO BE DIFFERENT.

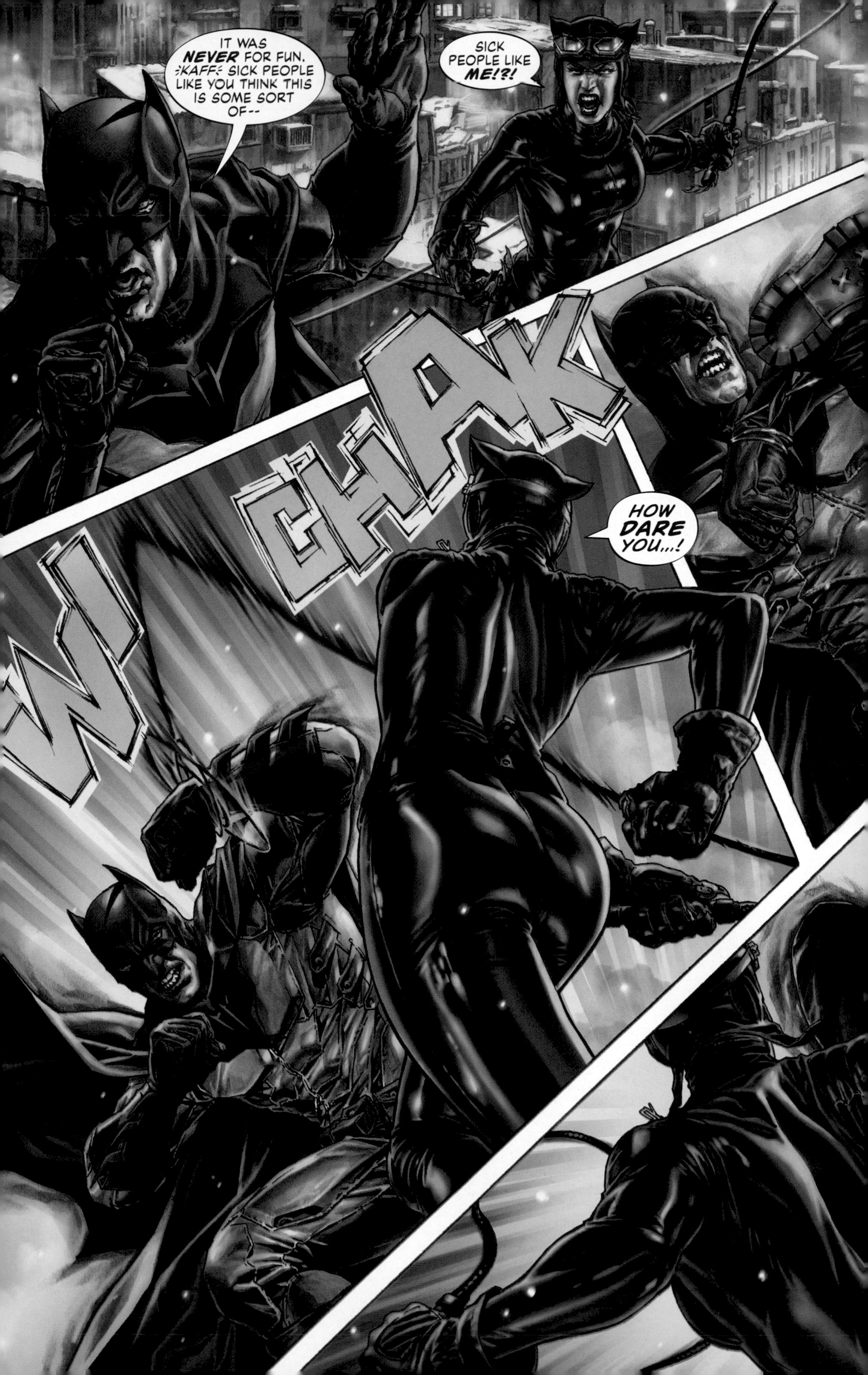

IT WAS NEVER FOR FUN. ⚡KAFF⚡ SICK PEOPLE LIKE YOU THINK THIS IS SOME SORT OF--
SICK PEOPLE LIKE ME!?!
WHACHAK
HOW DARE YOU...!

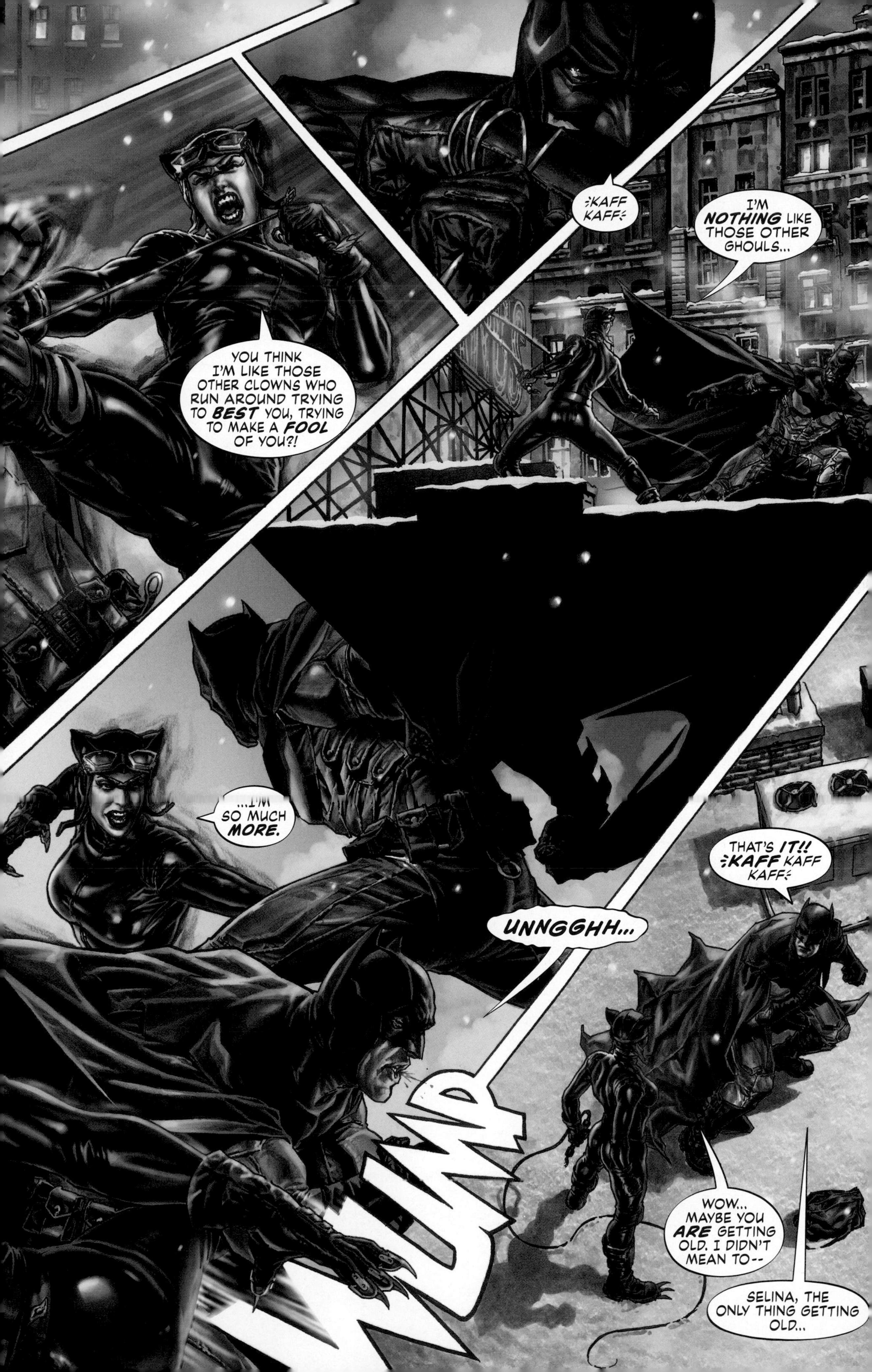

YOU THINK I'M LIKE THOSE OTHER CLOWNS WHO RUN AROUND TRYING TO BEST YOU, TRYING TO MAKE A FOOL OF YOU?!
KAFF KAFF
I'M NOTHING LIKE THOSE OTHER GHOULS...
...I'M SO MUCH MORE.
UNNGGHH...
WUMP
THAT'S IT!! KAFF KAFF KAFF
WOW... MAYBE YOU ARE GETTING OLD. I DIDN'T MEAN TO--
SELINA, THE ONLY THING GETTING OLD...

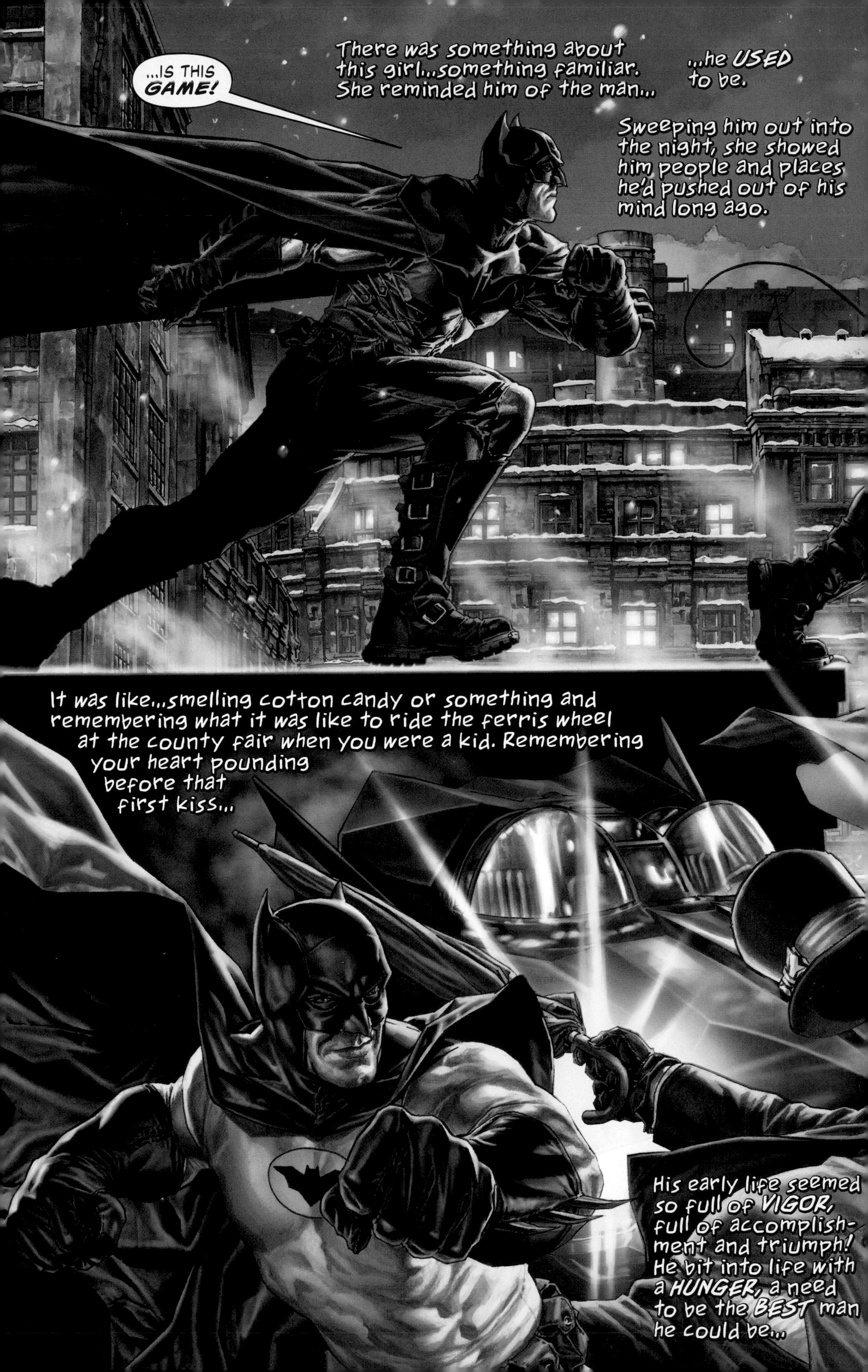

...IS THIS GAME!
There was something about this girl...something familiar. She reminded him of the man...
...he USED to be.
Sweeping him out into the night, she showed him people and places he'd pushed out of his mind long ago.
It was like...smelling cotton candy or something and remembering what it was like to ride the ferris wheel at the county fair when you were a kid. Remembering your heart pounding before that first kiss...
His early life seemed so full of VIGOR, full of accomplishment and triumph! He bit into life with a HUNGER, a need to be the BEST man he could be...

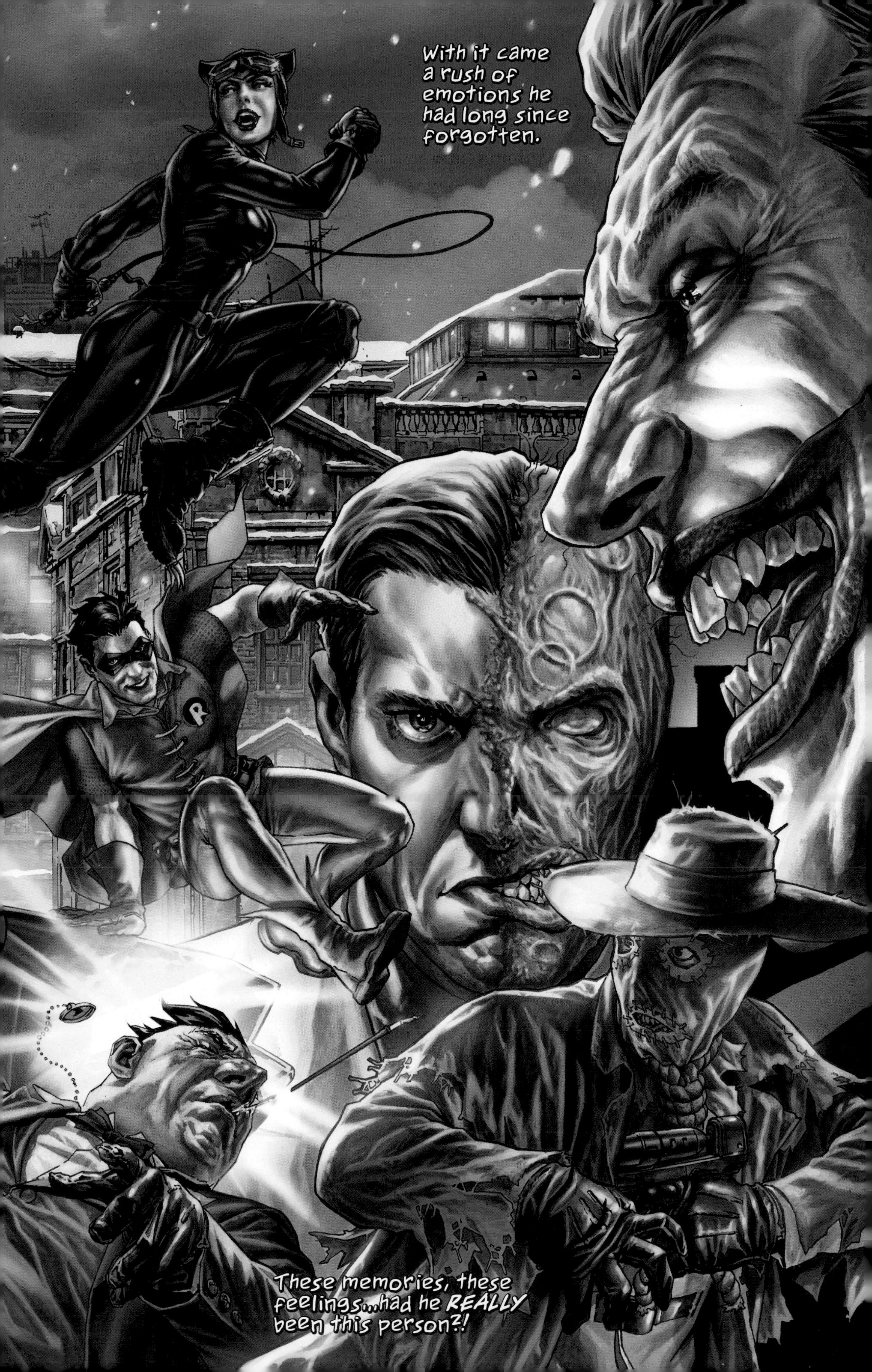
With it came a rush of emotions he had long since forgotten.
These memories, these feelings...had he REALLY been this person?!

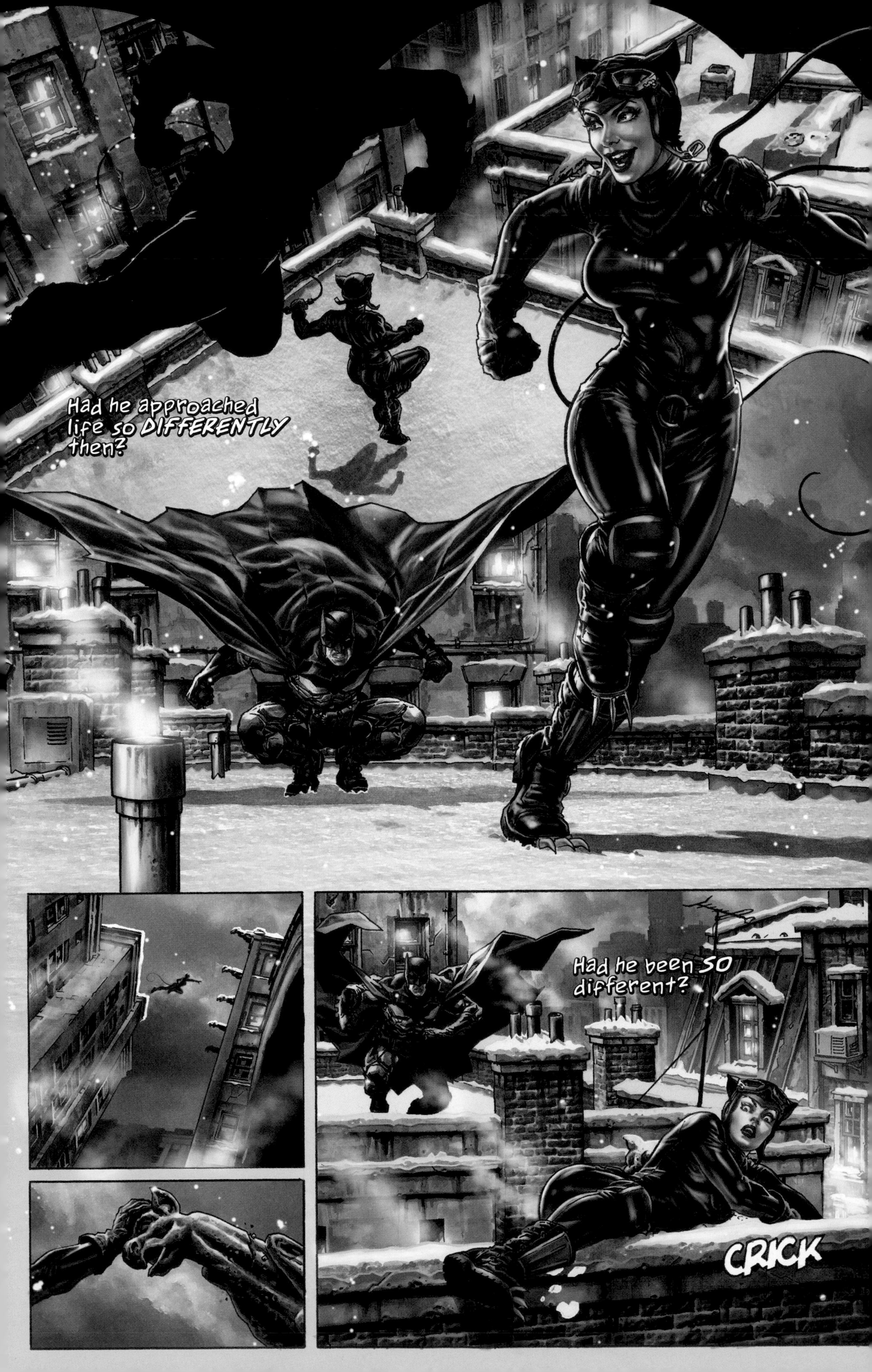

Had he approached life so DIFFERENTLY then?
Had he been SO different?
CRICK

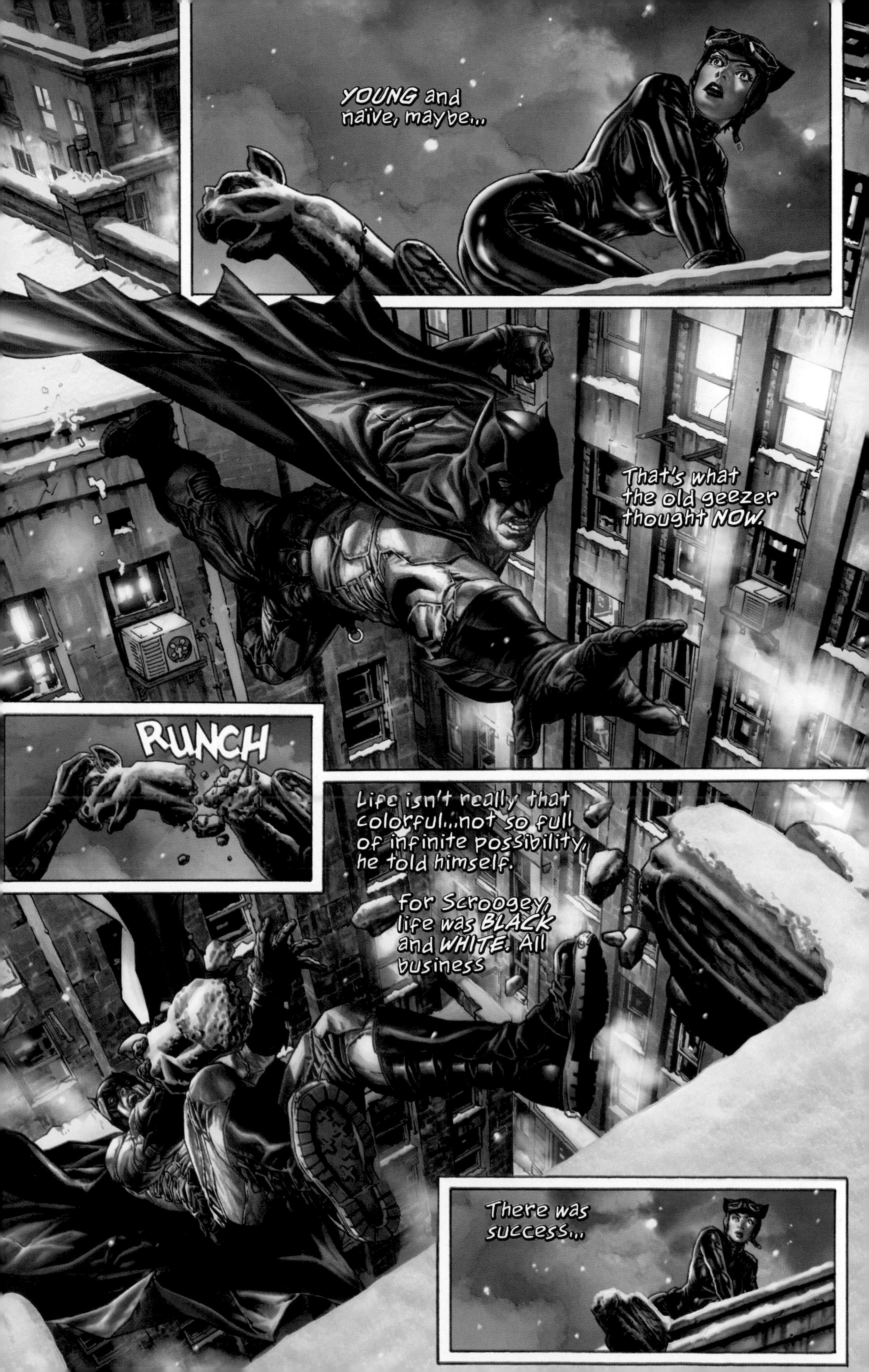
YOUNG and naive, maybe...
That's what the old geezer thought NOW.
RUNCH
Life isn't really that colorful...not so full of infinite possibility, he told himself.
For Scroogey, life was BLACK and WHITE. All business
There was success...

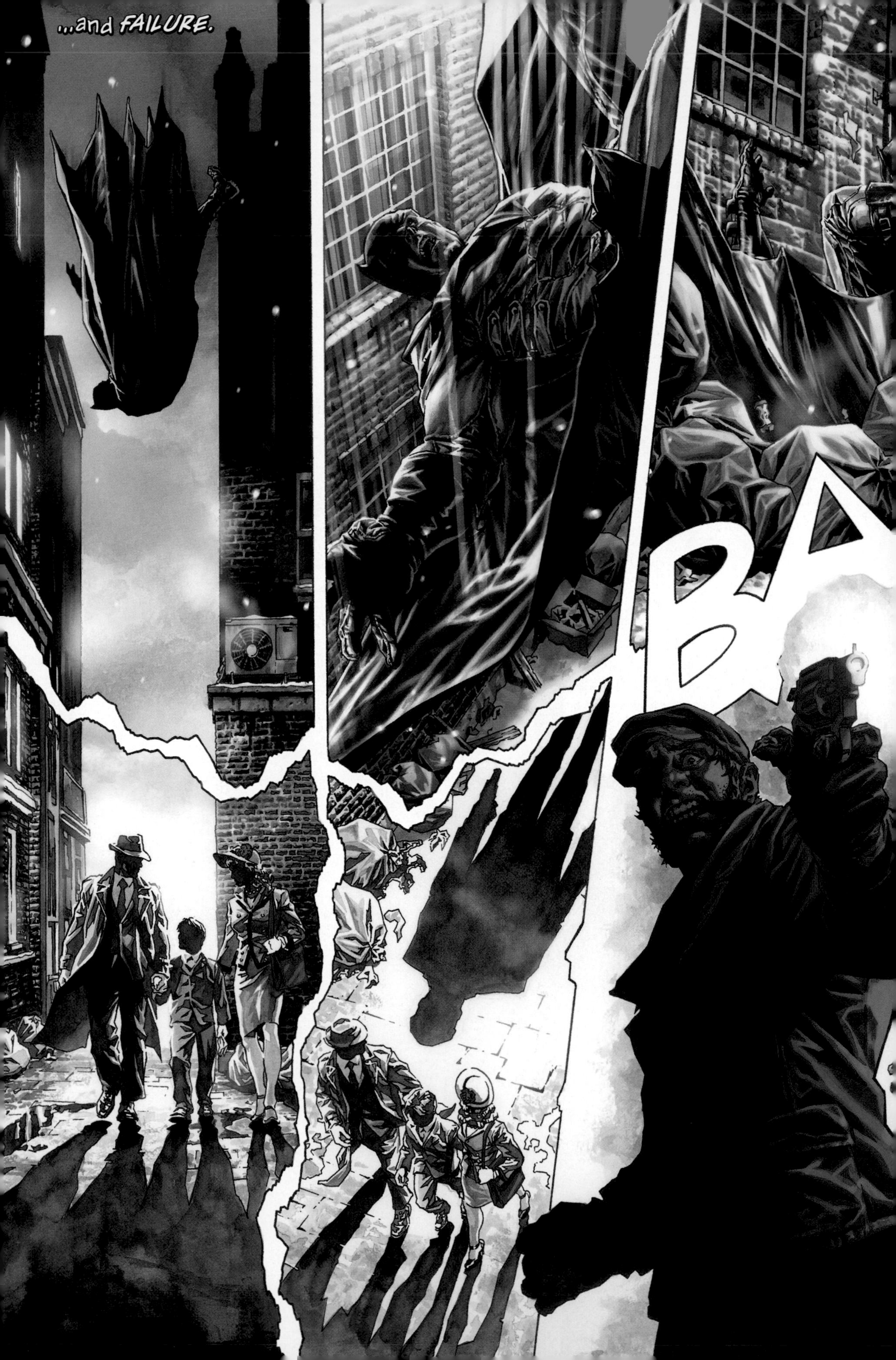
...and FAILURE.
BA

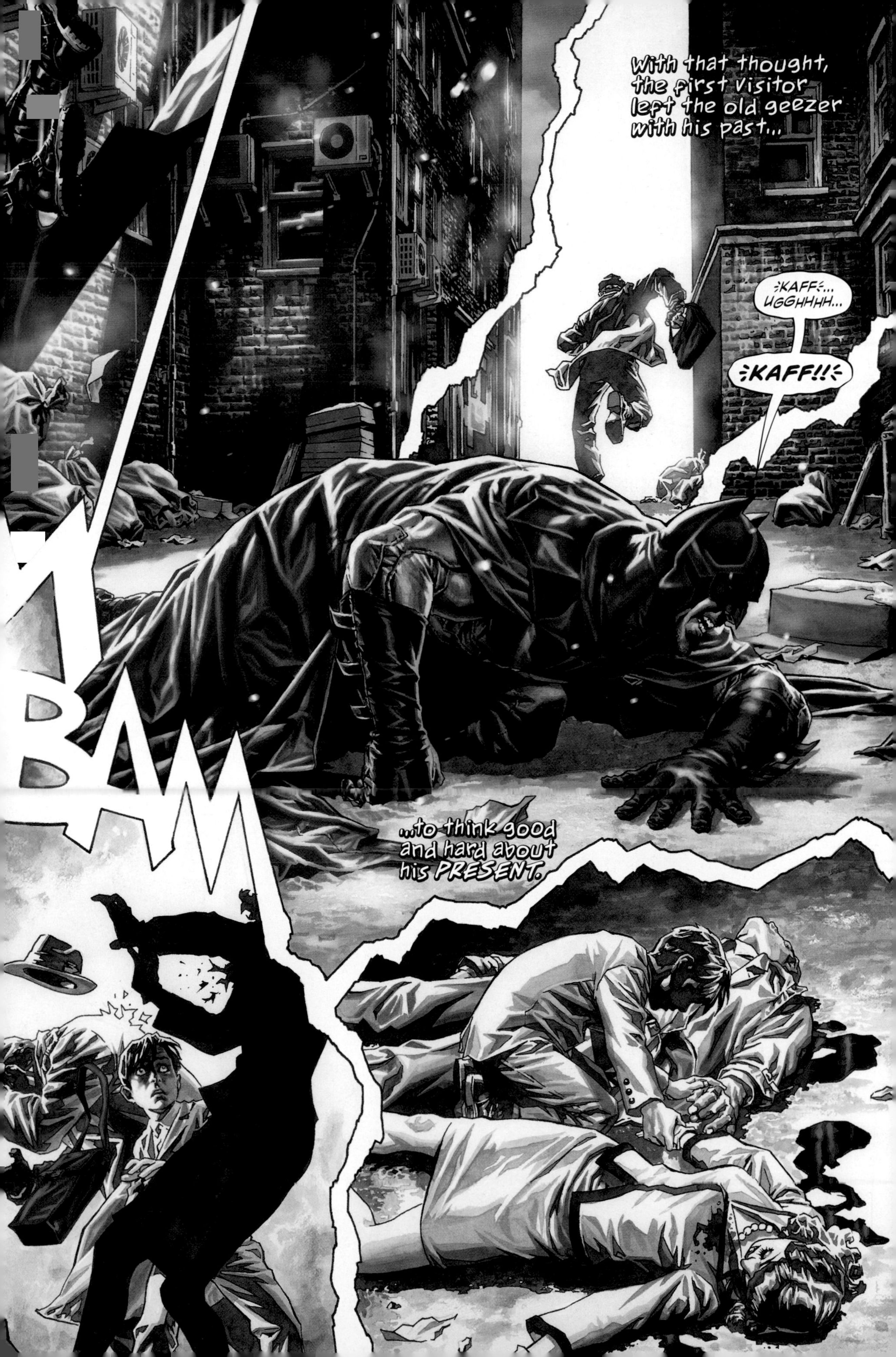
With that thought, the first visitor left the old geezer with his past...
KAFF... UGGHHHH...
KAFF!!
...to think good and hard about his PRESENT.
BAM

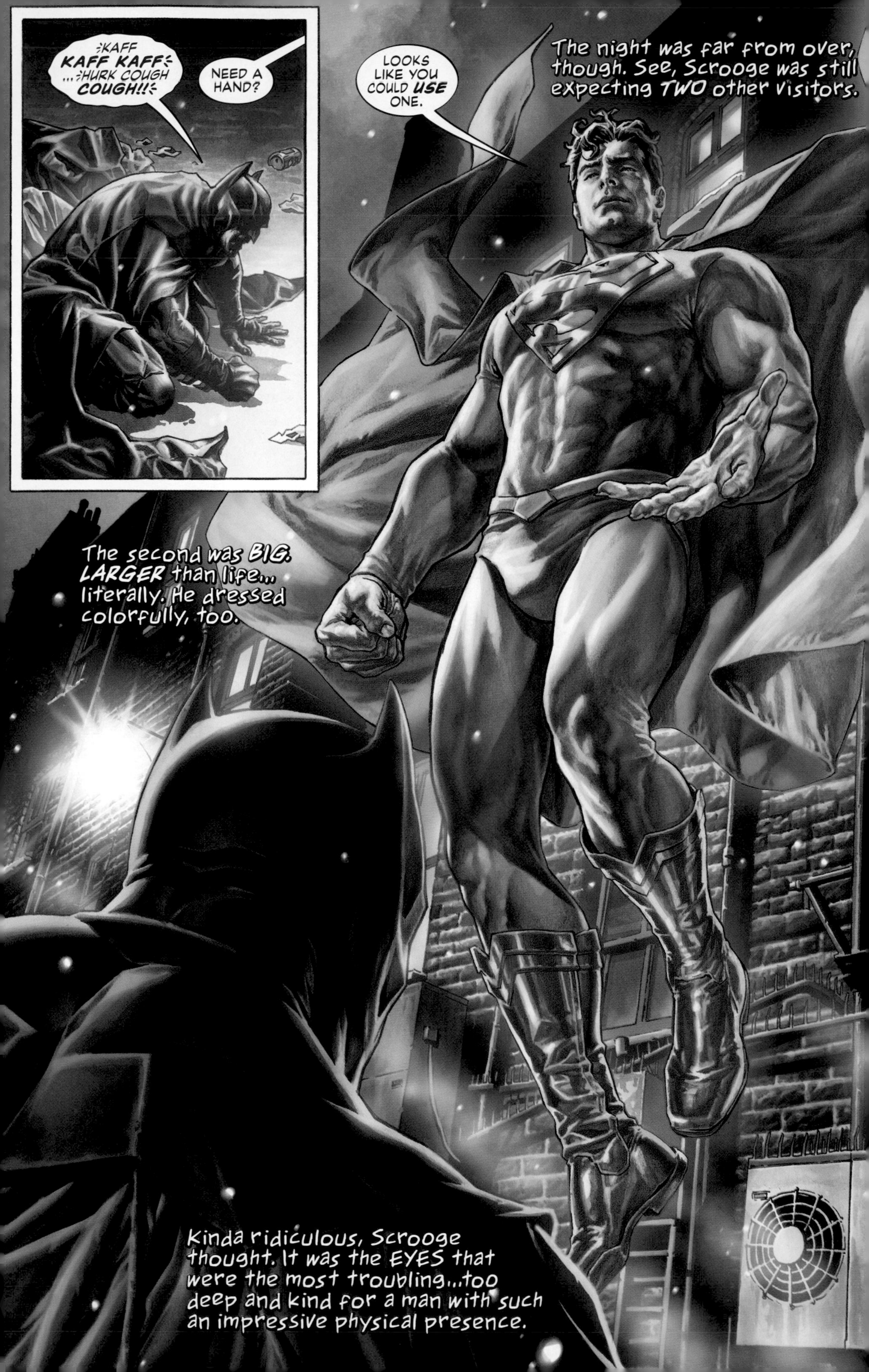

KAFF KAFF KAFF ...HURK COUGH COUGH!!
NEED A HAND?
LOOKS LIKE YOU COULD USE ONE.
The night was far from over, though. See, Scrooge was still expecting TWO other visitors.
The second was BIG. LARGER than life... literally. He dressed colorfully, too.
Kinda ridiculous, Scrooge thought. It was the EYES that were the most troubling...too deep and kind for a man with such an impressive physical presence.

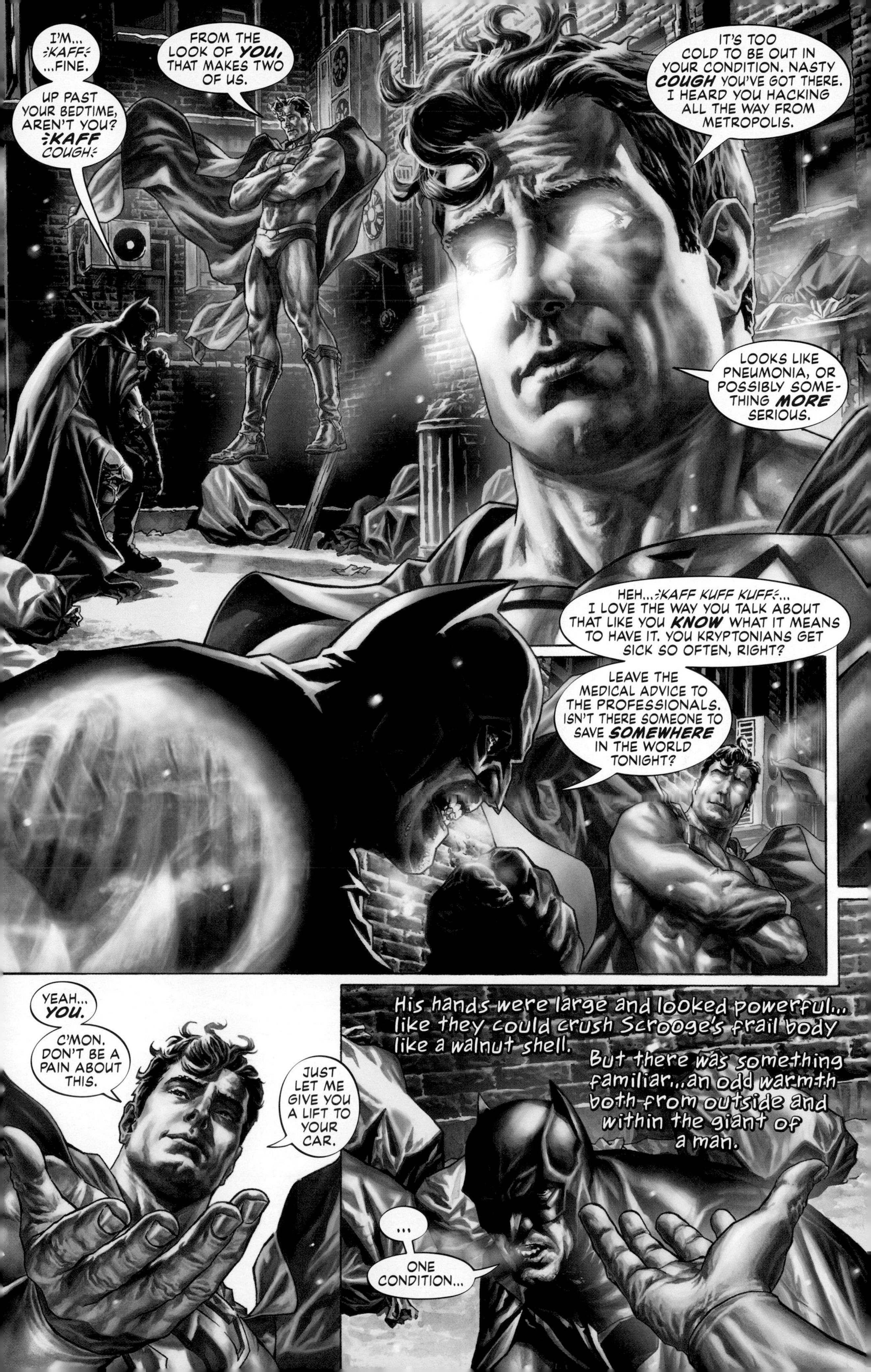
I'M... ≈KAFF≈ ...FINE.
UP PAST YOUR BEDTIME, AREN'T YOU? ≈KAFF COUGH≈
FROM THE LOOK OF YOU, THAT MAKES TWO OF US.
IT'S TOO COLD TO BE OUT IN YOUR CONDITION. NASTY COUGH YOU'VE GOT THERE. I HEARD YOU HACKING ALL THE WAY FROM METROPOLIS.
LOOKS LIKE PNEUMONIA, OR POSSIBLY SOMETHING MORE SERIOUS.
HEH...≈KAFF KUFF KUFF≈... I LOVE THE WAY YOU TALK ABOUT THAT LIKE YOU KNOW WHAT IT MEANS TO HAVE IT. YOU KRYPTONIANS GET SICK SO OFTEN, RIGHT?
LEAVE THE MEDICAL ADVICE TO THE PROFESSIONALS. ISN'T THERE SOMEONE TO SAVE SOMEWHERE IN THE WORLD TONIGHT?
YEAH... YOU.
C'MON. DON'T BE A PAIN ABOUT THIS.
JUST LET ME GIVE YOU A LIFT TO YOUR CAR.
His hands were large and looked powerful... like they could crush Scrooge's frail body like a walnut shell.
But there was something familiar...an odd warmth both from outside and within the giant of a man.
...
ONE CONDITION...

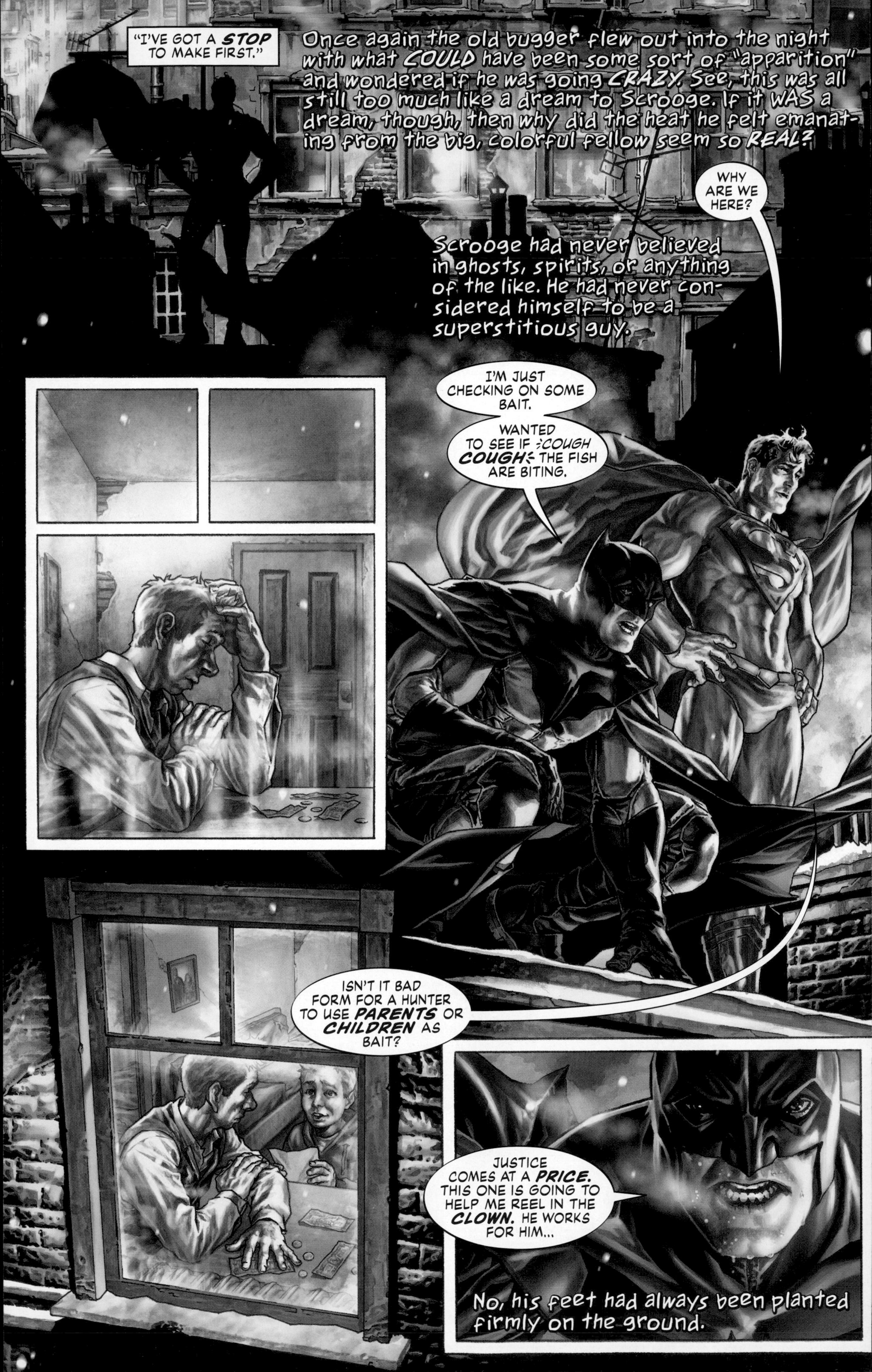

"I'VE GOT A STOP TO MAKE FIRST."
Once again the old bugger flew out into the night with what COULD have been some sort of "apparition" and wondered if he was going CRAZY. See, this was all still too much like a dream to Scrooge. If it WAS a dream, though, then why did the heat he felt emanating from the big, colorful fellow seem so REAL?
WHY ARE WE HERE?
Scrooge had never believed in ghosts, spirits, or anything of the like. He had never considered himself to be a superstitious guy.
I'M JUST CHECKING ON SOME BAIT.
WANTED TO SEE IF :COUGH COUGH: THE FISH ARE BITING.
ISN'T IT BAD FORM FOR A HUNTER TO USE PARENTS OR CHILDREN AS BAIT?
JUSTICE COMES AT A PRICE. THIS ONE IS GOING TO HELP ME REEL IN THE CLOWN. HE WORKS FOR HIM...
No, his feet had always been planted firmly on the ground.

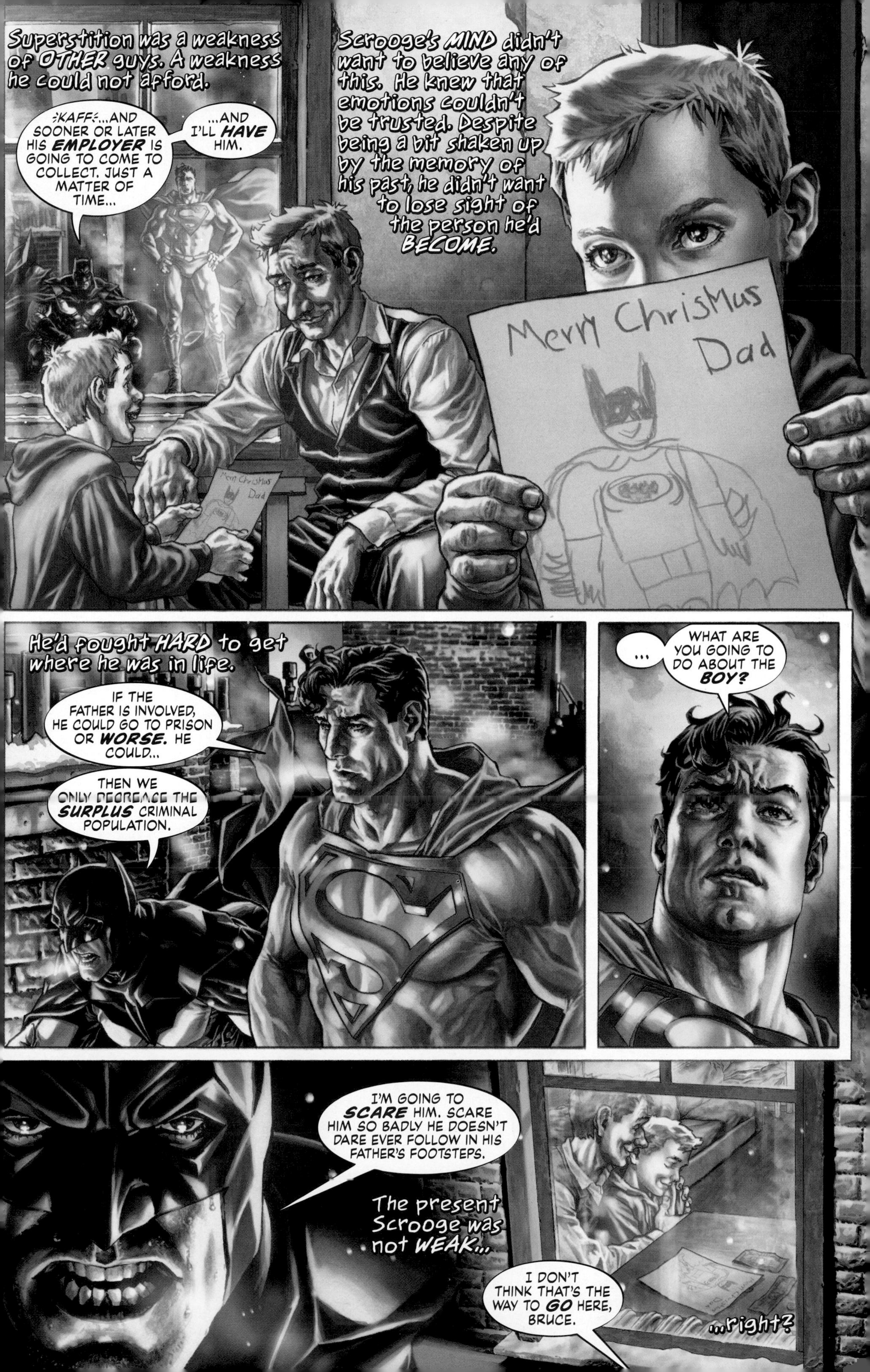
Superstition was a weakness of OTHER guys. A weakness he could not afford.
KAFF...AND SOONER OR LATER HIS EMPLOYER IS GOING TO COME TO COLLECT. JUST A MATTER OF TIME...
...AND I'LL HAVE HIM.
Scrooge's MIND didn't want to believe any of this. He knew that emotions couldn't be trusted. Despite being a bit shaken up by the memory of his past, he didn't want to lose sight of the person he'd BECOME.
Merry ChrisMus Dad
He'd fought HARD to get where he was in life.
IF THE FATHER IS INVOLVED, HE COULD GO TO PRISON OR WORSE. HE COULD...
THEN WE ONLY DECREASE THE SURPLUS CRIMINAL POPULATION.
...
WHAT ARE YOU GOING TO DO ABOUT THE BOY?
I'M GOING TO SCARE HIM. SCARE HIM SO BADLY HE DOESN'T DARE EVER FOLLOW IN HIS FATHER'S FOOTSTEPS.
The present Scrooge was not WEAK...
I DON'T THINK THAT'S THE WAY TO GO HERE, BRUCE.
...right?

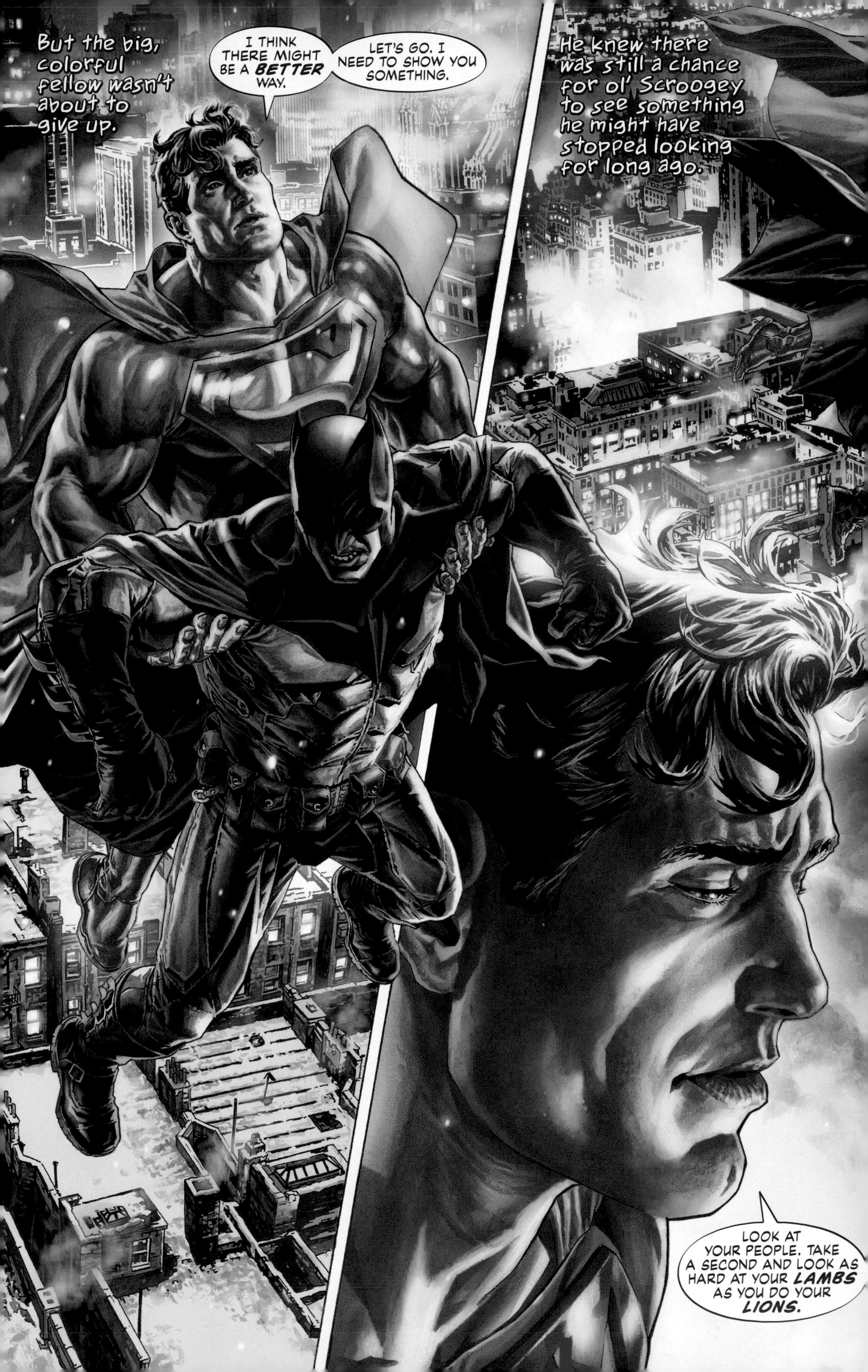
But the big, colorful fellow wasn't about to give up.
I THINK THERE MIGHT BE A BETTER WAY.
LET'S GO. I NEED TO SHOW YOU SOMETHING.
He knew there was still a chance for ol' Scroogey to see something he might have stopped looking for long ago.
LOOK AT YOUR PEOPLE. TAKE A SECOND AND LOOK AS HARD AT YOUR LAMBS AS YOU DO YOUR LIONS.

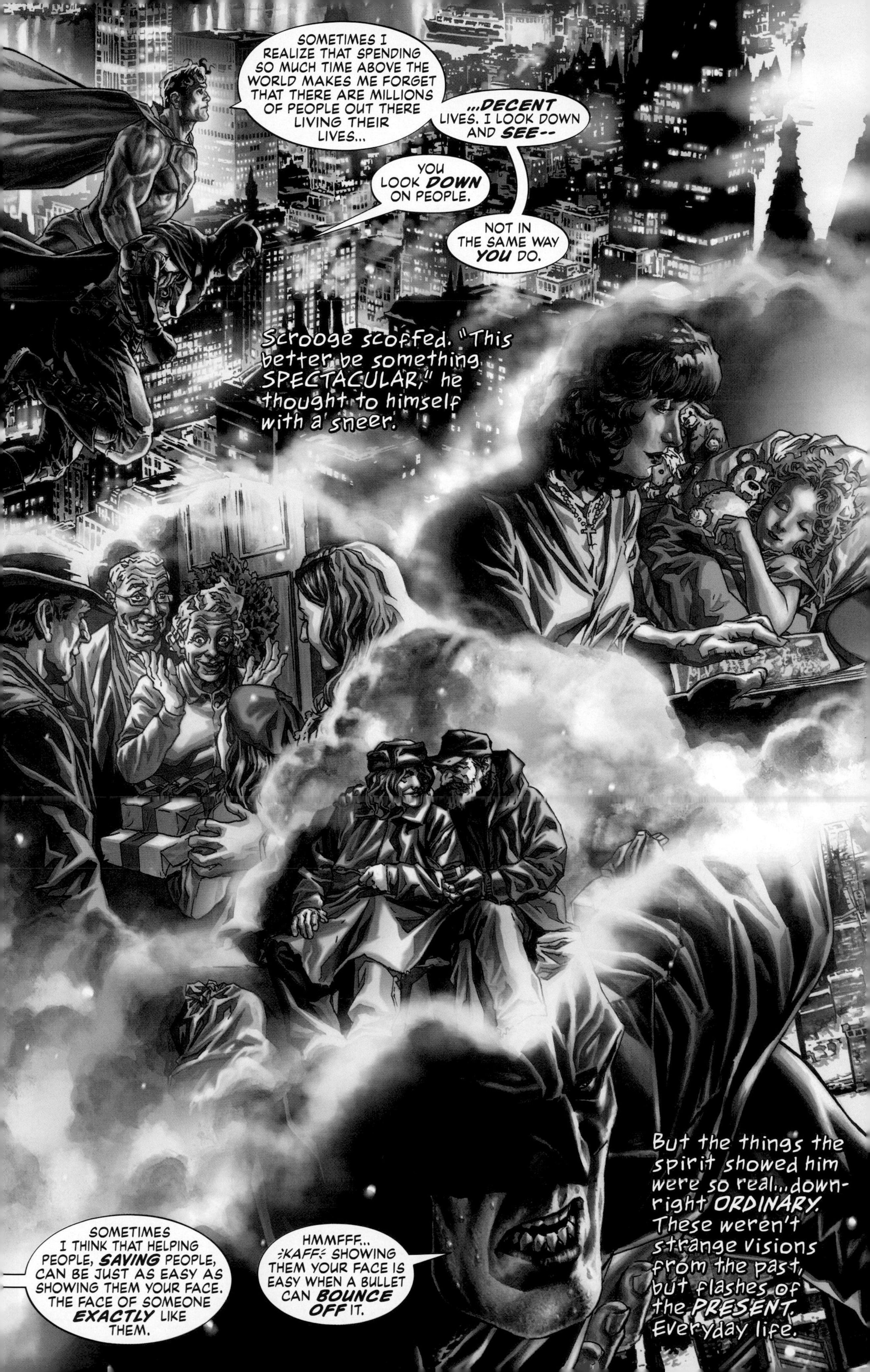
SOMETIMES I REALIZE THAT SPENDING SO MUCH TIME ABOVE THE WORLD MAKES ME FORGET THAT THERE ARE MILLIONS OF PEOPLE OUT THERE LIVING THEIR LIVES...
...DECENT LIVES. I LOOK DOWN AND SEE--
YOU LOOK DOWN ON PEOPLE.
NOT IN THE SAME WAY YOU DO.
Scrooge scoffed. "This better be something SPECTACULAR," he thought to himself with a sneer.
SOMETIMES I THINK THAT HELPING PEOPLE, SAVING PEOPLE, CAN BE JUST AS EASY AS SHOWING THEM YOUR FACE. THE FACE OF SOMEONE EXACTLY LIKE THEM.
HMMFFF... KAFF SHOWING THEM YOUR FACE IS EASY WHEN A BULLET CAN BOUNCE OFF IT.
But the things the spirit showed him were so real...downright ORDINARY. These weren't strange visions from the past, but flashes of the PRESENT. Everyday life.

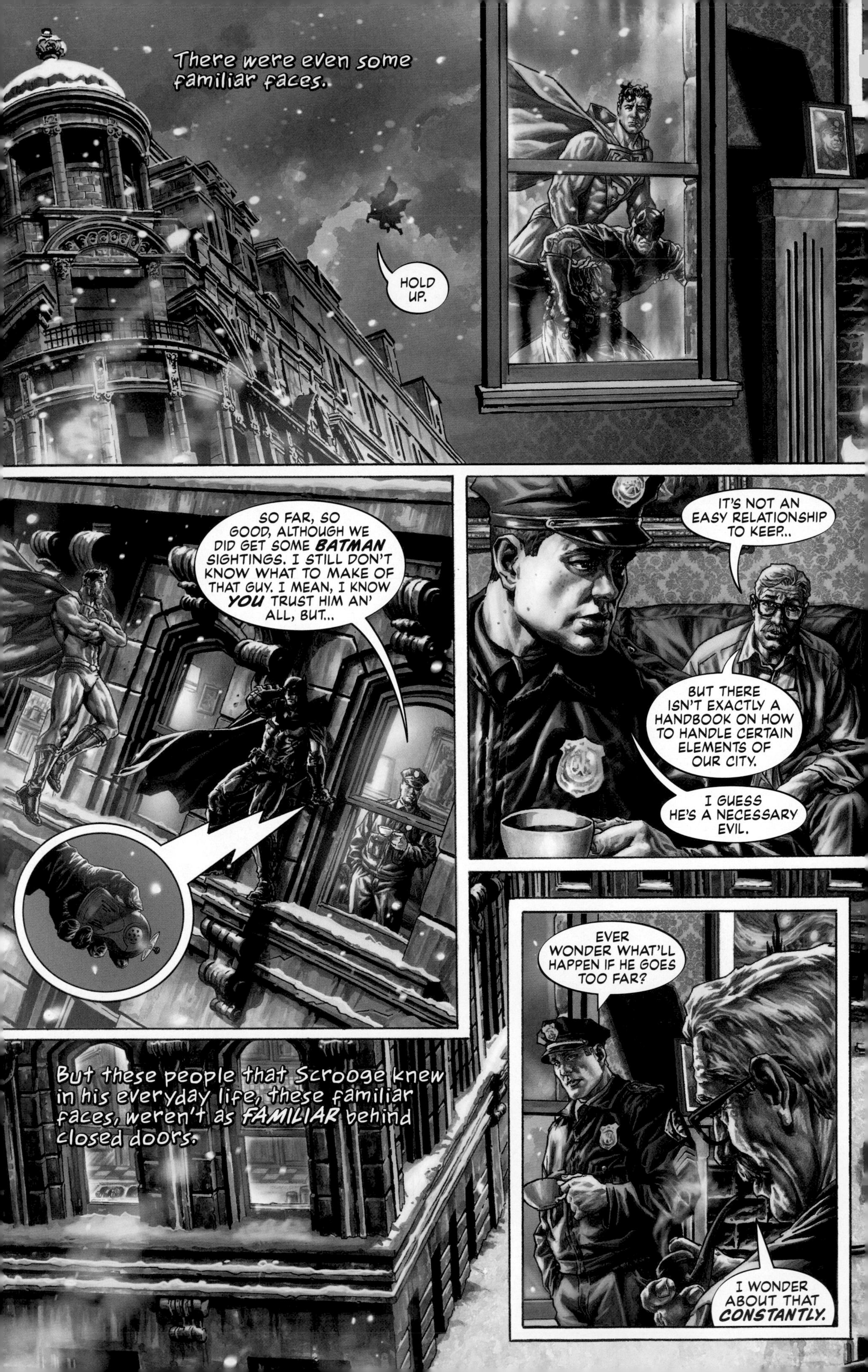

There were even some familiar faces.
HOLD UP.
SO FAR, SO GOOD, ALTHOUGH WE DID GET SOME BATMAN SIGHTINGS. I STILL DON'T KNOW WHAT TO MAKE OF THAT GUY. I MEAN, I KNOW YOU TRUST HIM AN' ALL, BUT...
IT'S NOT AN EASY RELATIONSHIP TO KEEP...
BUT THERE ISN'T EXACTLY A HANDBOOK ON HOW TO HANDLE CERTAIN ELEMENTS OF OUR CITY.
I GUESS HE'S A NECESSARY EVIL.
But these people that Scrooge knew in his everyday life, these familiar faces, weren't as FAMILIAR behind closed doors.
EVER WONDER WHAT'LL HAPPEN IF HE GOES TOO FAR?
I WONDER ABOUT THAT CONSTANTLY.

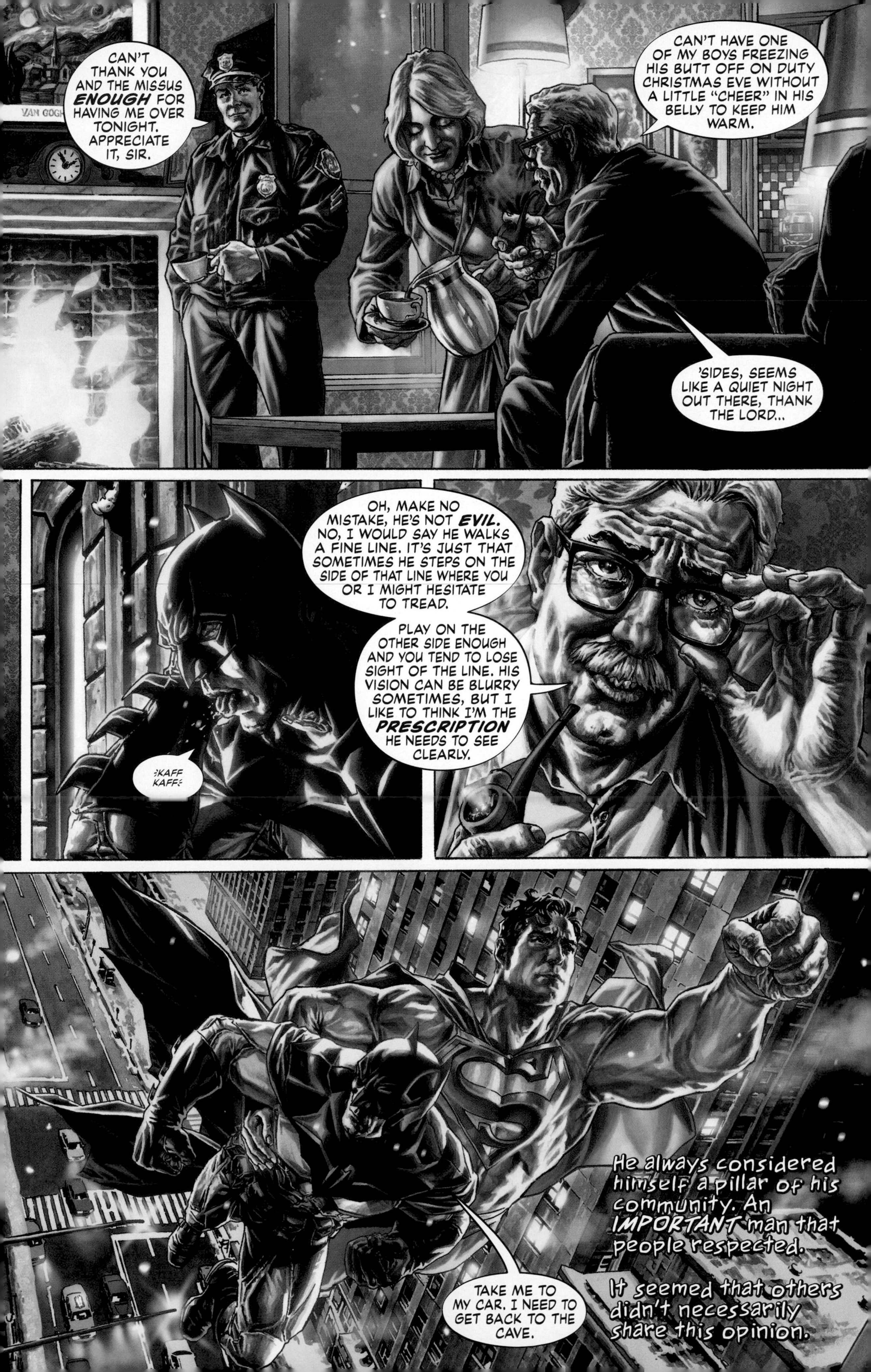

VAN GOGH
CAN'T THANK YOU AND THE MISSUS ENOUGH FOR HAVING ME OVER TONIGHT. APPRECIATE IT, SIR.
CAN'T HAVE ONE OF MY BOYS FREEZING HIS BUTT OFF ON DUTY CHRISTMAS EVE WITHOUT A LITTLE "CHEER" IN HIS BELLY TO KEEP HIM WARM.
'SIDES, SEEMS LIKE A QUIET NIGHT OUT THERE, THANK THE LORD...
OH, MAKE NO MISTAKE, HE'S NOT EVIL. NO, I WOULD SAY HE WALKS A FINE LINE. IT'S JUST THAT SOMETIMES HE STEPS ON THE SIDE OF THAT LINE WHERE YOU OR I MIGHT HESITATE TO TREAD.
PLAY ON THE OTHER SIDE ENOUGH AND YOU TEND TO LOSE SIGHT OF THE LINE. HIS VISION CAN BE BLURRY SOMETIMES, BUT I LIKE TO THINK I'M THE PRESCRIPTION HE NEEDS TO SEE CLEARLY.
KAFF KAFF
He always considered himself a pillar of his community. An IMPORTANT man that people respected.
It seemed that others didn't necessarily share this opinion.
TAKE ME TO MY CAR. I NEED TO GET BACK TO THE CAVE.

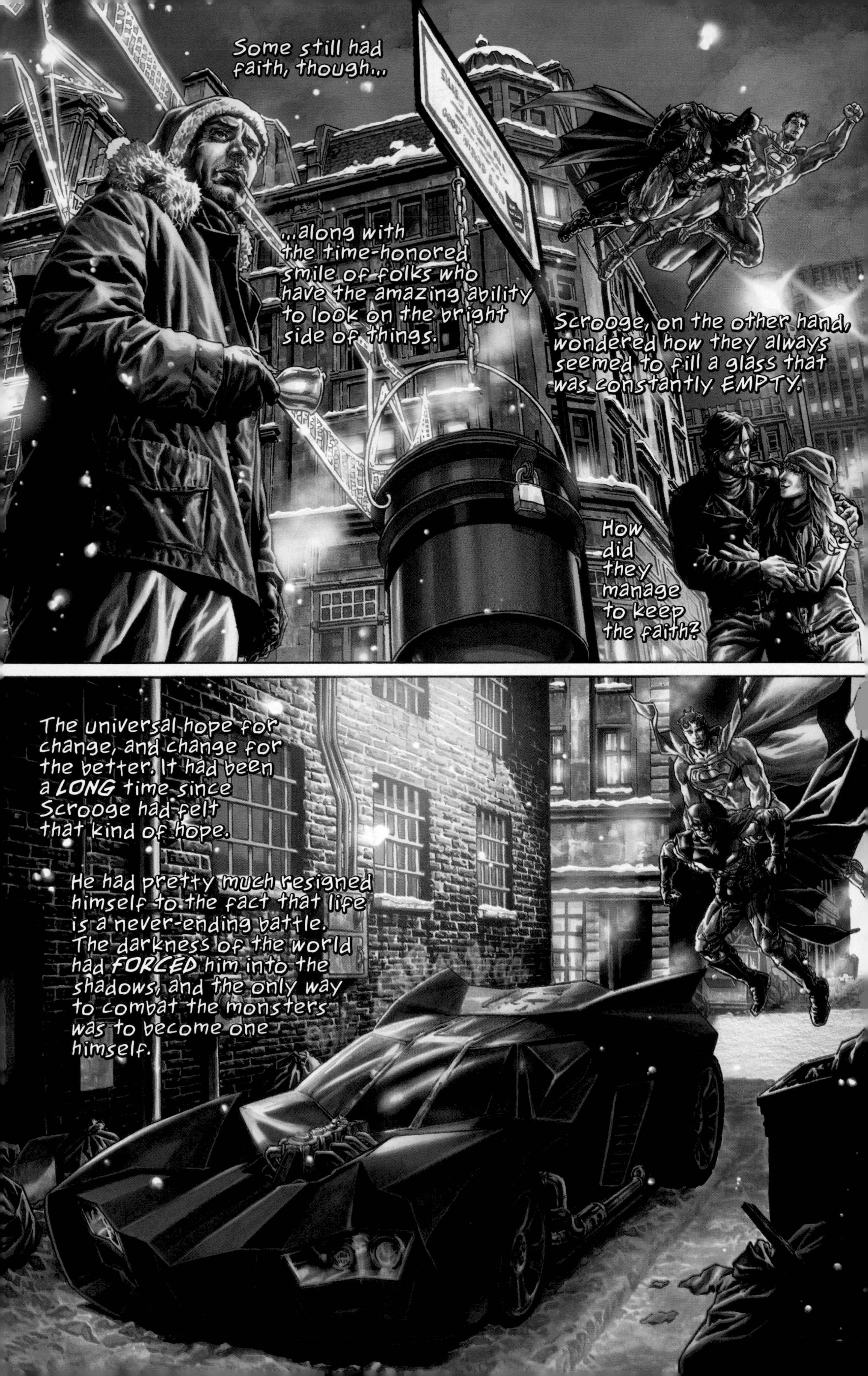
Some still had faith, though...
...along with the time-honored smile of folks who have the amazing ability to look on the bright side of things.
Scrooge, on the other hand, wondered how they always seemed to fill a glass that was constantly EMPTY.
How did they manage to keep the faith?
The universal hope for change, and change for the better. It had been a LONG time since Scrooge had felt that kind of hope.
He had pretty much resigned himself to the fact that life is a never-ending battle. The darkness of the world had FORCED him into the shadows, and the only way to combat the monsters was to become one himself.

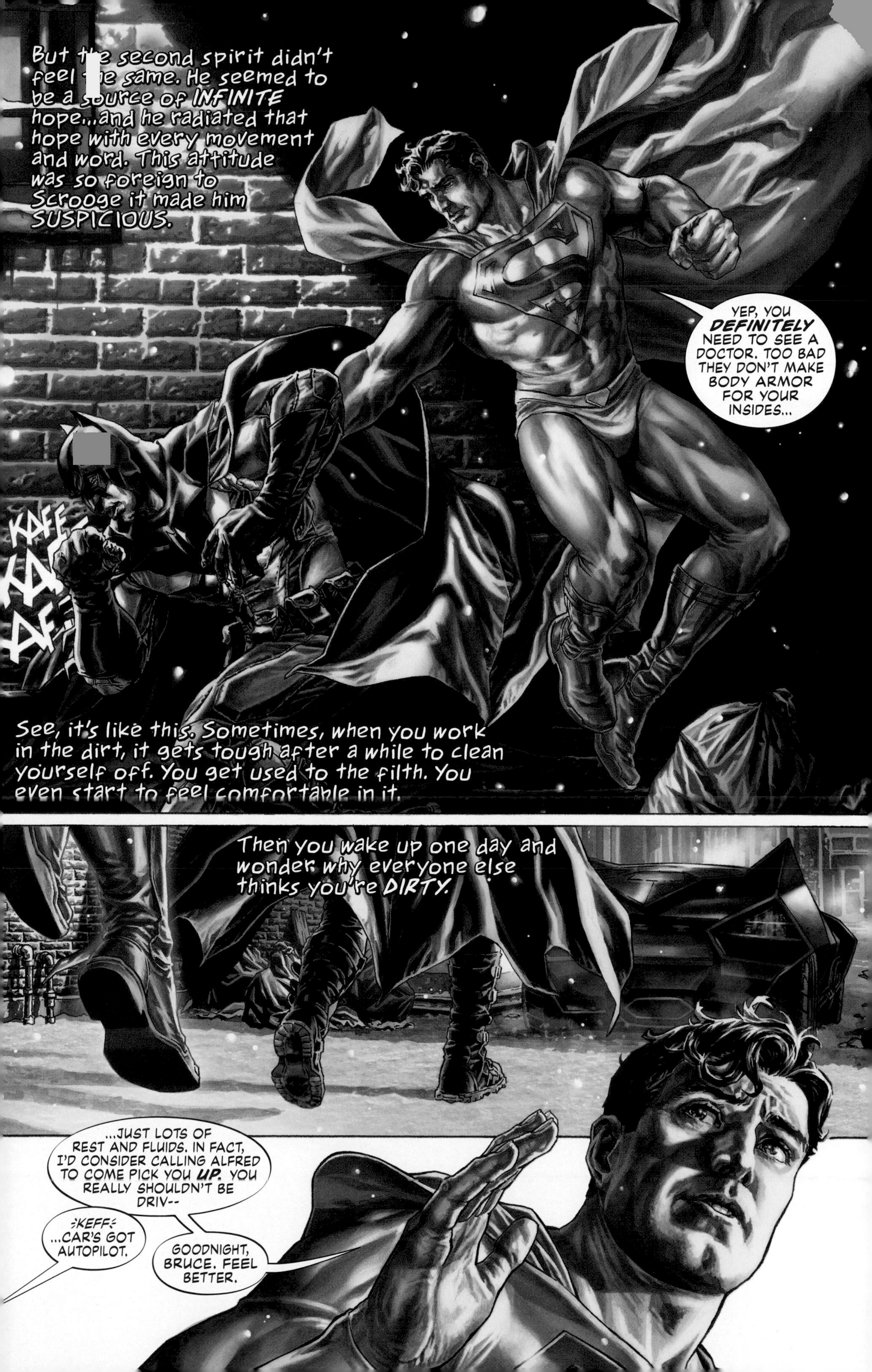

But the second spirit didn't feel the same. He seemed to be a source of INFINITE hope...and he radiated that hope with every movement and word. This attitude was so foreign to Scrooge it made him SUSPICIOUS.
YEP, YOU DEFINITELY NEED TO SEE A DOCTOR. TOO BAD THEY DON'T MAKE BODY ARMOR FOR YOUR INSIDES...
See, it's like this. Sometimes, when you work in the dirt, it gets tough after a while to clean yourself off. You get used to the filth. You even start to feel comfortable in it.
Then you wake up one day and wonder why everyone else thinks you're DIRTY.
...JUST LOTS OF REST AND FLUIDS. IN FACT, I'D CONSIDER CALLING ALFRED TO COME PICK YOU UP. YOU REALLY SHOULDN'T BE DRIV--
KEFF ...CAR'S GOT AUTOPILOT.
GOODNIGHT, BRUCE. FEEL BETTER.

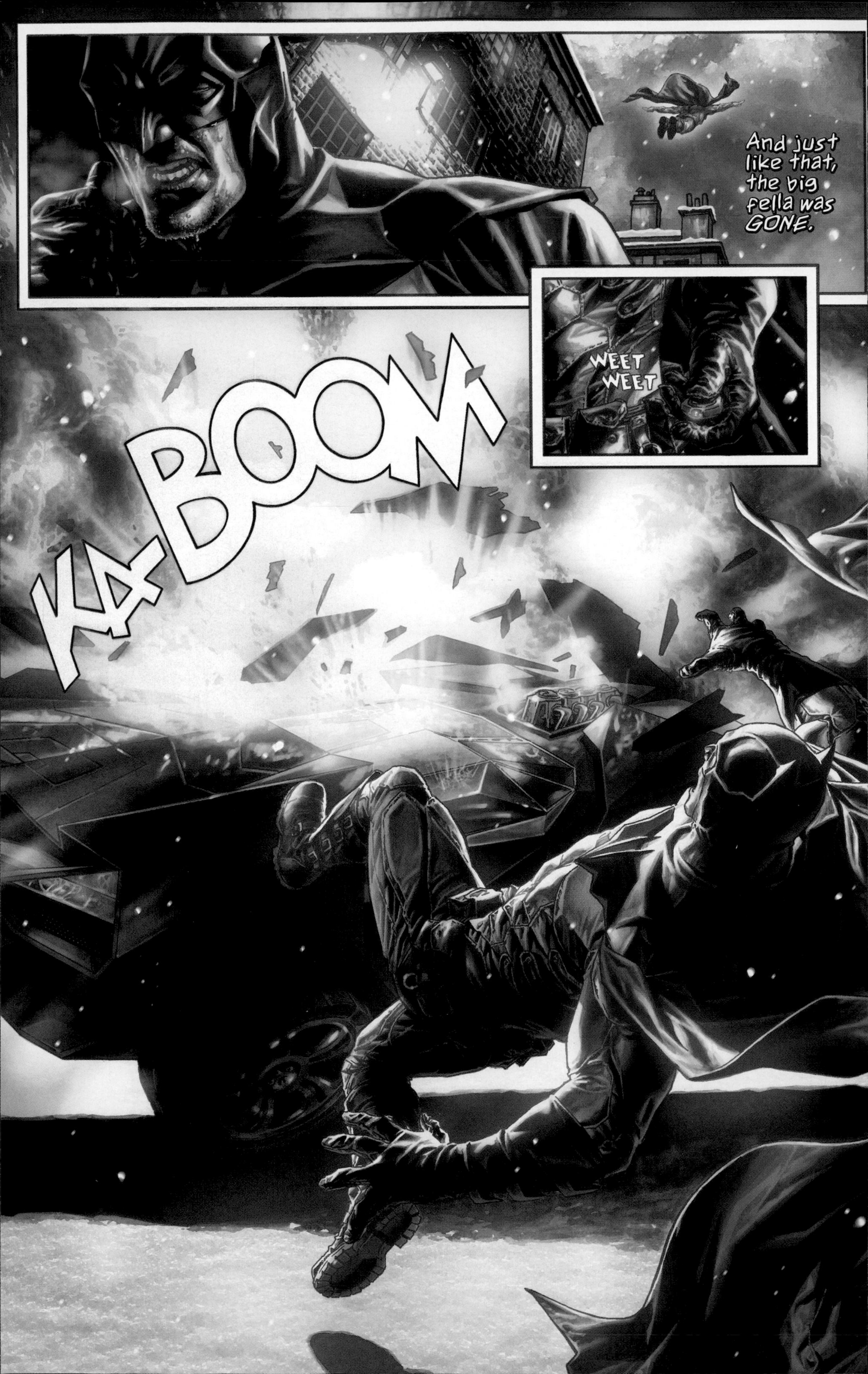
And just like that, the big fella was GONE.
WEET WEET
KA-BOOM

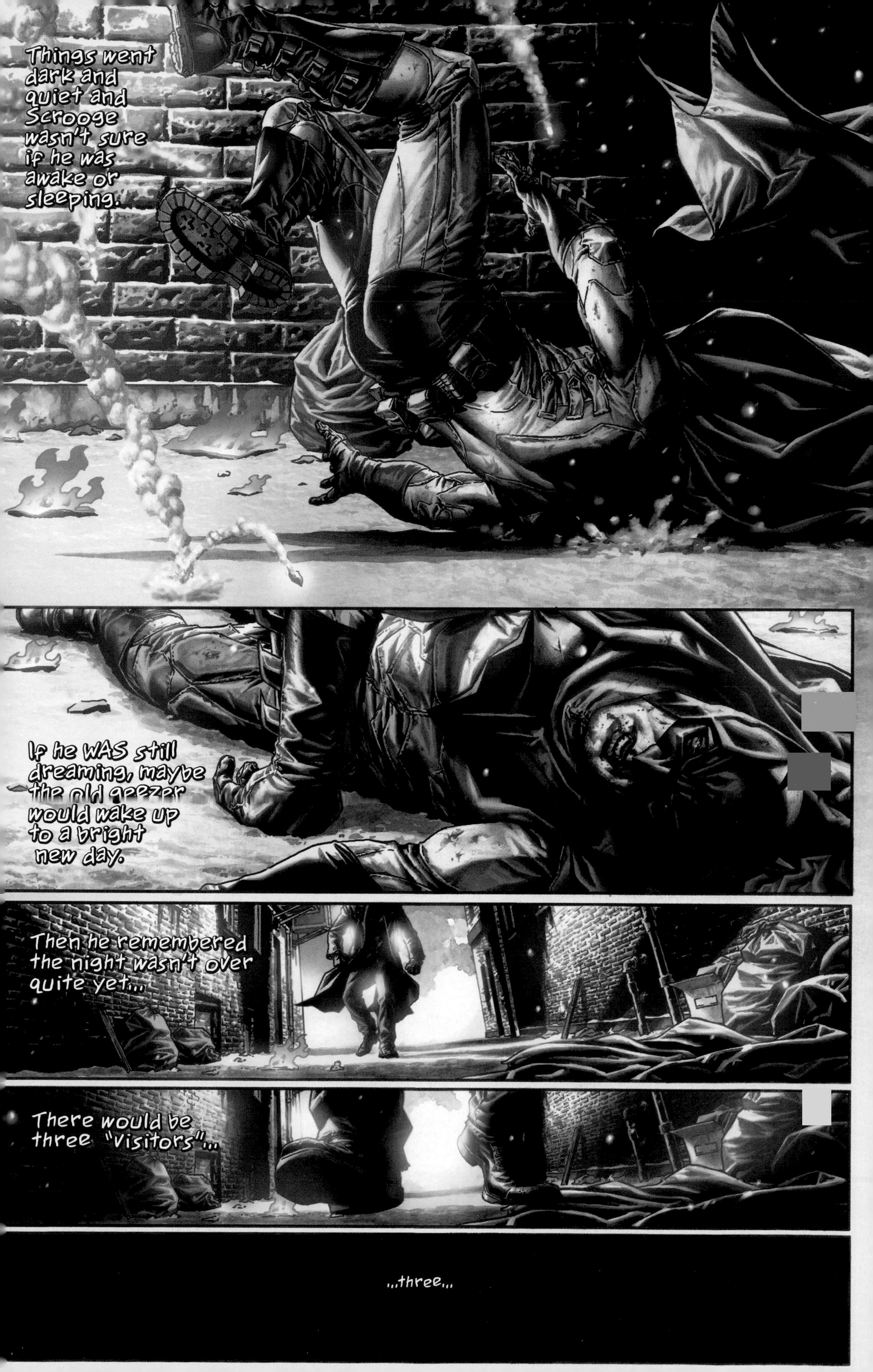
Things went dark and quiet and Scrooge wasn't sure if he was awake or sleeping.
If he WAS still dreaming, maybe the old geezer would wake up to a bright new day.
Then he remembered the night wasn't over quite yet...
There would be three "visitors"...
...three...

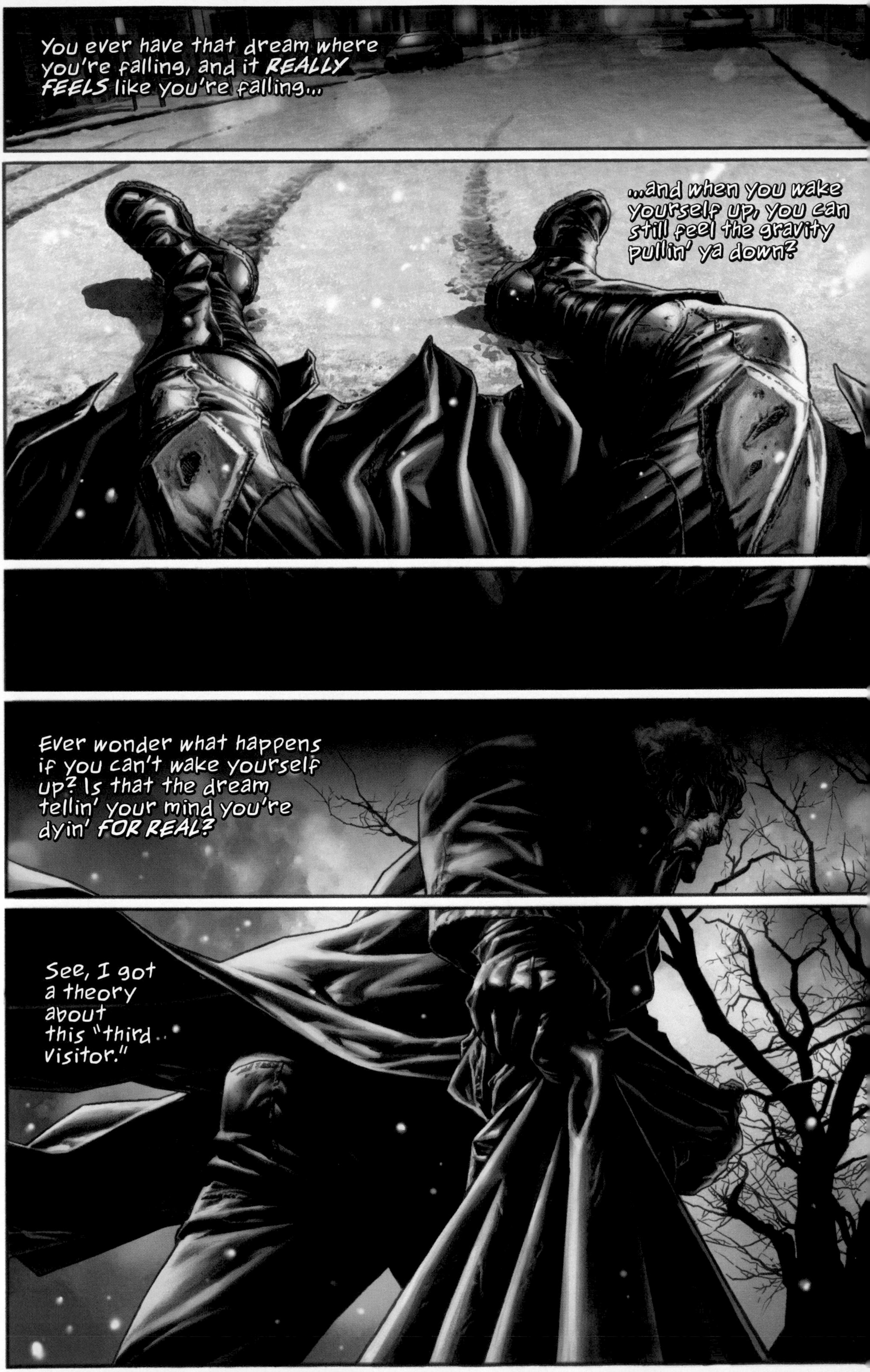
You ever have that dream where you're falling, and it REALLY FEELS like you're falling...
...and when you wake yourself up, you can still feel the gravity pullin' ya down?
Ever wonder what happens if you can't wake yourself up? Is that the dream tellin' your mind you're dyin' FOR REAL?
See, I got a theory about this "third visitor."

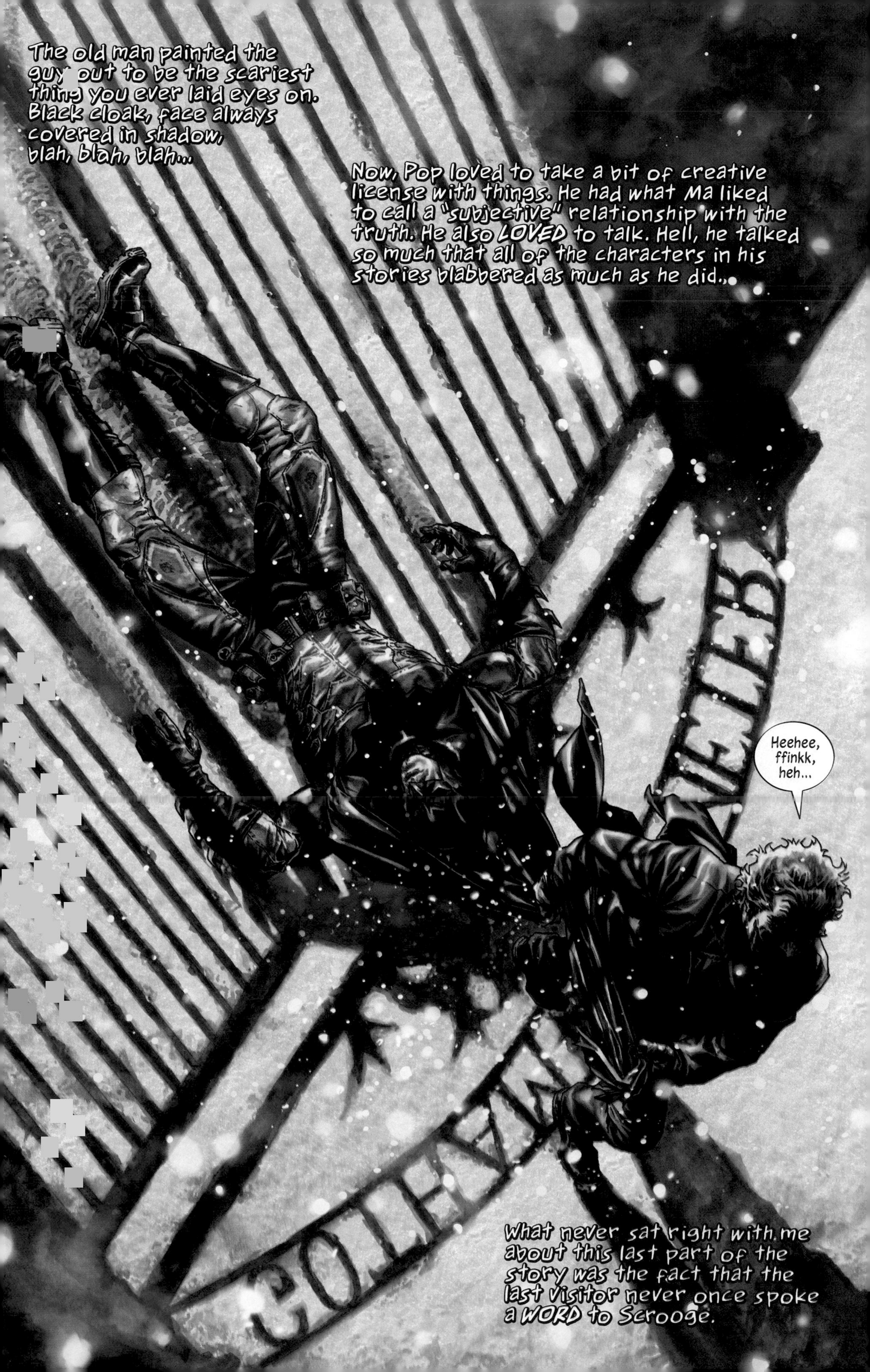
The old man painted the guy out to be the scariest thing you ever laid eyes on. Black cloak, face always covered in shadow, blah, blah, blah...
Now, Pop loved to take a bit of creative license with things. He had what Ma liked to call a "subjective" relationship with the truth. He also LOVED to talk. Hell, he talked so much that all of the characters in his stories blabbered as much as he did..
Heehee, ffinkk, heh...
What never sat right with me about this last part of the story was the fact that the last visitor never once spoke a WORD to Scrooge.

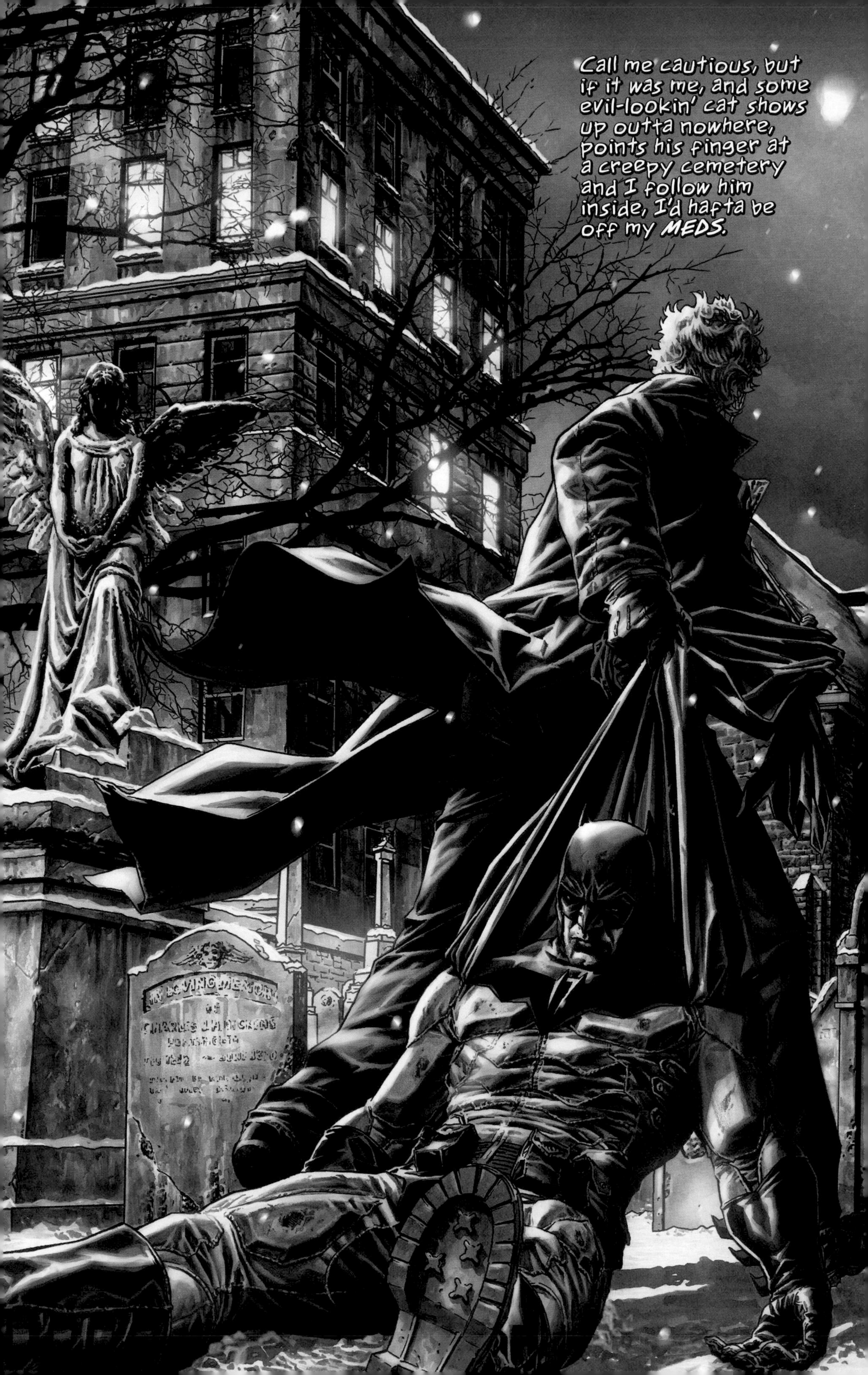
Call me cautious, but if it was me, and some evil-lookin' cat shows up outta nowhere, points his finger at a creepy cemetery and I follow him inside, I'd hafta be off my MEDS.

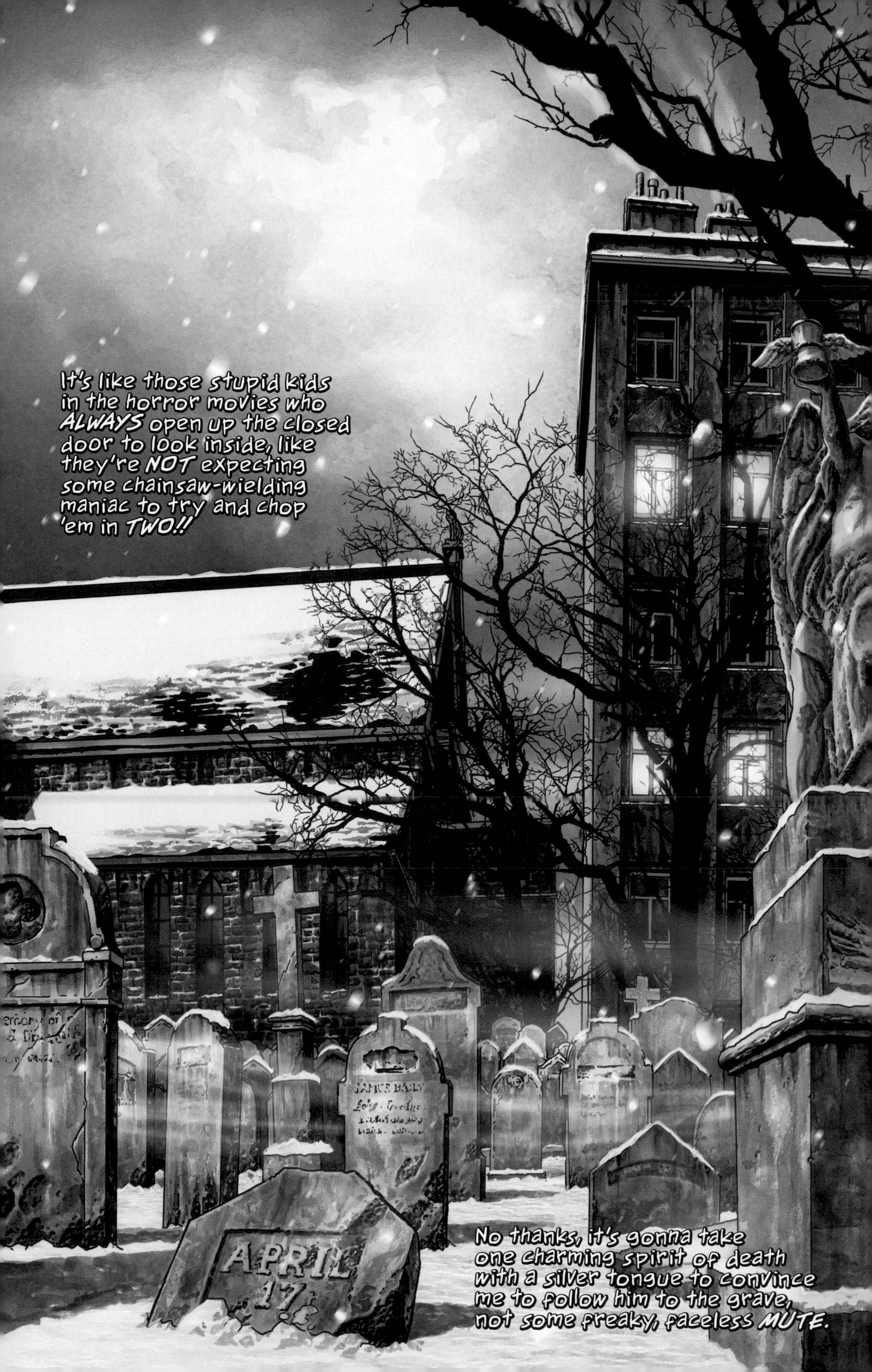
It's like those stupid kids in the horror movies who ALWAYS open up the closed door to look inside, like they're NOT expecting some chainsaw-wielding maniac to try and chop 'em in TWO!!
APRIL 17
No thanks, it's gonna take one charming spirit of death with a silver tongue to convince me to follow him to the grave, not some freaky, faceless MUTE.

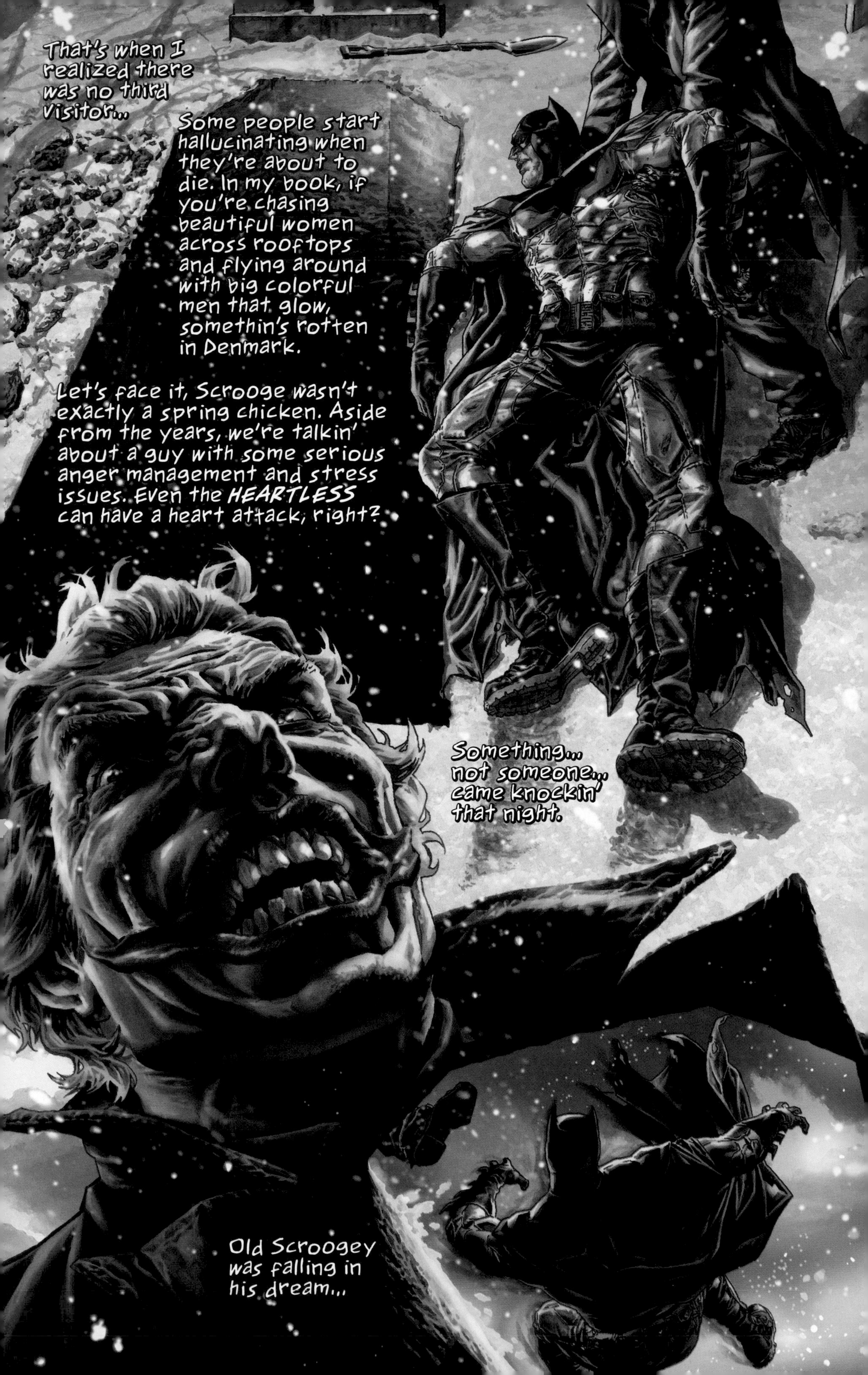
That's when I realized there was no third visitor...
Some people start hallucinating when they're about to die. In my book, if you're chasing beautiful women across rooftops and flying around with big colorful men that glow, somethin's rotten in Denmark.
Let's face it, Scrooge wasn't exactly a spring chicken. Aside from the years, we're talkin' about a guy with some serious anger management and stress issues. Even the HEARTLESS can have a heart attack, right?
Something... not someone... came knockin' that night.
Old Scroogey was falling in his dream...

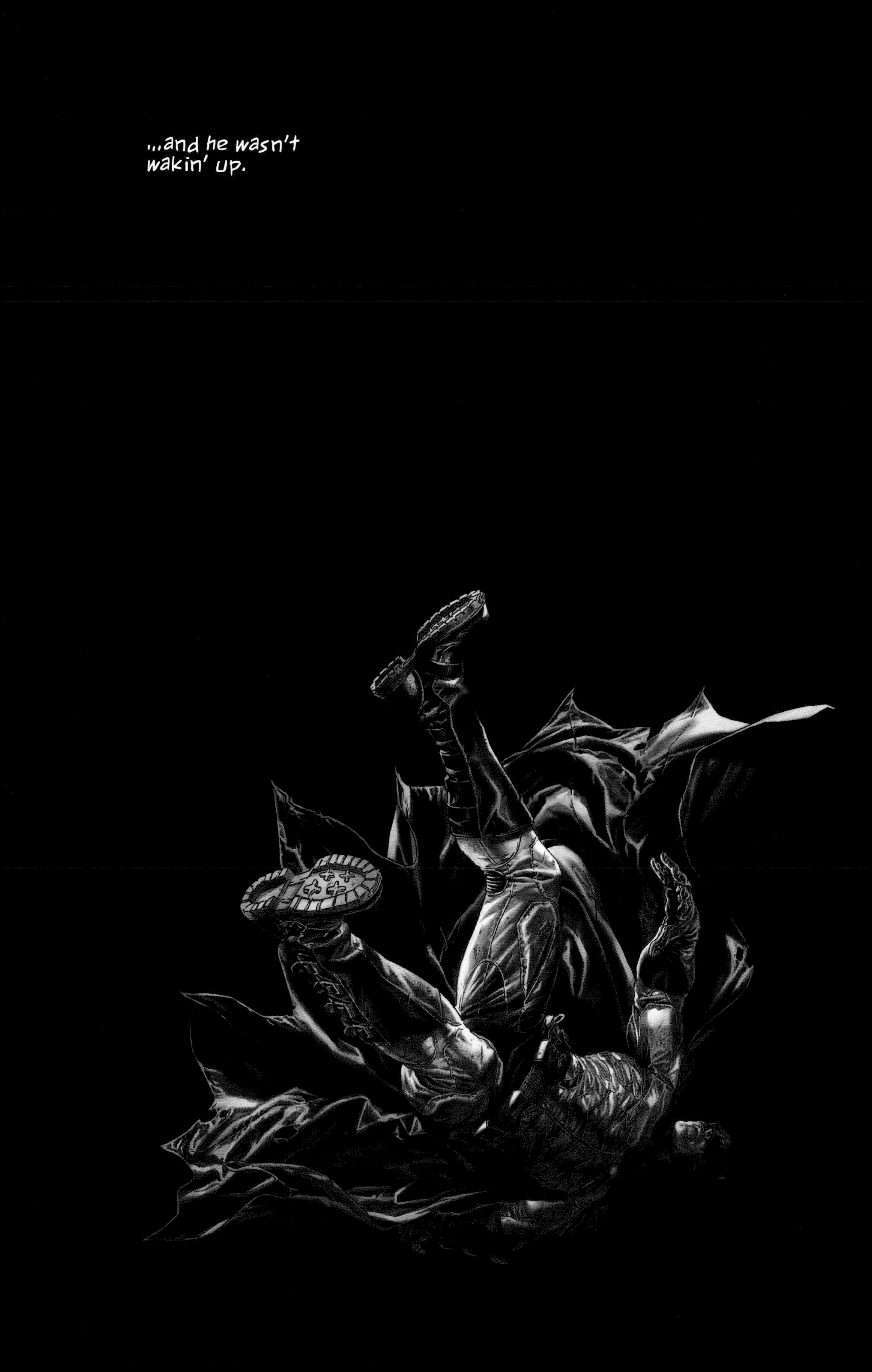
...and he wasn't wakin' up.

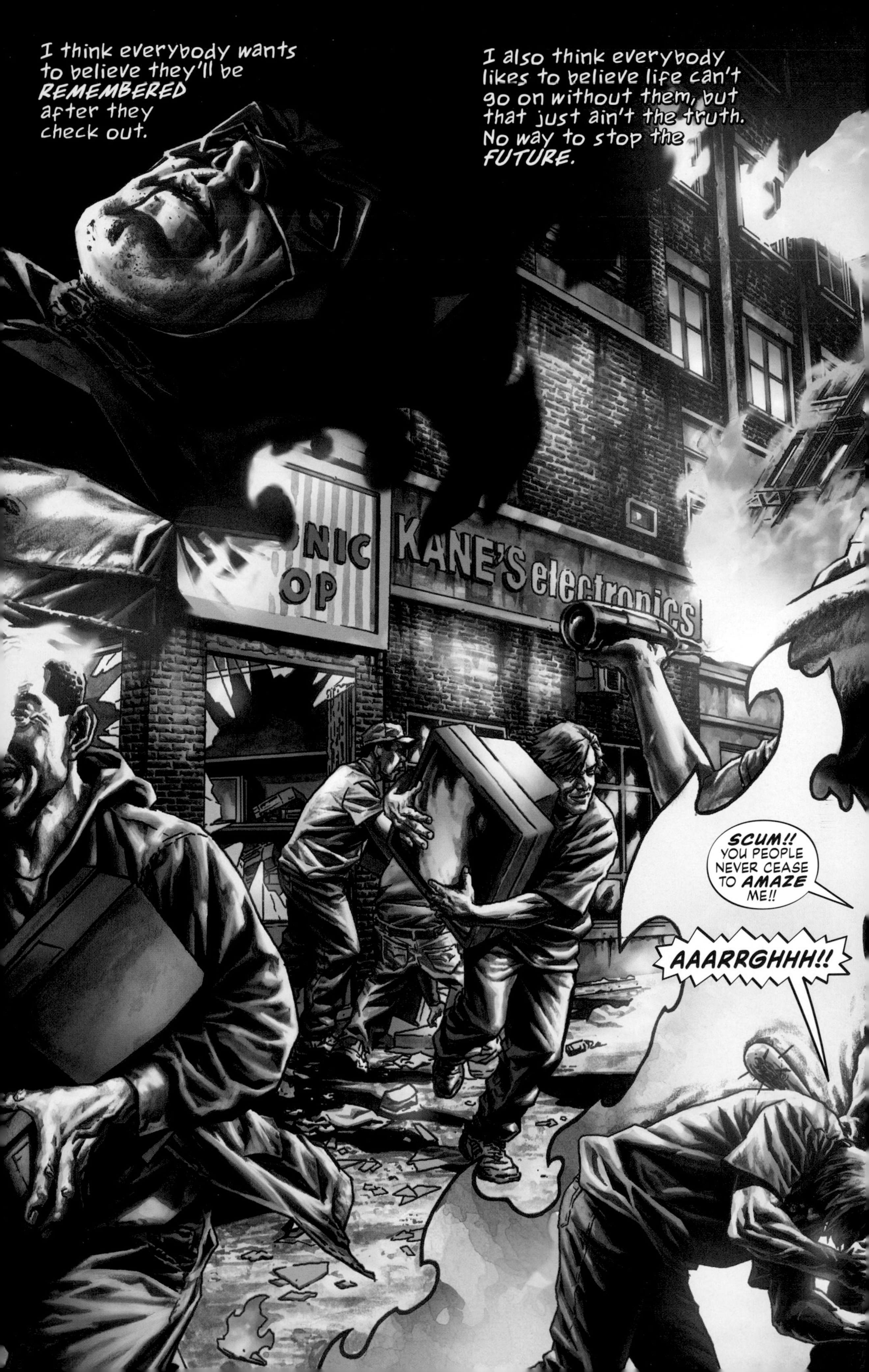
I think everybody wants to believe they'll be REMEMBERED after they check out.
I also think everybody likes to believe life can't go on without them, but that just ain't the truth. No way to stop the FUTURE.
NIC
OP
KANE'S electronics
SCUM!! YOU PEOPLE NEVER CEASE TO AMAZE ME!!
AAARRGHHH!!

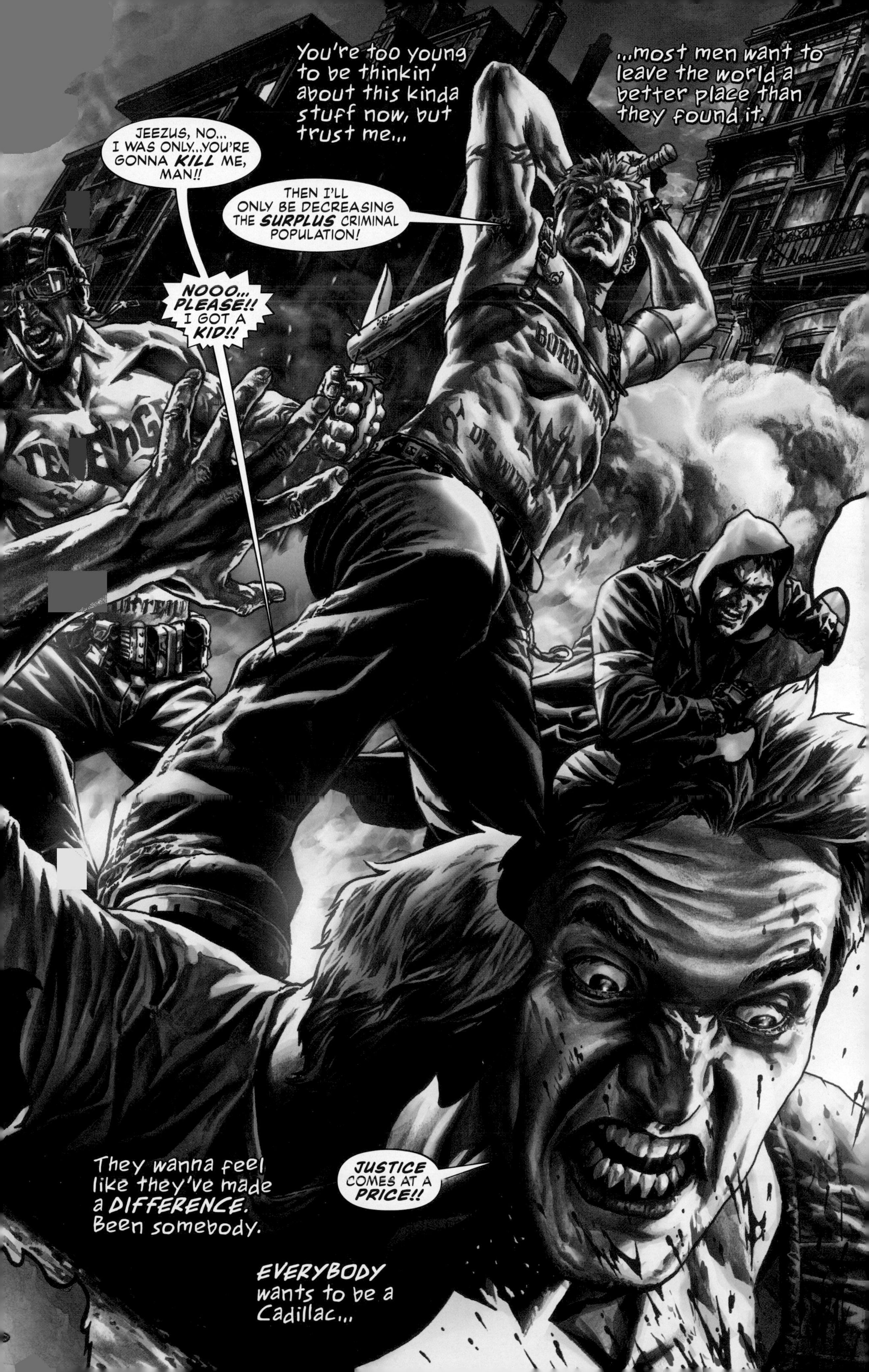

You're too young to be thinkin' about this kinda stuff now, but trust me...
...most men want to leave the world a better place than they found it.
JEEZUS, NO... I WAS ONLY...YOU'RE GONNA KILL ME, MAN!!
THEN I'LL ONLY BE DECREASING THE SURPLUS CRIMINAL POPULATION!
NOOO... PLEASE!! I GOT A KID!!
They wanna feel like they've made a DIFFERENCE. Been somebody.
JUSTICE COMES AT A PRICE!!
EVERYBODY wants to be a Cadillac...

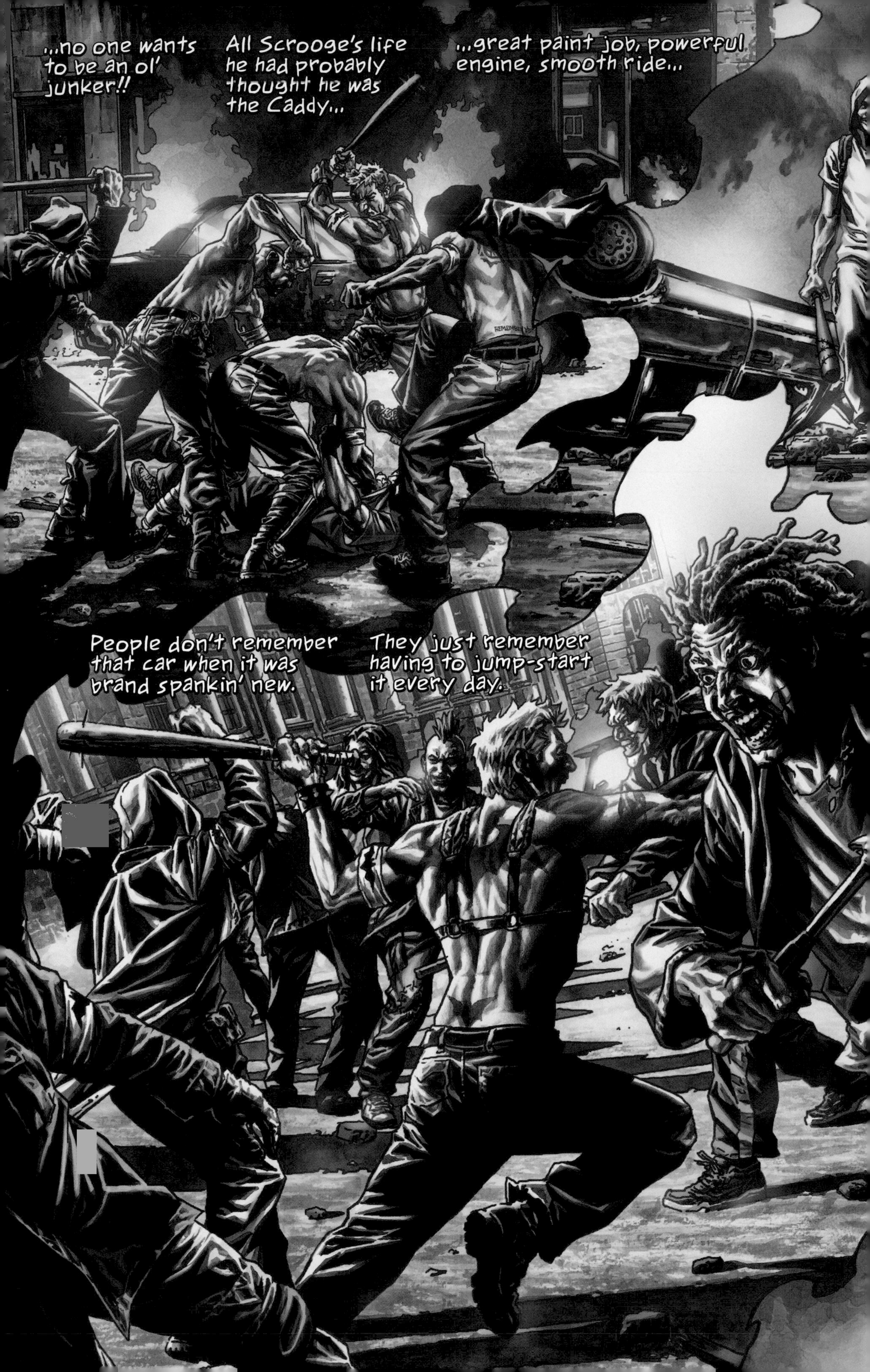

...no one wants to be an ol' junker!!
All Scrooge's life he had probably thought he was the Caddy...
...great paint job, powerful engine, smooth ride...
People don't remember that car when it was brand spankin' new.
They just remember having to jump-start it every day.

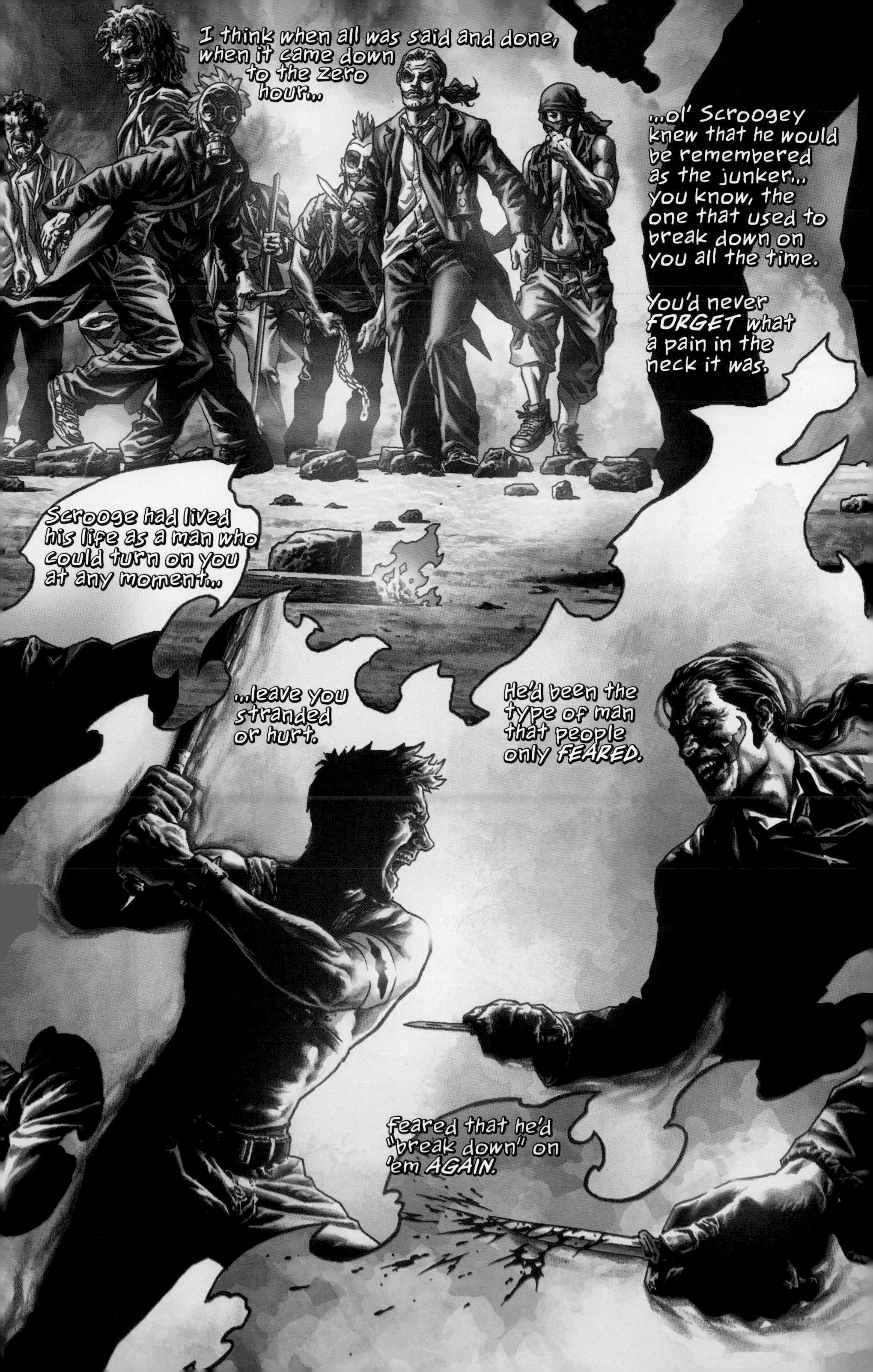

I think when all was said and done, when it came down to the zero hour...
...ol' Scroogey knew that he would be remembered as the junker... you know, the one that used to break down on you all the time.
You'd never FORGET what a pain in the neck it was.
Scrooge had lived his life as a man who could turn on you at any moment...
...leave you stranded or hurt.
He'd been the type of man that people only FEARED.
Feared that he'd "break down" on 'em AGAIN.

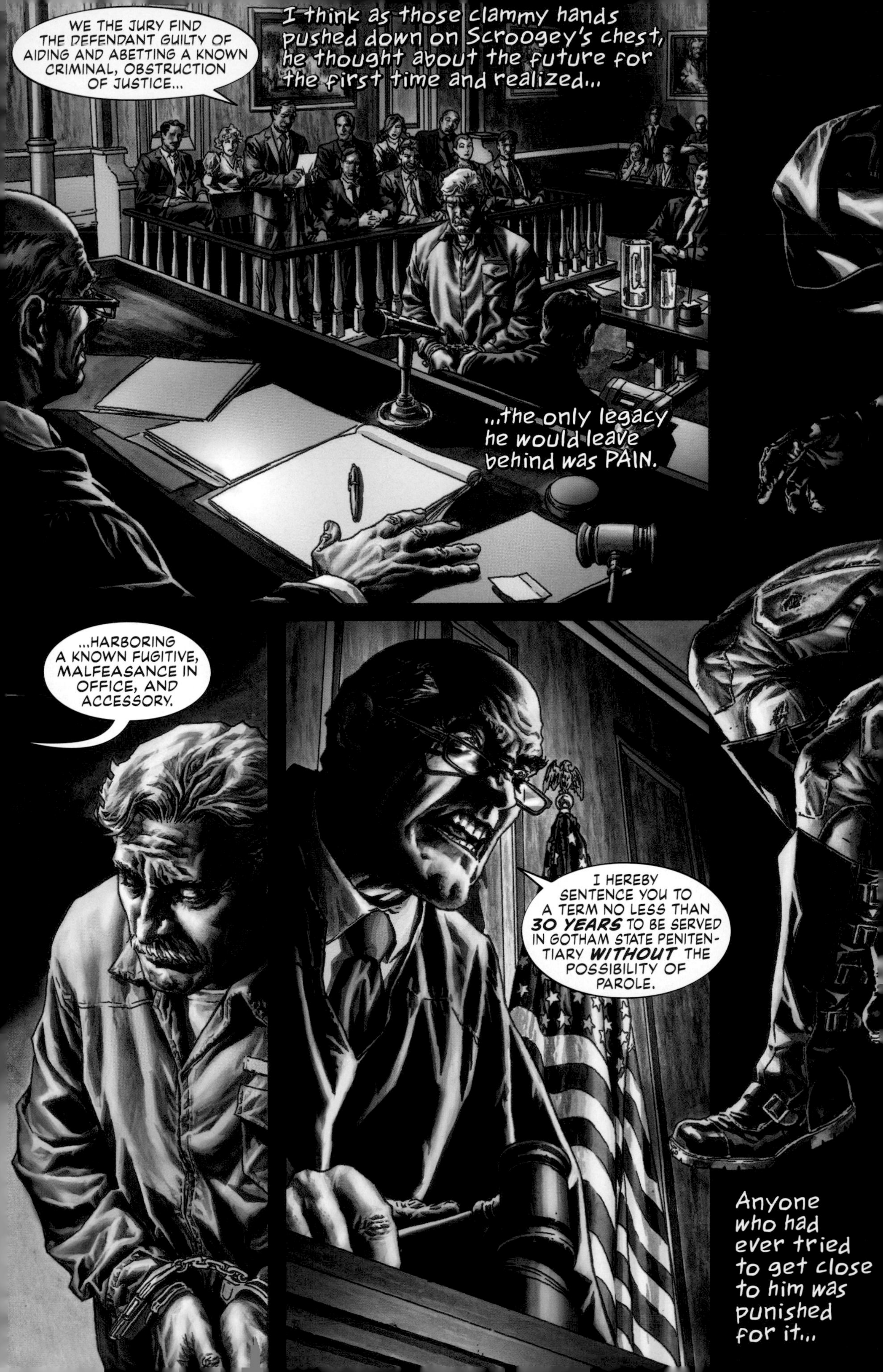
WE THE JURY FIND THE DEFENDANT GUILTY OF AIDING AND ABETTING A KNOWN CRIMINAL, OBSTRUCTION OF JUSTICE...
I think as those clammy hands pushed down on Scroogey's chest, he thought about the future for the first time and realized...
...the only legacy he would leave behind was PAIN.
...HARBORING A KNOWN FUGITIVE, MALFEASANCE IN OFFICE, AND ACCESSORY.
I HEREBY SENTENCE YOU TO A TERM NO LESS THAN **30 YEARS** TO BE SERVED IN GOTHAM STATE PENITENTIARY ***WITHOUT*** THE POSSIBILITY OF PAROLE.
Anyone who had ever tried to get close to him was punished for it...

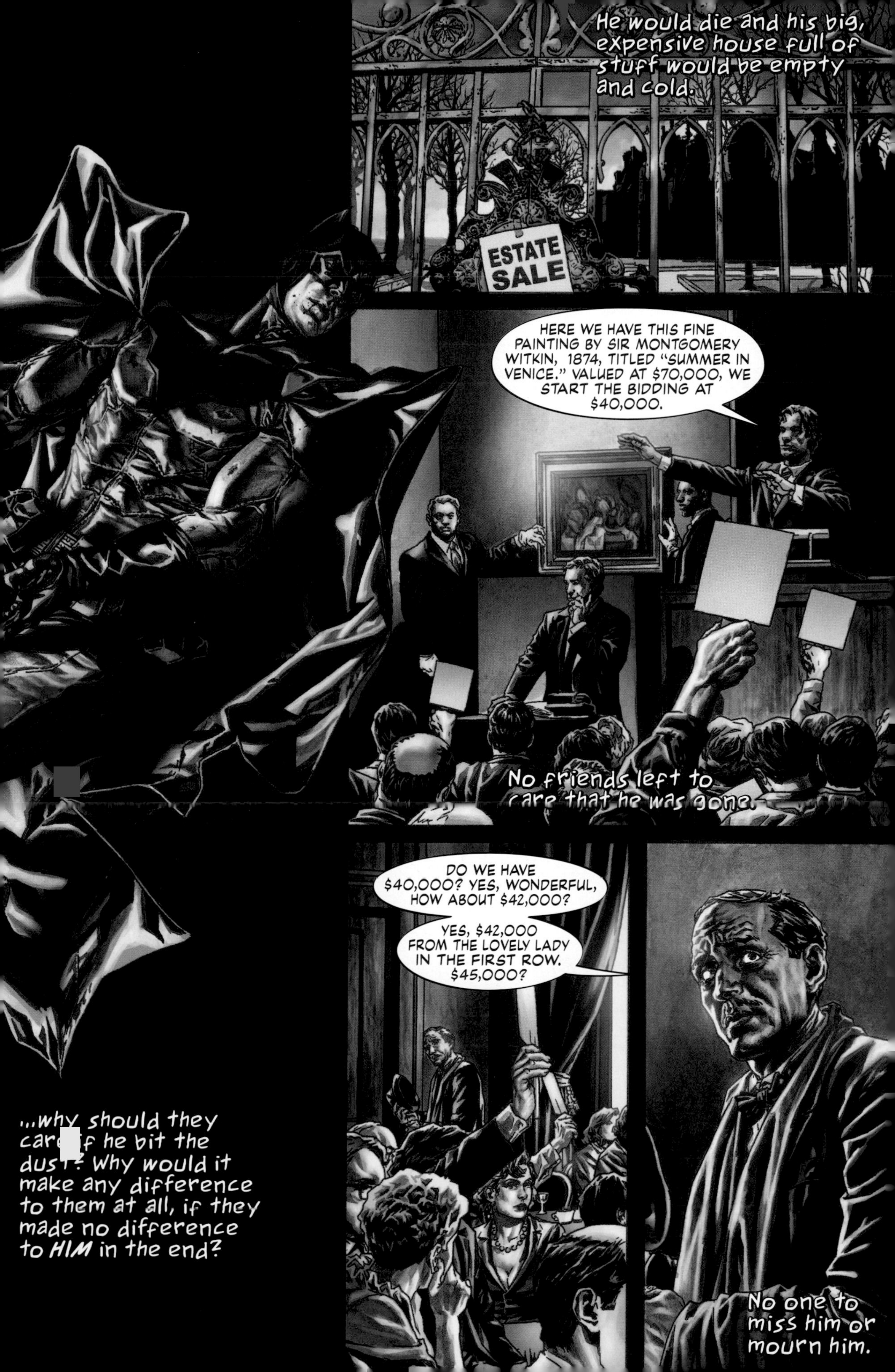

He would die and his big, expensive house full of stuff would be empty and cold.
ESTATE SALE
HERE WE HAVE THIS FINE PAINTING BY SIR MONTGOMERY WITKIN, 1874, TITLED "SUMMER IN VENICE." VALUED AT $70,000, WE START THE BIDDING AT $40,000.
No friends left to care that he was gone.
DO WE HAVE $40,000? YES, WONDERFUL, HOW ABOUT $42,000?
YES, $42,000 FROM THE LOVELY LADY IN THE FIRST ROW. $45,000?
No one to miss him or mourn him.
...why should they car f he bit the dust? Why would it make any difference to them at all, if they made no difference to *HIM* in the end?

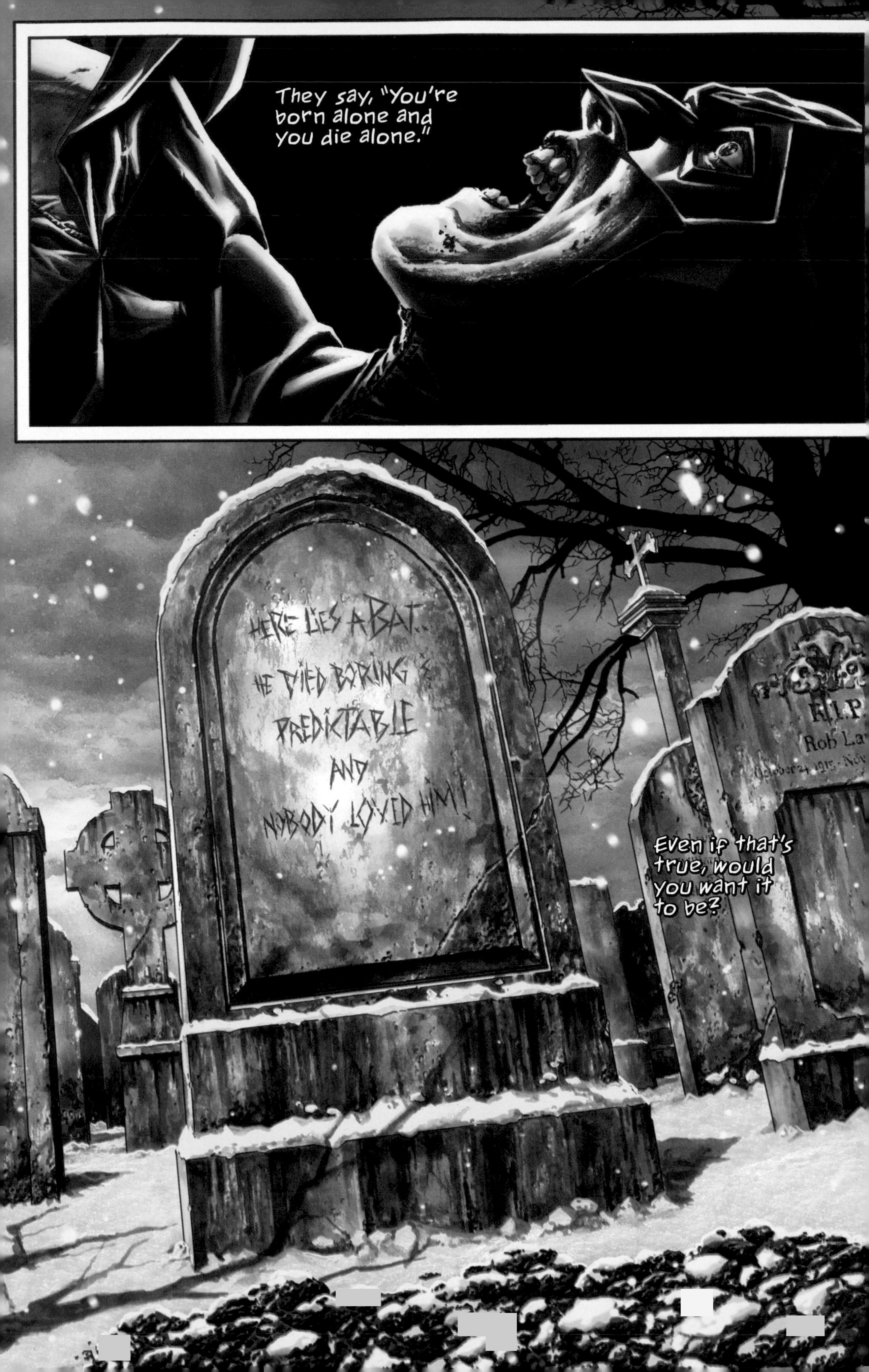
They say, "You're born alone and you die alone."
HERE LIES A BAT...
HE DIED BORING & PREDICTABLE AND NOBODY LOVED HIM!
Even if that's true, would you want it to be?

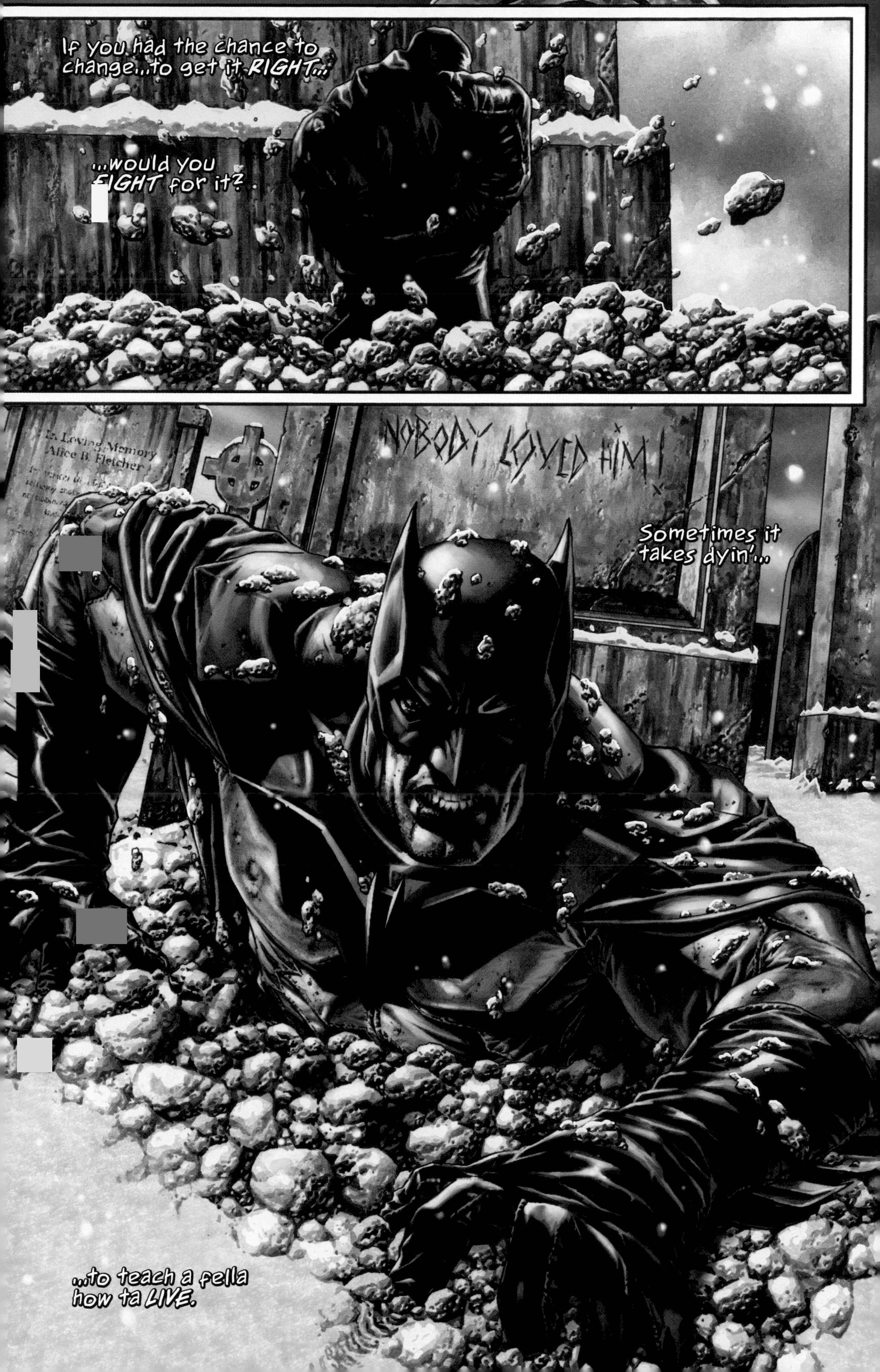
If you had the chance to change...to get it RIGHT...
...would you FIGHT for it?
In Loving Memory
Alice B. Fletcher
NOBODY LOVED HIM!
Sometimes it takes dyin'...
...to teach a fella how ta LIVE.

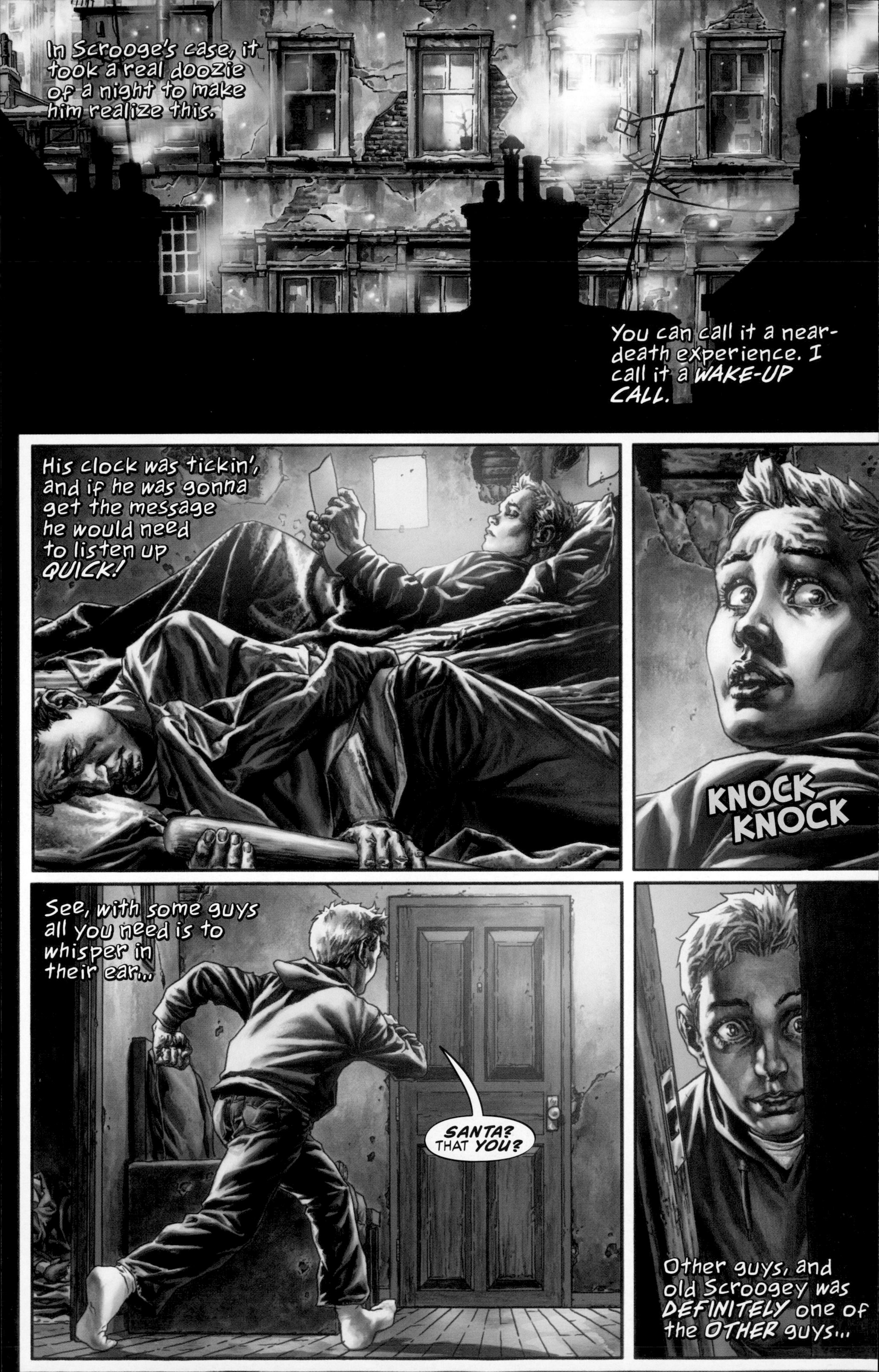
In Scrooge's case, it took a real doozie of a night to make him realize this.
You can call it a near-death experience. I call it a WAKE-UP CALL.
His clock was tickin', and if he was gonna get the message he would need to listen up QUICK!
KNOCK KNOCK
See, with some guys all you need is to whisper in their ear...
SANTA? THAT YOU?
Other guys, and old Scroogey was DEFINITELY one of the OTHER guys...

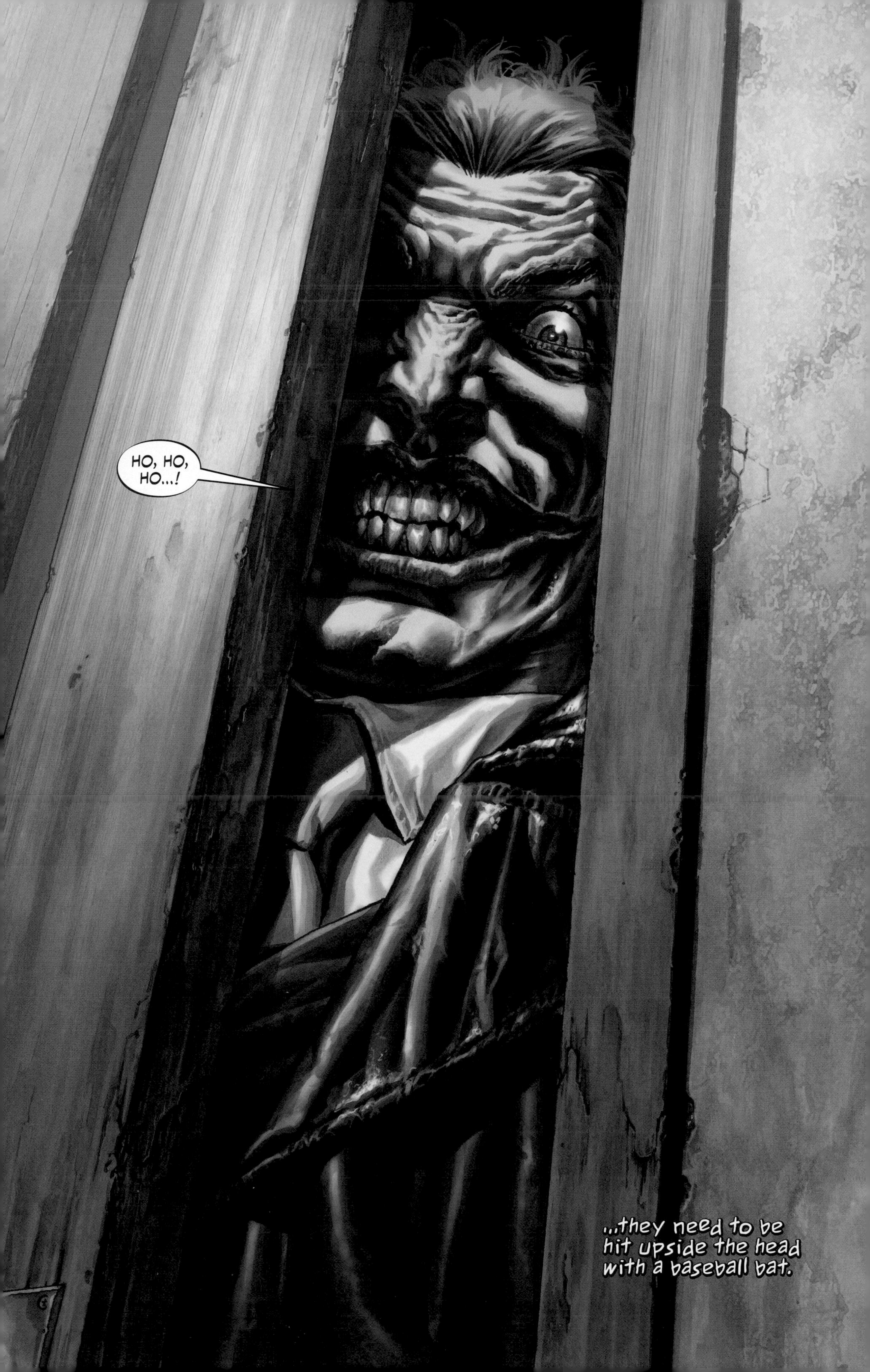
HO, HO, HO...!
...they need to be hit upside the head with a baseball bat.

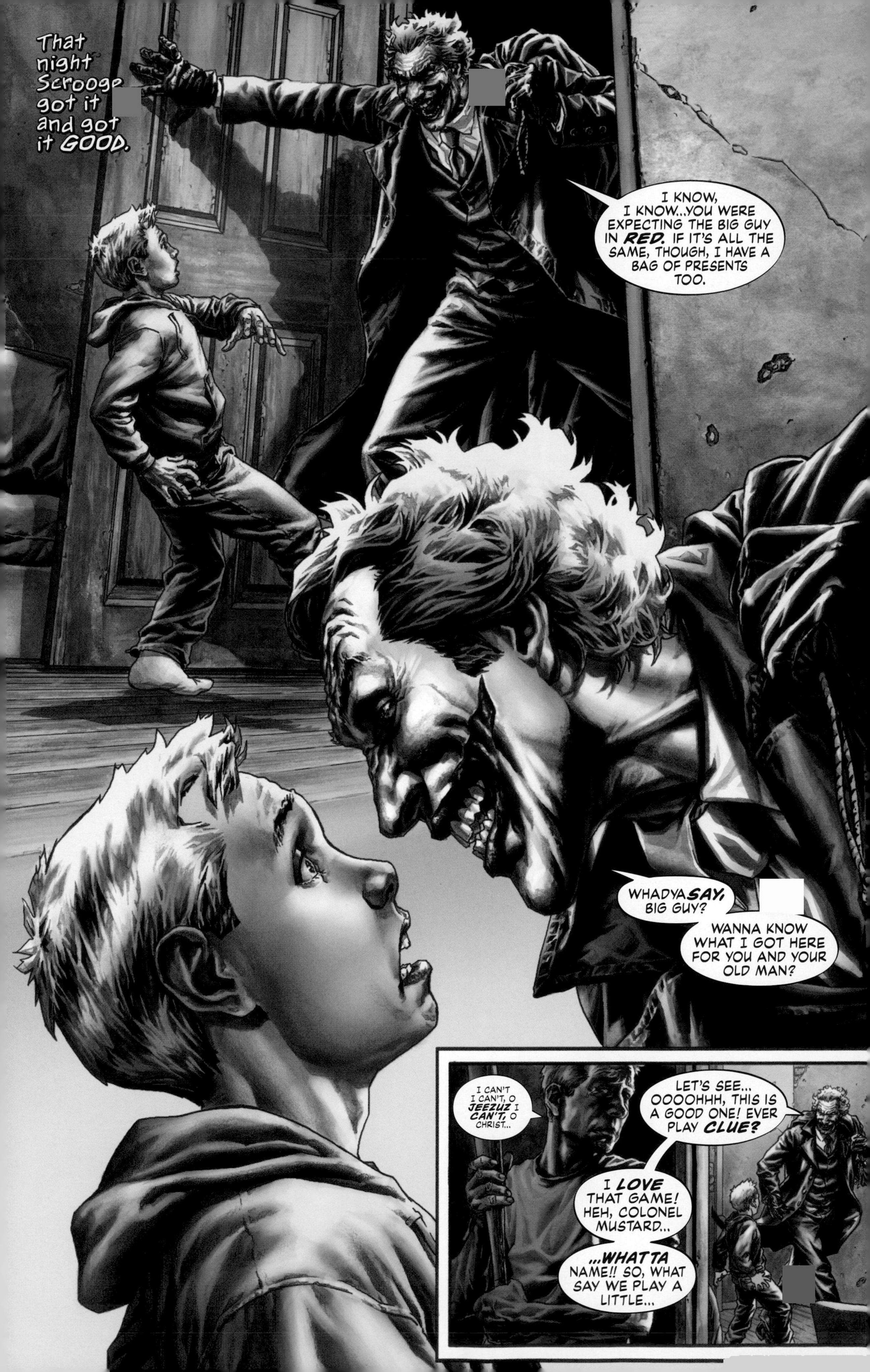
That night Scrooge got it and got it GOOD.
I KNOW, I KNOW...YOU WERE EXPECTING THE BIG GUY IN RED. IF IT'S ALL THE SAME, THOUGH, I HAVE A BAG OF PRESENTS TOO.
WHADYA SAY, BIG GUY?
WANNA KNOW WHAT I GOT HERE FOR YOU AND YOUR OLD MAN?
I CAN'T I CAN'T, O JEEZUZ I CAN'T, O CHRIST...
LET'S SEE... OOOOHHH, THIS IS A GOOD ONE! EVER PLAY CLUE?
I LOVE THAT GAME! HEH, COLONEL MUSTARD...
...WHATTA NAME!! SO, WHAT SAY WE PLAY A LITTLE...

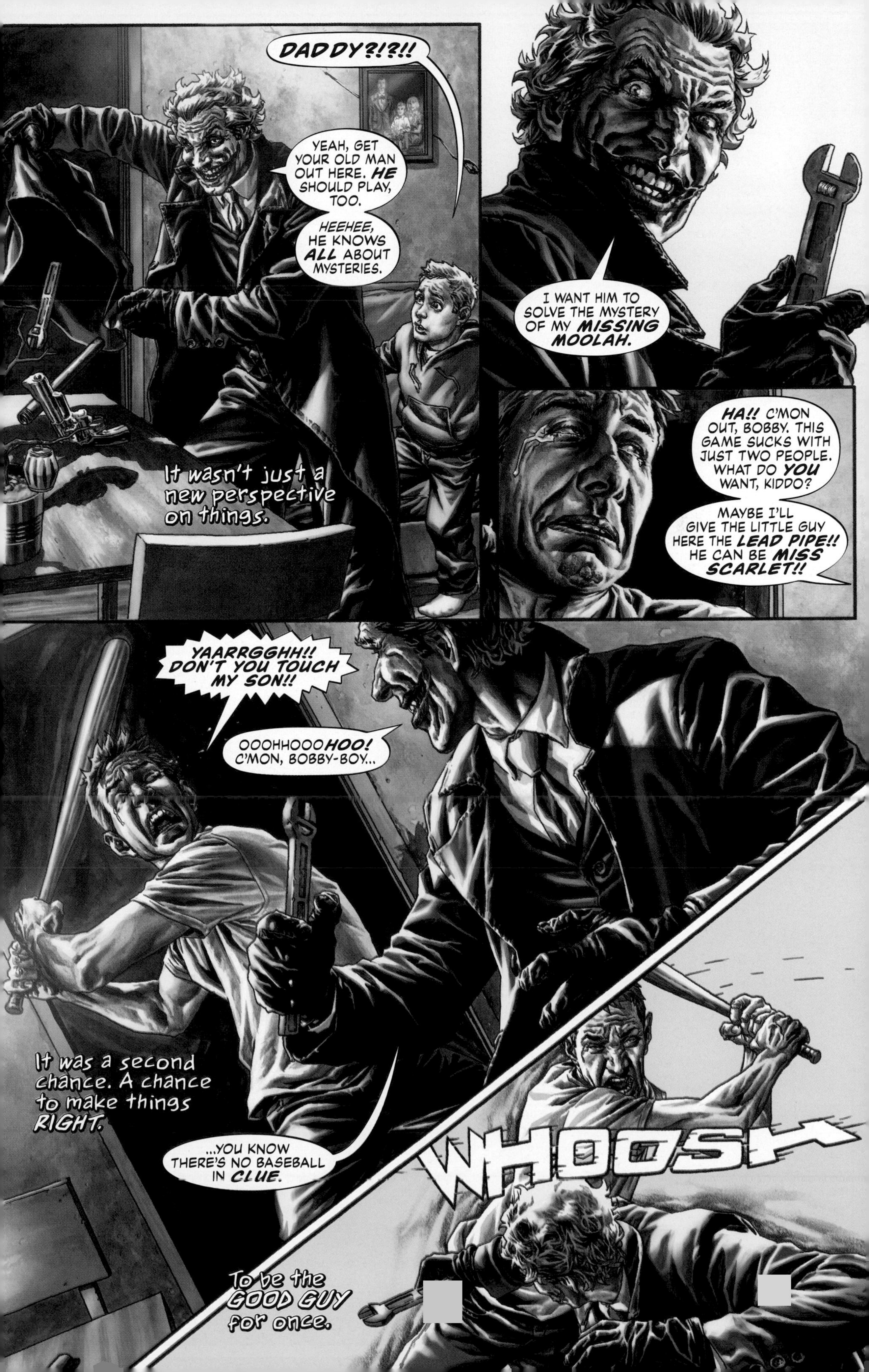
DADDY?!?!!
YEAH, GET YOUR OLD MAN OUT HERE. HE SHOULD PLAY, TOO.
HEEHEE, HE KNOWS ALL ABOUT MYSTERIES.
It wasn't just a new perspective on things.
I WANT HIM TO SOLVE THE MYSTERY OF MY MISSING MOOLAH.
HA!! C'MON OUT, BOBBY. THIS GAME SUCKS WITH JUST TWO PEOPLE. WHAT DO YOU WANT, KIDDO?
MAYBE I'LL GIVE THE LITTLE GUY HERE THE LEAD PIPE!! HE CAN BE MISS SCARLET!!
YAARRGGHH!! DON'T YOU TOUCH MY SON!!
OOOHHOOOHOO! C'MON, BOBBY-BOY...
It was a second chance. A chance to make things RIGHT.
...YOU KNOW THERE'S NO BASEBALL IN CLUE.
WHOOSH
To be the GOOD GUY for once.

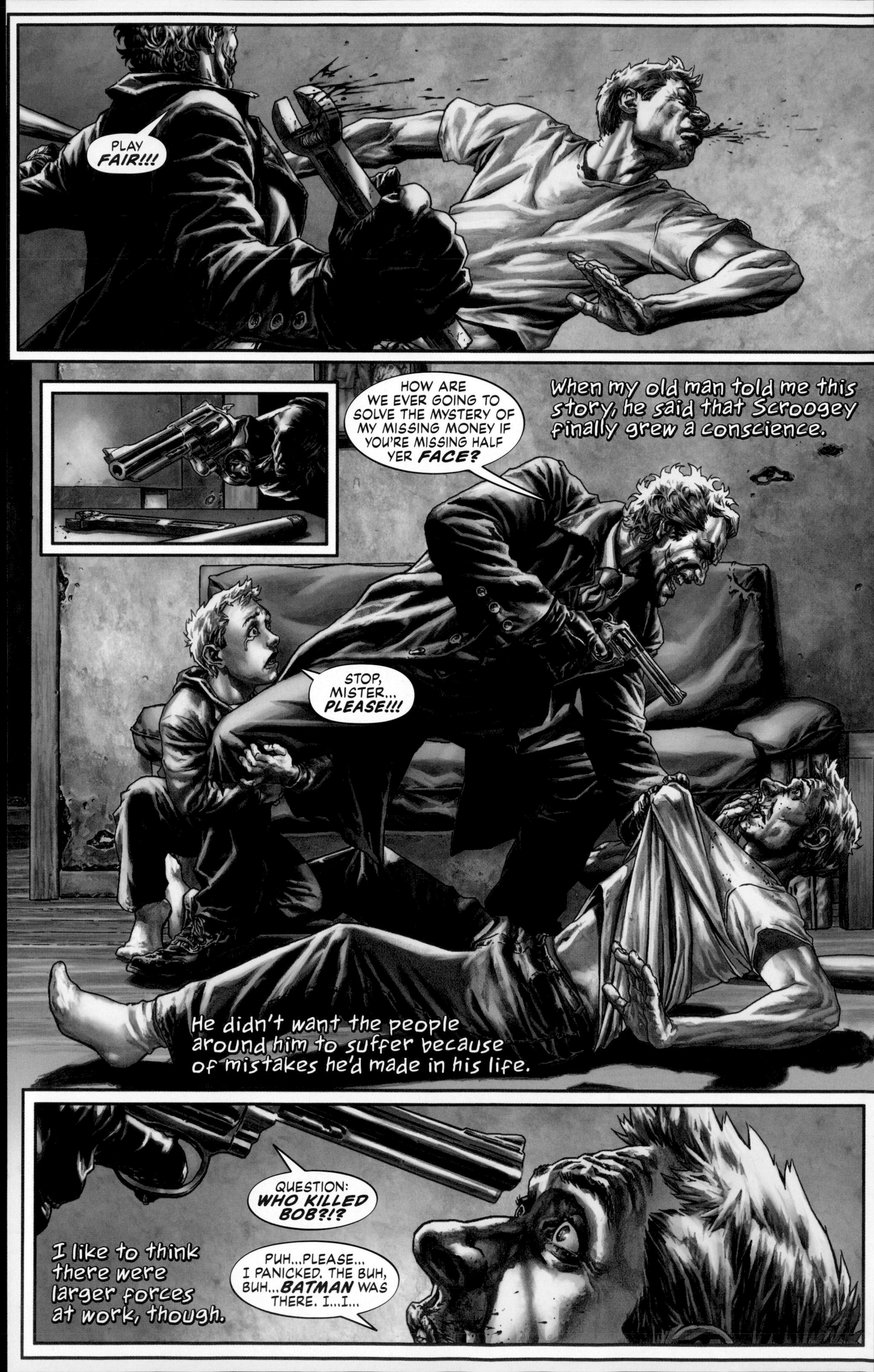
PLAY FAIR!!!
HOW ARE WE EVER GOING TO SOLVE THE MYSTERY OF MY MISSING MONEY IF YOU'RE MISSING HALF YER FACE?
When my old man told me this story, he said that Scroogey finally grew a conscience.
STOP, MISTER... PLEASE!!!
He didn't want the people around him to suffer because of mistakes he'd made in his life.
QUESTION: WHO KILLED BOB?!?
I like to think there were larger forces at work, though.
PUH...PLEASE... I PANICKED. THE BUH, BUH...BATMAN WAS THERE. I...I...

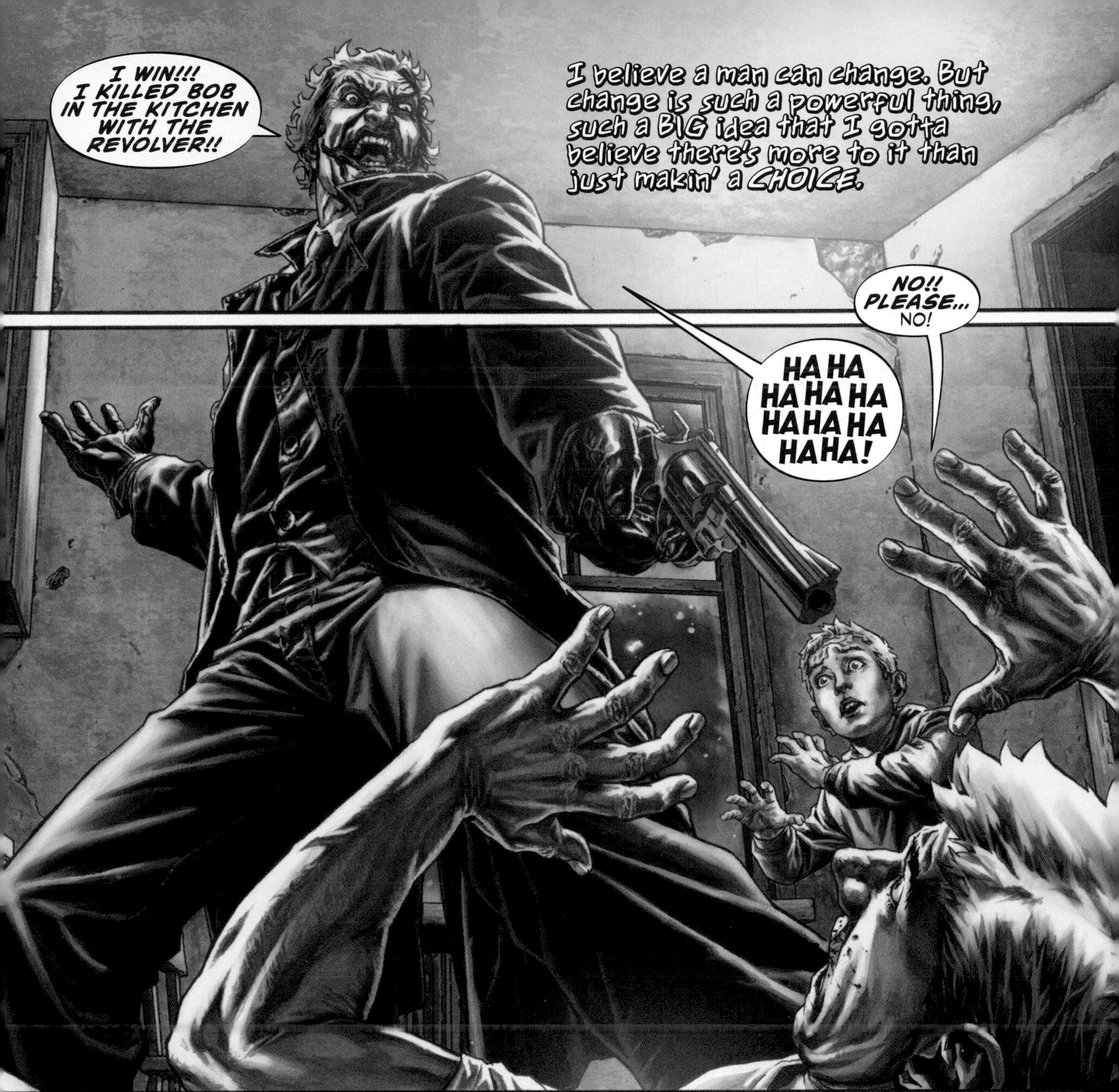
I WIN!!! I KILLED BOB IN THE KITCHEN WITH THE REVOLVER!!
I believe a man can change. But change is such a powerful thing, such a BIG idea that I gotta believe there's more to it than just makin' a CHOICE.
HA HA HA HA HA HA HA HA HA HA!
NO!! PLEASE... NO!
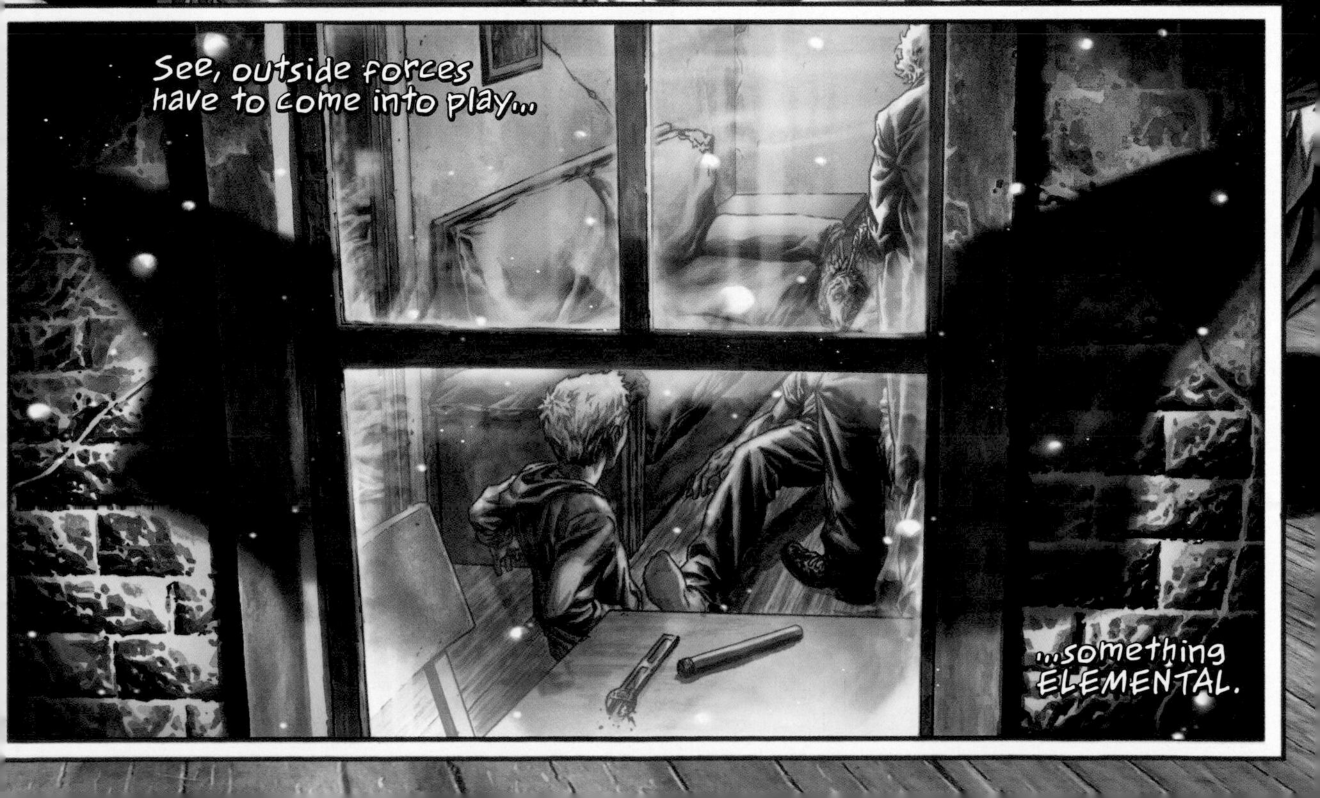
See, outside forces have to come into play...
...something ELEMENTAL.

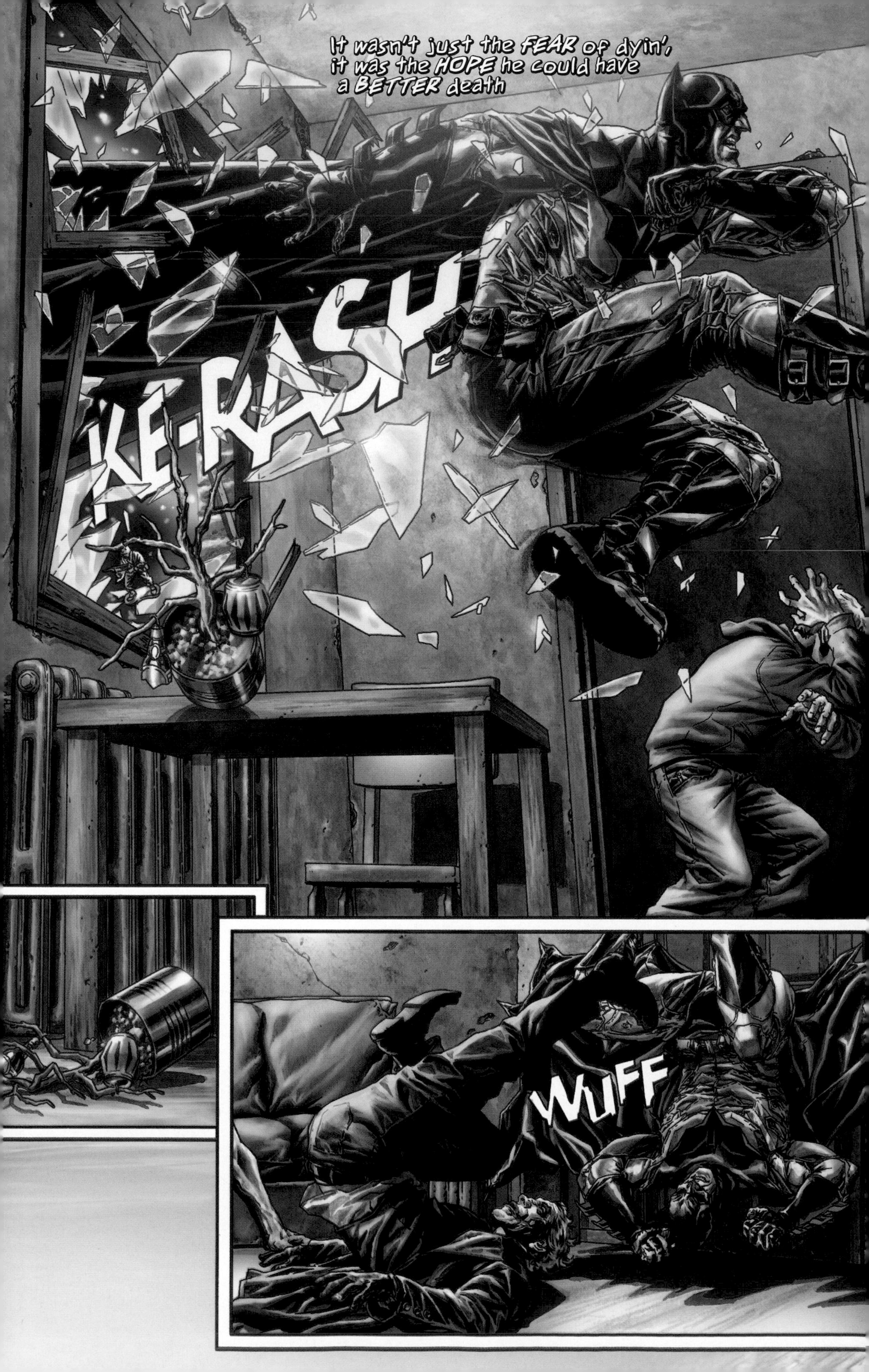
It wasn't just the FEAR of dyin', it was the HOPE he could have a BETTER death
KE-RASH
WUFF

You gotta make the leap, take the chance that you'll fail, but go down tryin' anyway.

After a lifetime of HURTING and BULLYING people...making people afraid of him...

THUD

...ol' Scrooge had the chance to make sure that when he finally DID check out...

KLUNK

...when all was said and done...

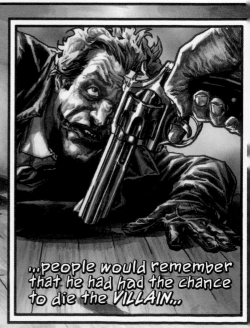

...people would remember that he had had the chance to die the VILLAIN...

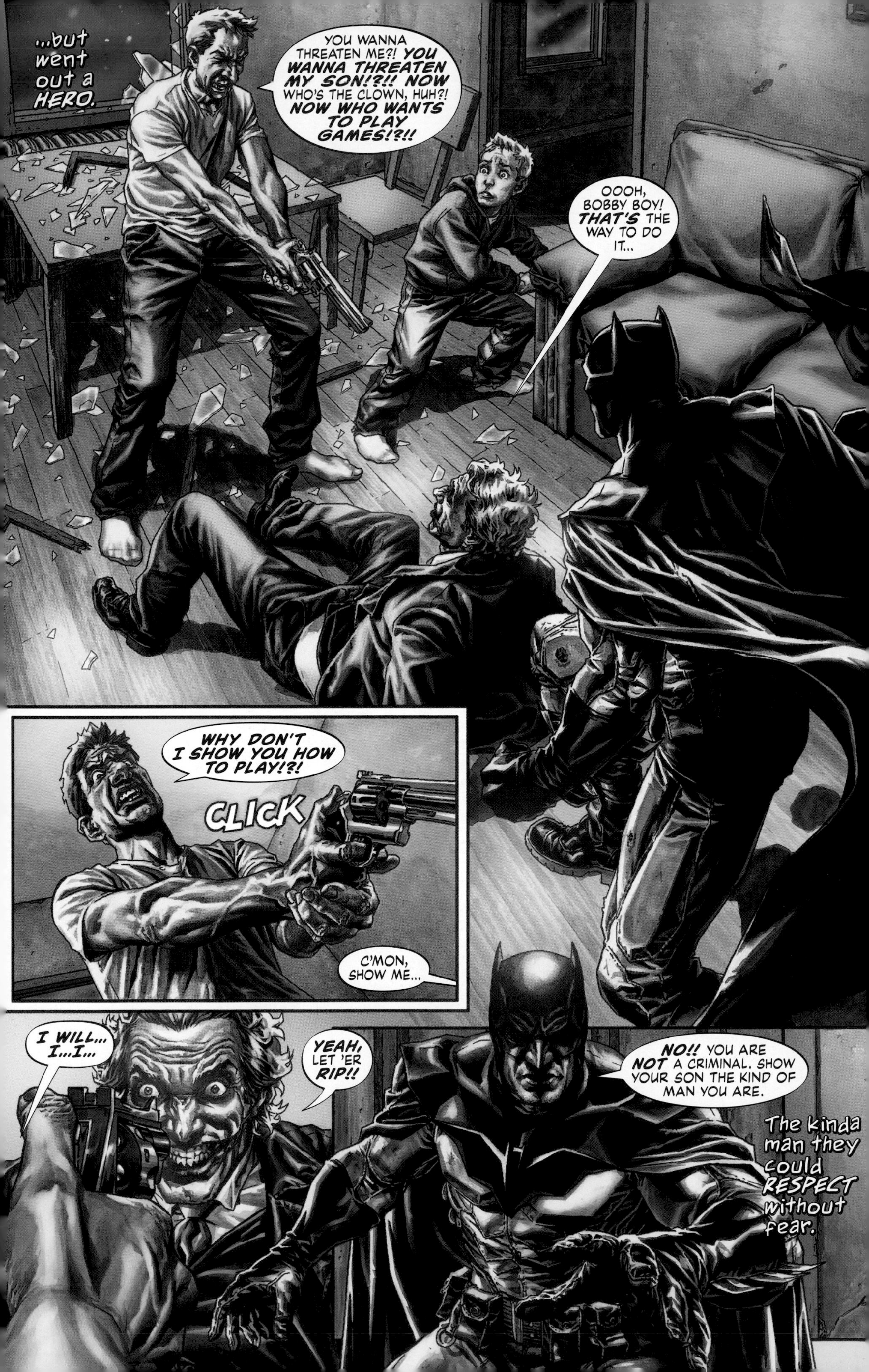

...but went out a HERO.
YOU WANNA THREATEN ME?! YOU WANNA THREATEN MY SON!?!! NOW WHO'S THE CLOWN, HUH?! NOW WHO WANTS TO PLAY GAMES!?!!
OOOH, BOBBY BOY! THAT'S THE WAY TO DO IT...
WHY DON'T I SHOW YOU HOW TO PLAY!?!
CLICK
C'MON, SHOW ME...
I WILL... I...I...
YEAH, LET 'ER RIP!!
NO!! YOU ARE NOT A CRIMINAL. SHOW YOUR SON THE KIND OF MAN YOU ARE.
The kinda man they could RESPECT without fear.

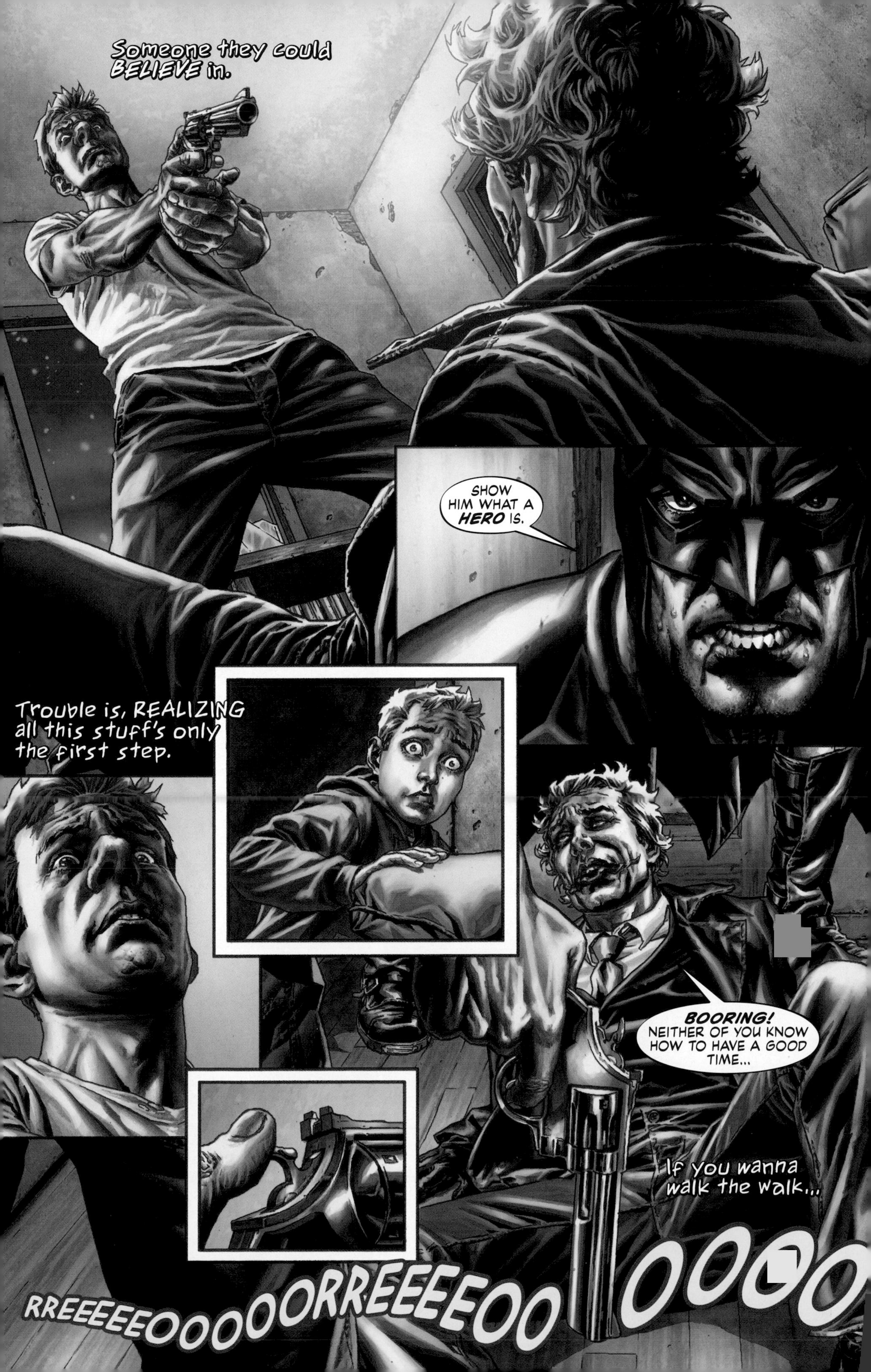
Someone they could BELIEVE in.
SHOW HIM WHAT A HERO IS.
Trouble is, REALIZING all this stuff's only the first step.
BOORING! NEITHER OF YOU KNOW HOW TO HAVE A GOOD TIME...
If you wanna walk the walk...
RREEEEEEOOOOOORREEEEEOO OOOO

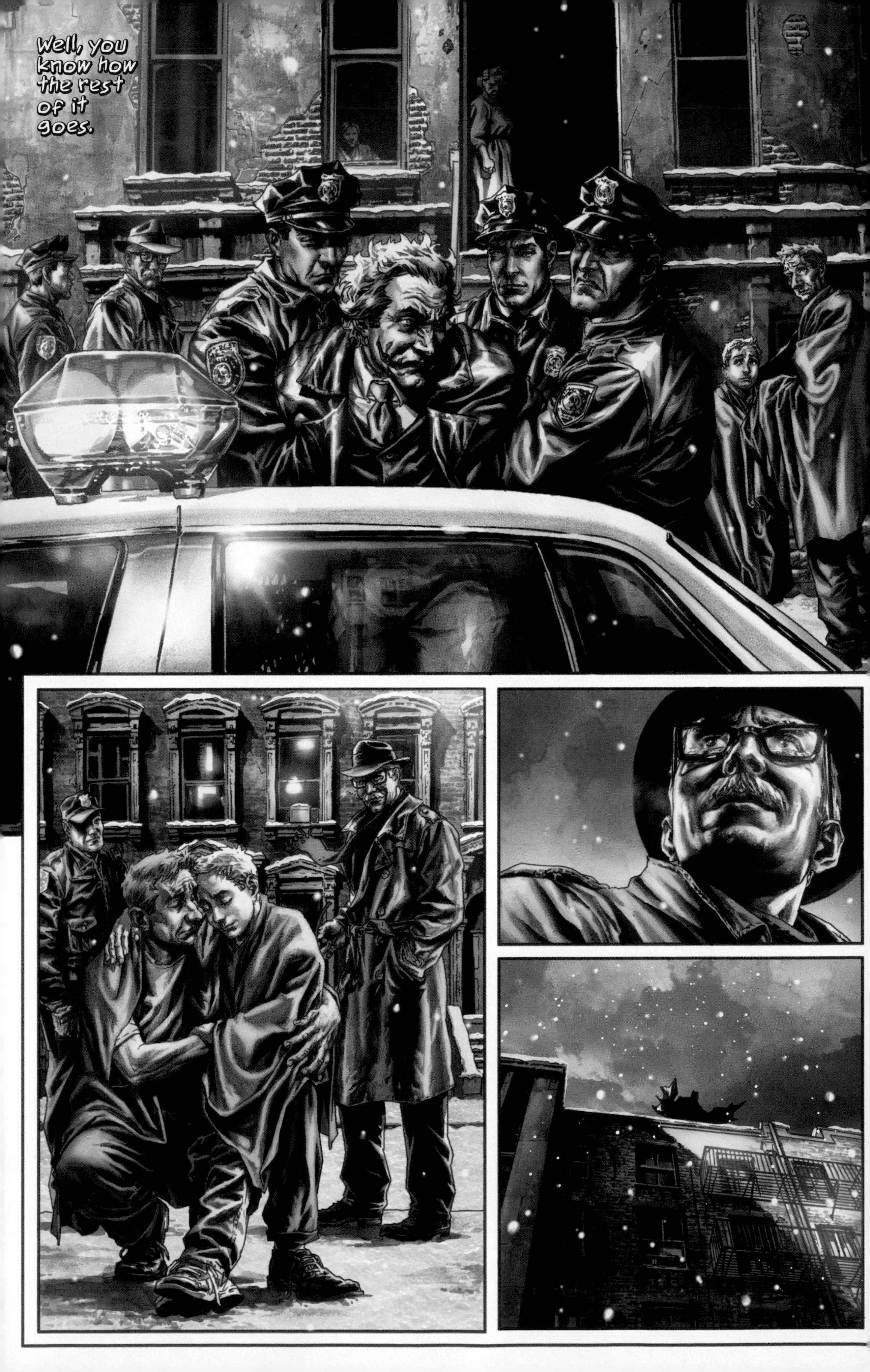
Well, you know how the rest of it goes.

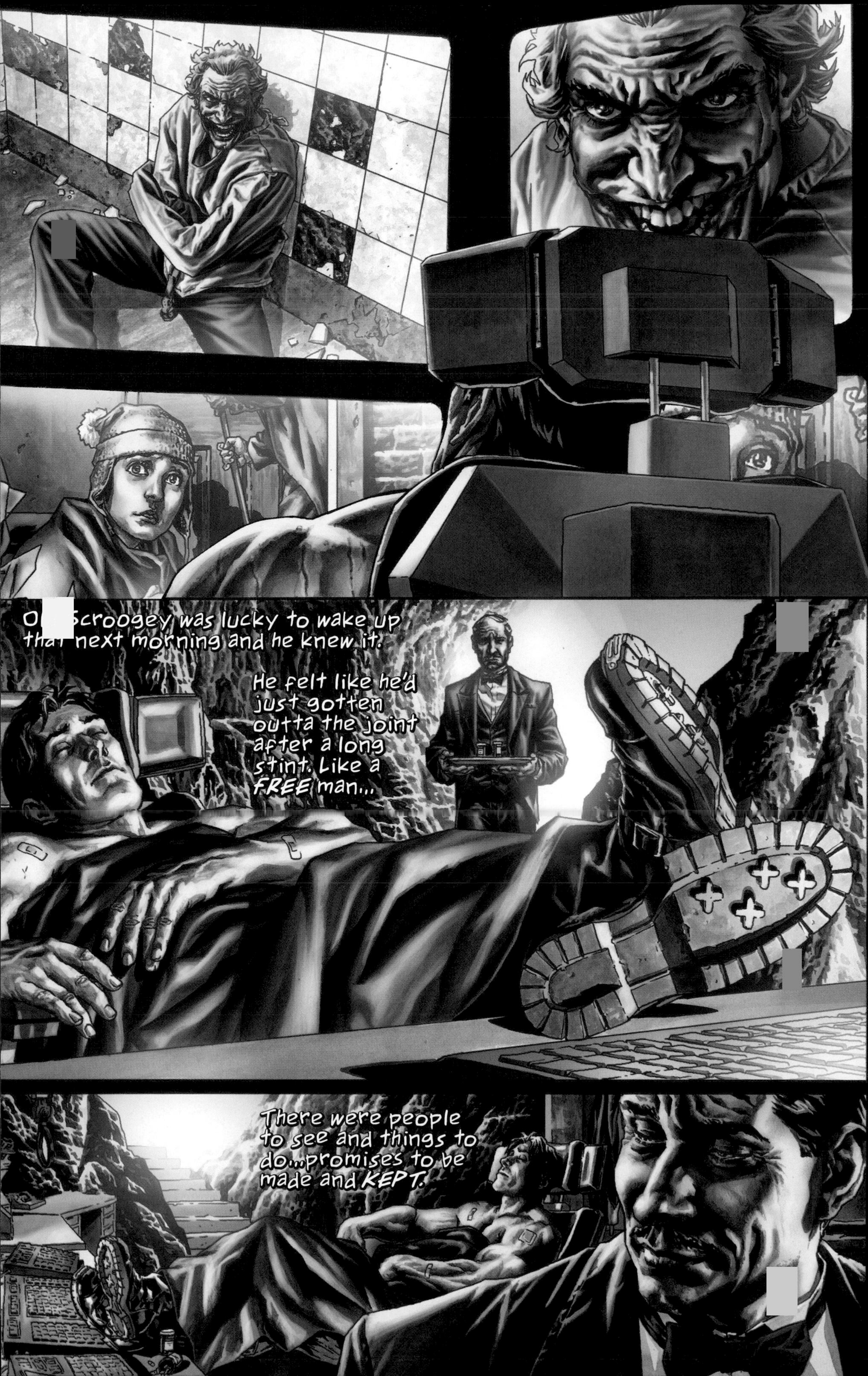
O Scroogey was lucky to wake up that next morning and he knew it.
He felt like he'd just gotten outta the joint after a long stint. Like a FREE man...
There were people to see and things to do...promises to be made and KEPT.

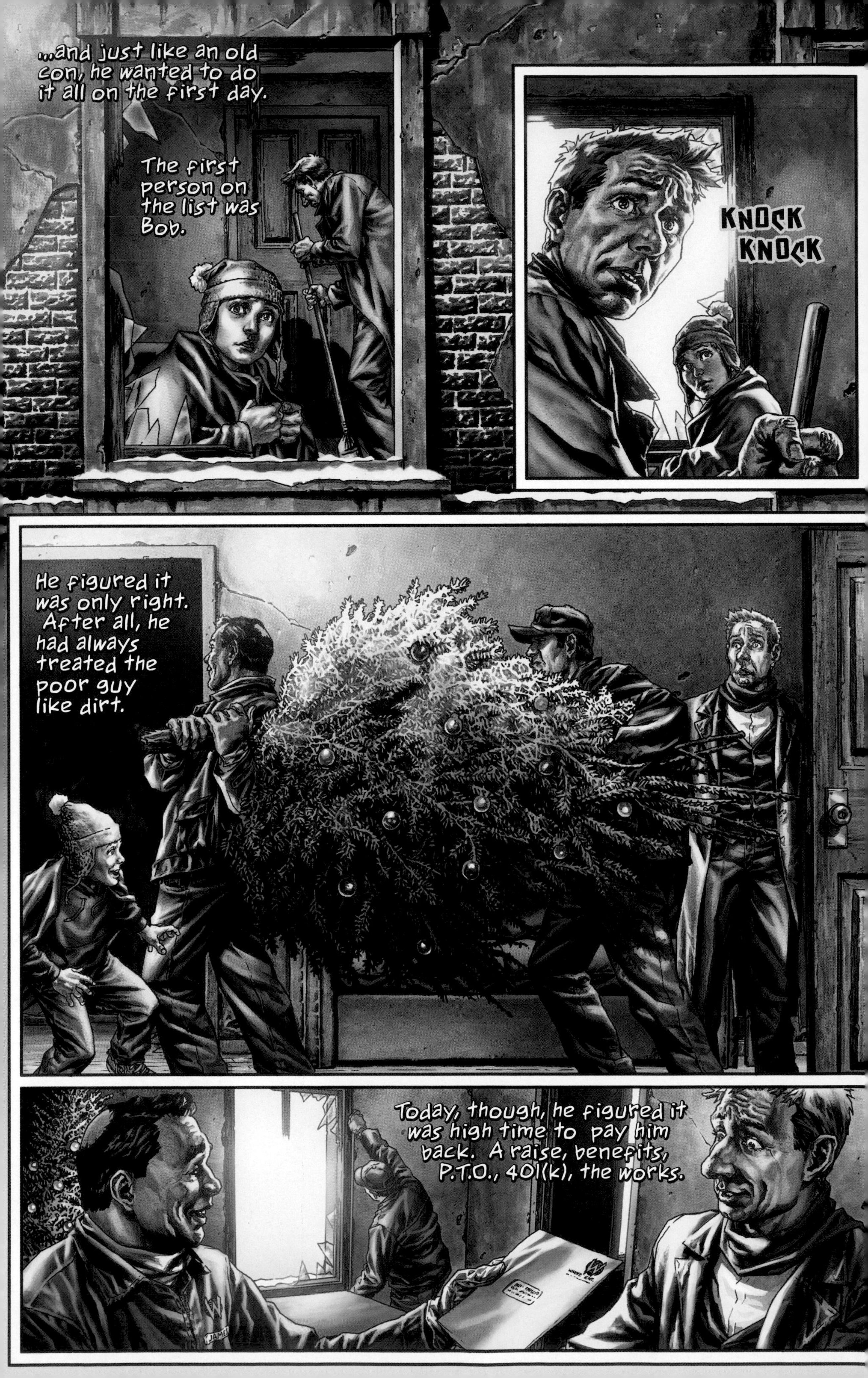
...and just like an old con, he wanted to do it all on the first day.
The first person on the list was Bob.
KNOCK KNOCK
He figured it was only right. After all, he had always treated the poor guy like dirt.
Today, though, he figured it was high time to pay him back. A raise, benefits, P.T.O., 401(k), the works.

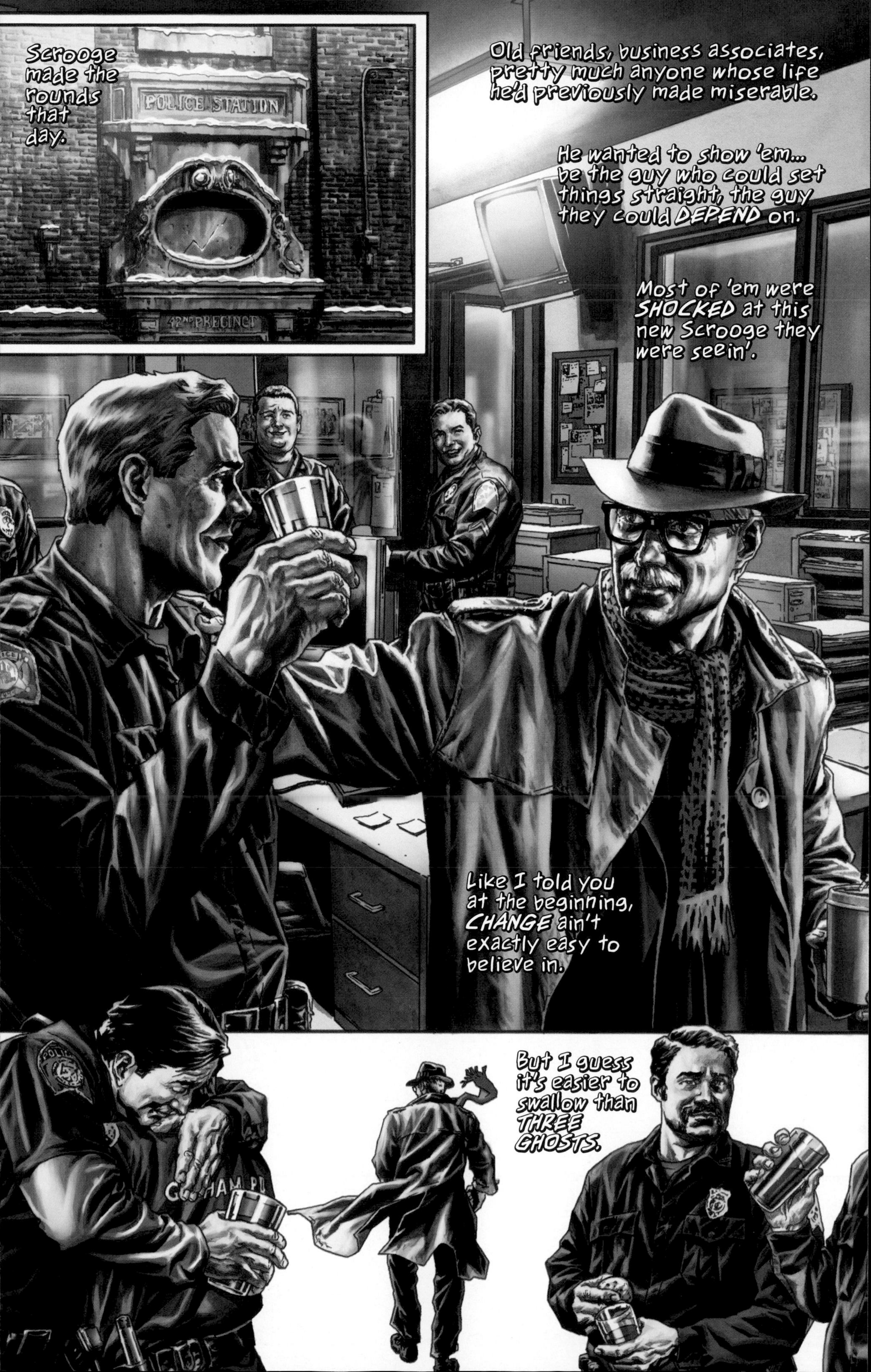

POLICE STATION
42ND PRECINCT
Scrooge made the rounds that day.
Old friends, business associates, pretty much anyone whose life he'd previously made miserable.
He wanted to show 'em... be the guy who could set things straight, the guy they could DEPEND on.
Most of 'em were SHOCKED at this new Scrooge they were seein'.
Like I told you at the beginning, CHANGE ain't exactly easy to believe in.
But I guess it's easier to swallow than THREE GHOSTS.

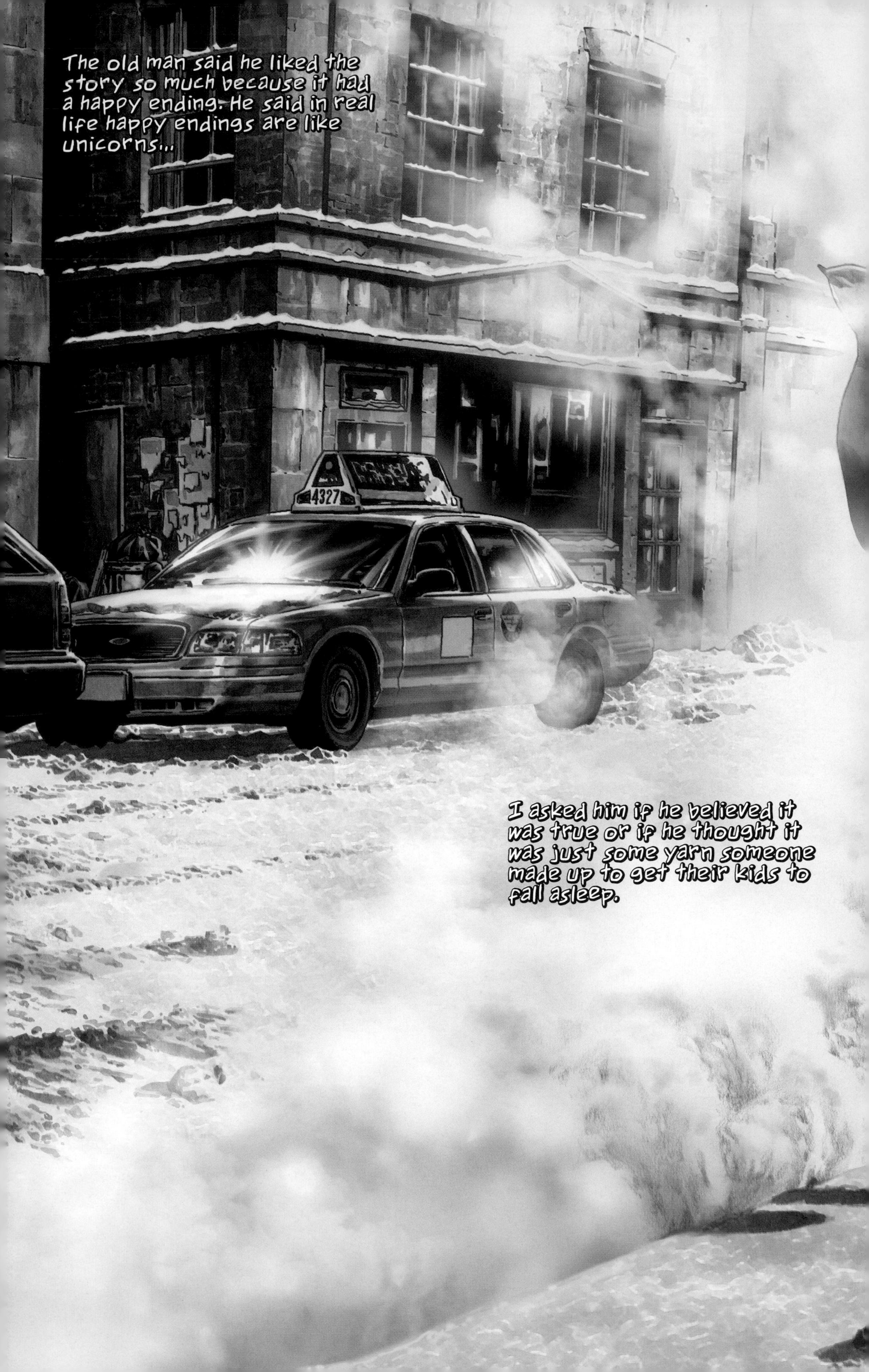
The old man said he liked the story so much because it had a happy ending. He said in real life happy endings are like unicorns...
4327
I asked him if he believed it was true or if he thought it was just some yarn someone made up to get their kids to fall asleep.

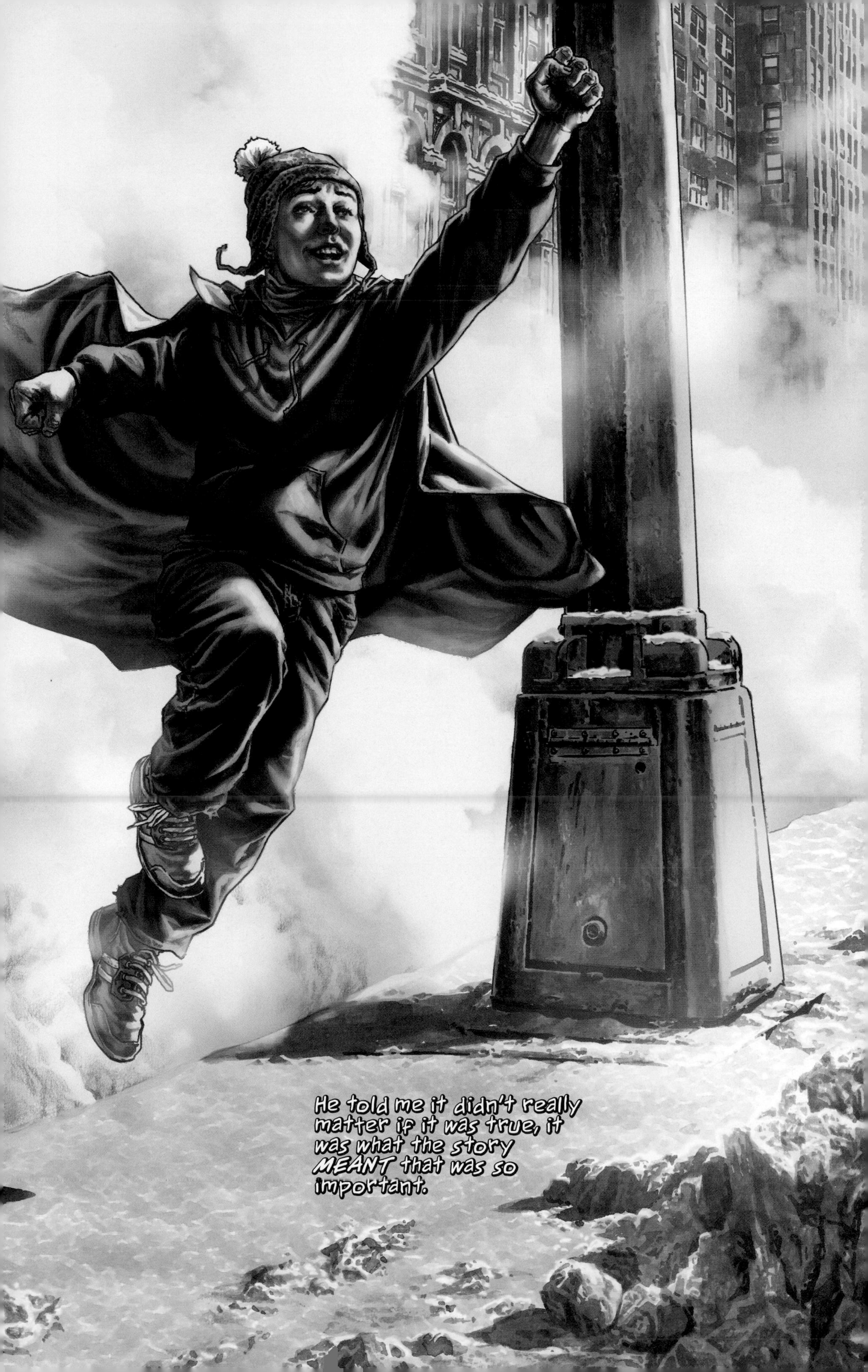
He told me it didn't really matter if it was true, it was what the story MEANT that was so important.

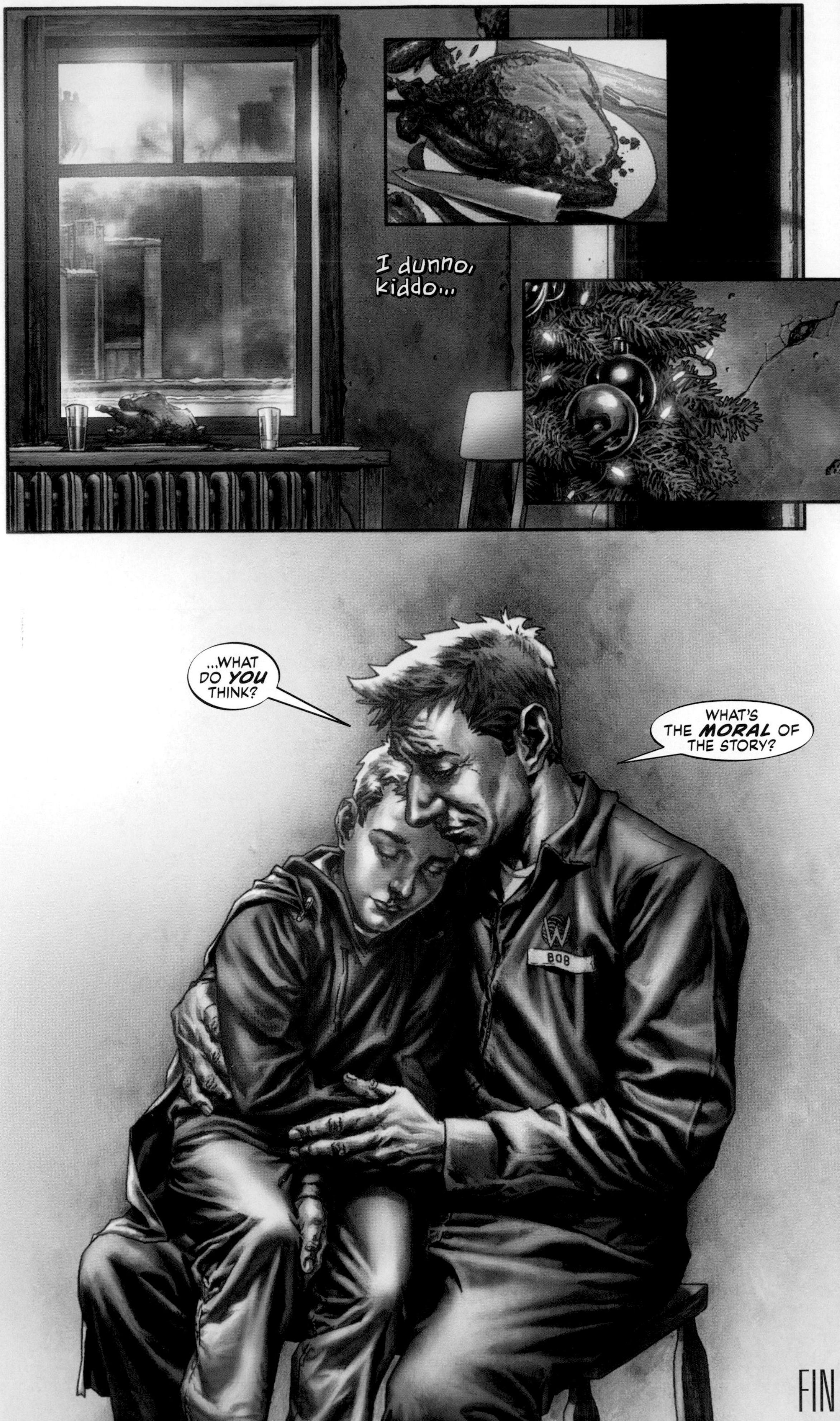
I dunno, kiddo...
...WHAT DO YOU THINK?
WHAT'S THE MORAL OF THE STORY?
FIN

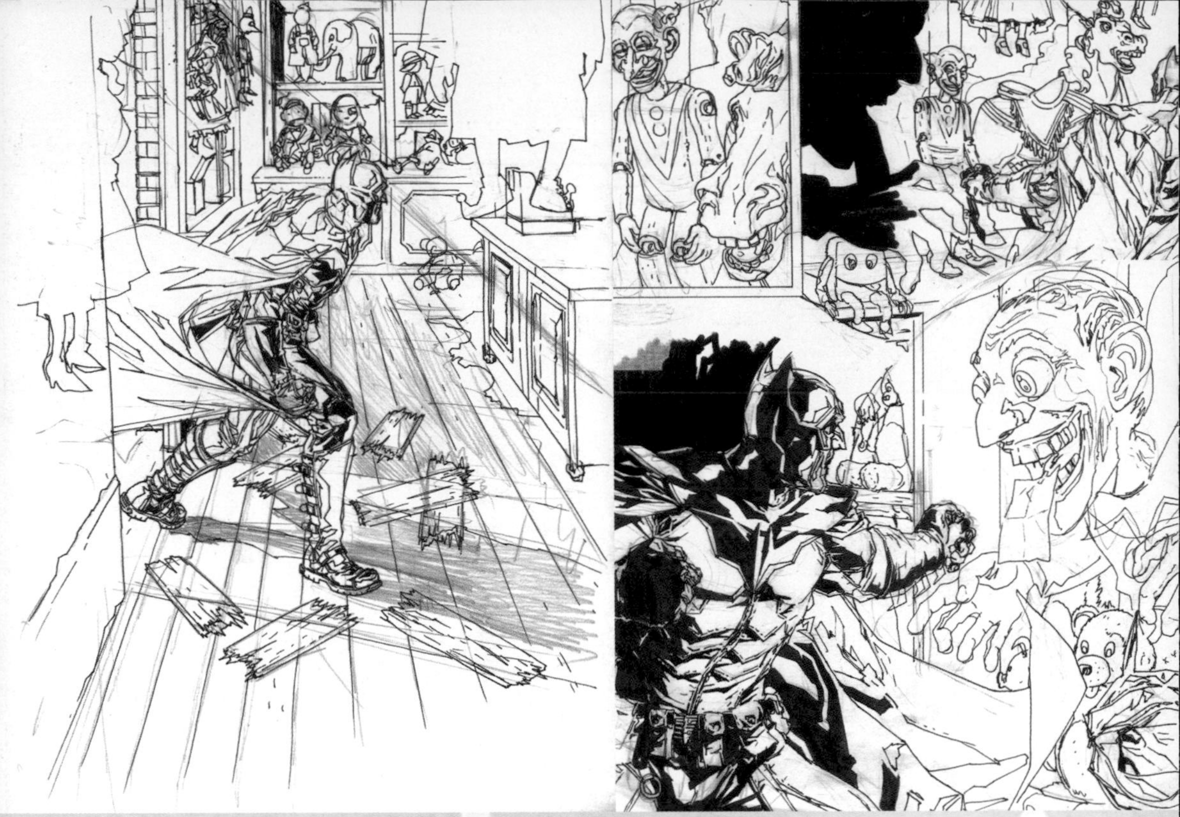

Some preliminary sketches for pages 22 and 23. I normally don't block in shadow areas in the layout and sketch process. Since lighting was such a big part of making this particular sequence feel atmospheric, though, I took the sketches a little further just to figure out where elements would cast shadows or fade to black.

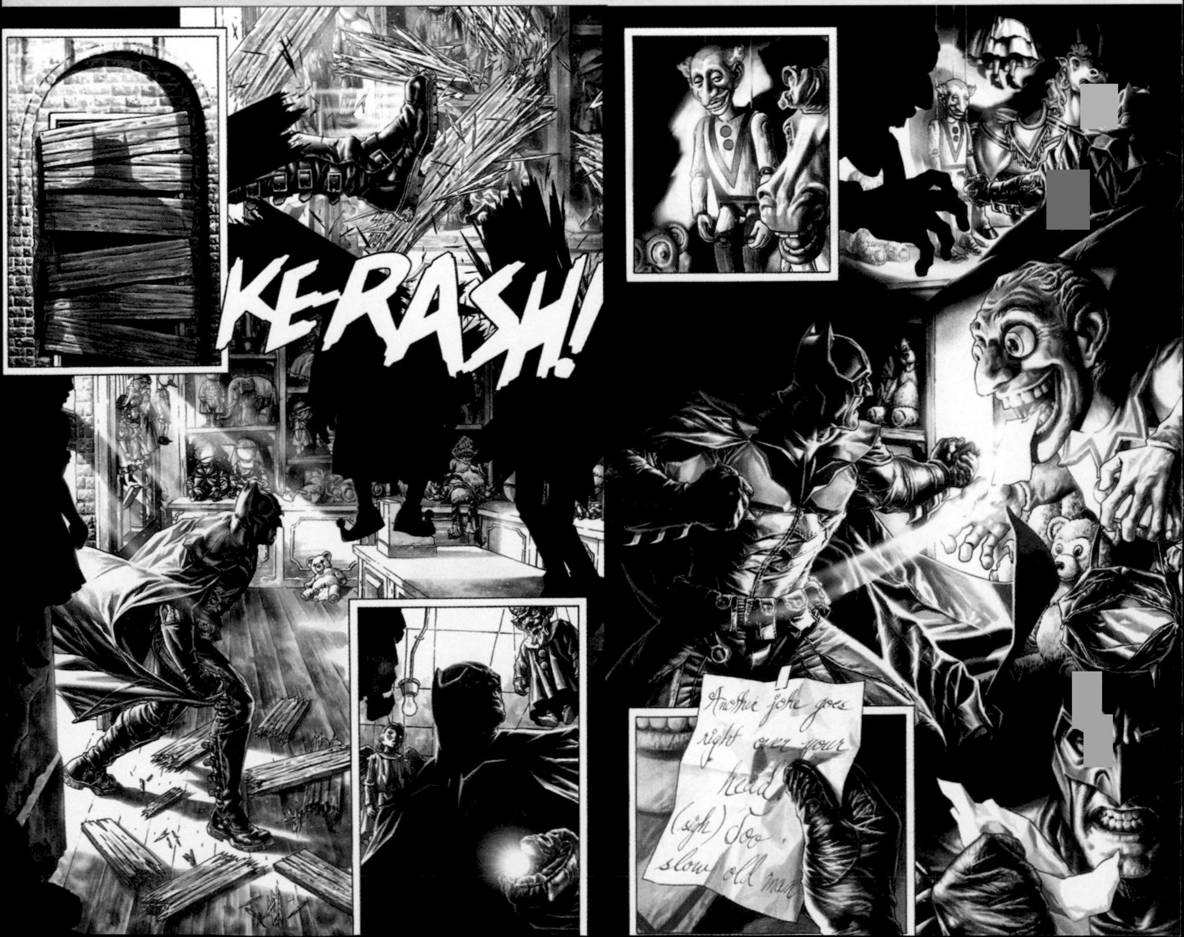
KE-RASH!
Another joke goes right over your head (sigh) Joe. slow old man

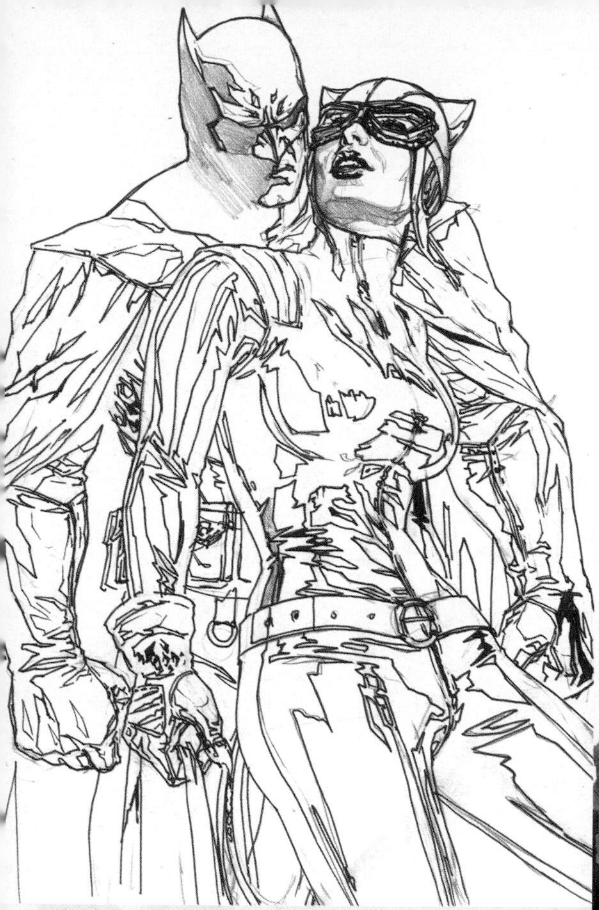

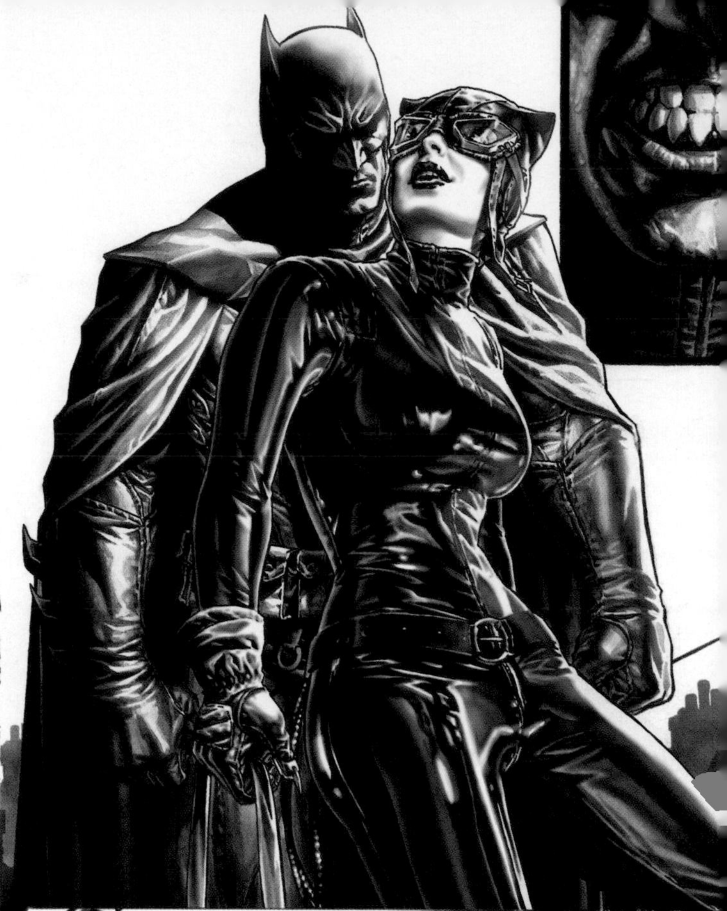

Catwoman was the character I looked forward to drawing the most in this book. I knew I wanted her costume to look slick and reflective, almost like a piece of obsidian. The relationship between Batman and Selina has always interested me because of the love/hate dynamic. Plus, the fact that she's been interpreted visually throughout the years in many different ways made her a great candidate for the "ghost of Christmas past."

The Batman TV show of the '60s had a big impact on me as a child. I wanted to introduce some of the more "ridiculous" scenarios that were commonplace in that series as a way to emphasize the change from the lighthearted Batman of the past to the darker, violent vigilante of today. This of course mirrored the narrative structure of A CHRISTMAS CAROL as well.

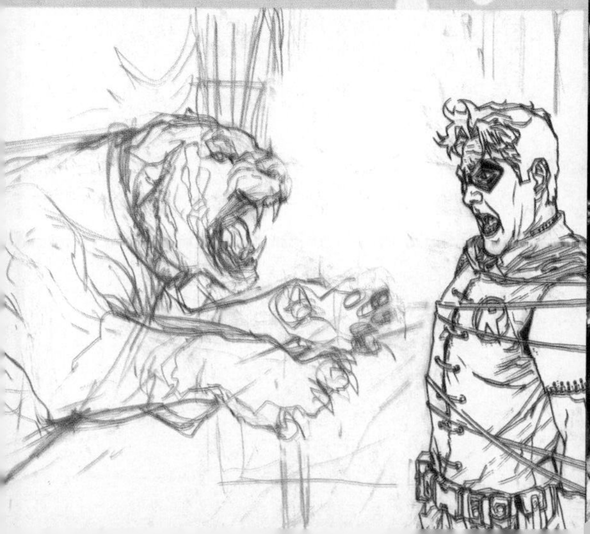

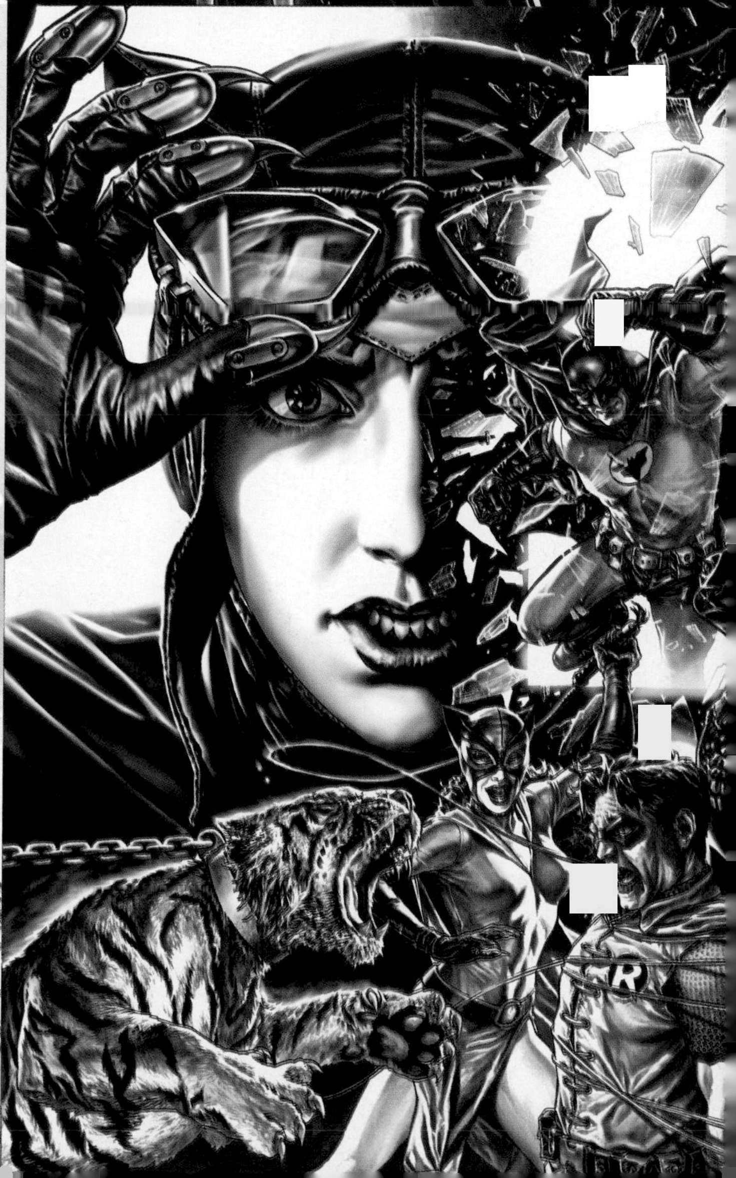

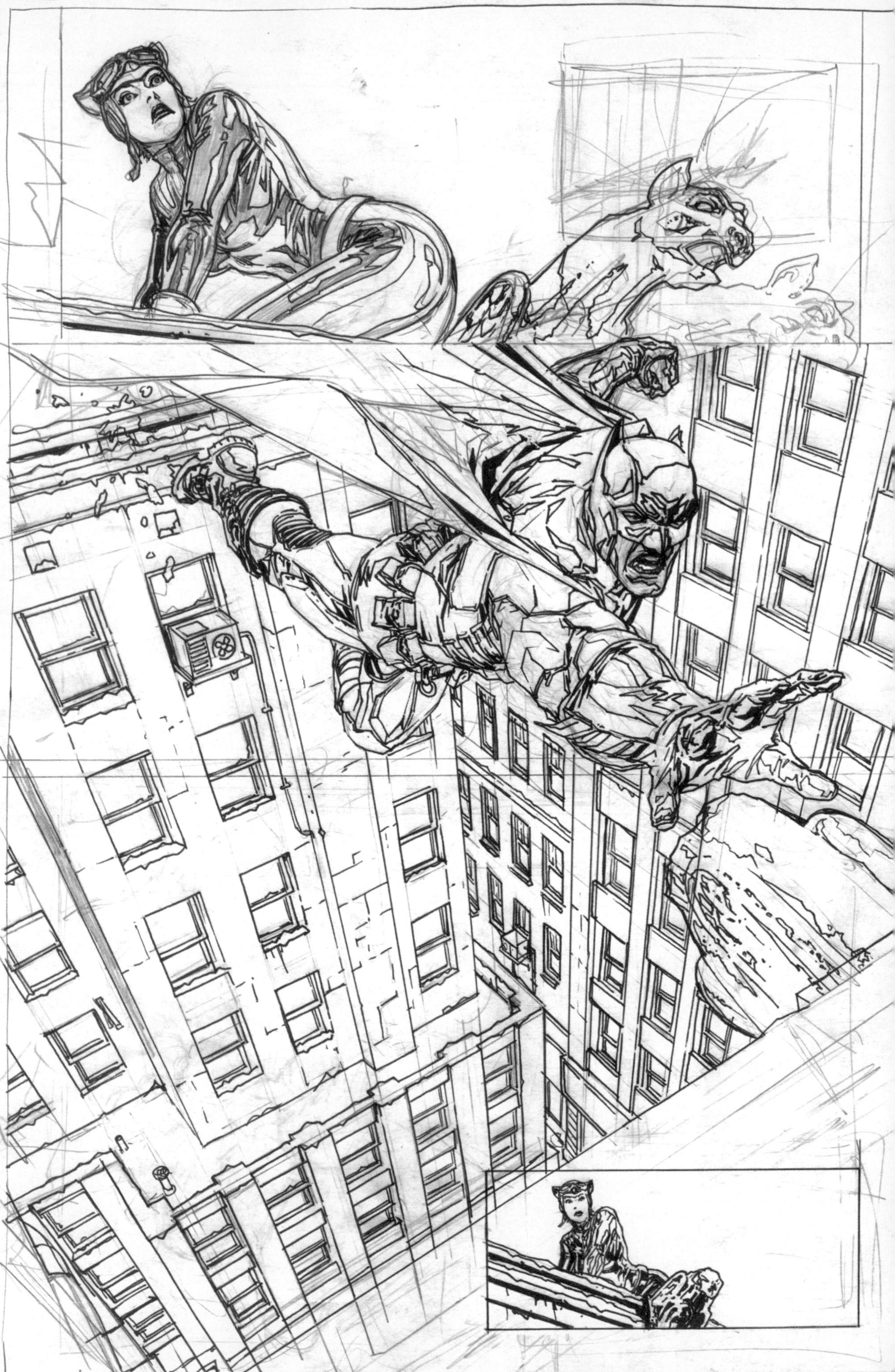

Nearly finished pencils...I added an inset panel and falling Batman figure after getting the perspective right on the background buildings.

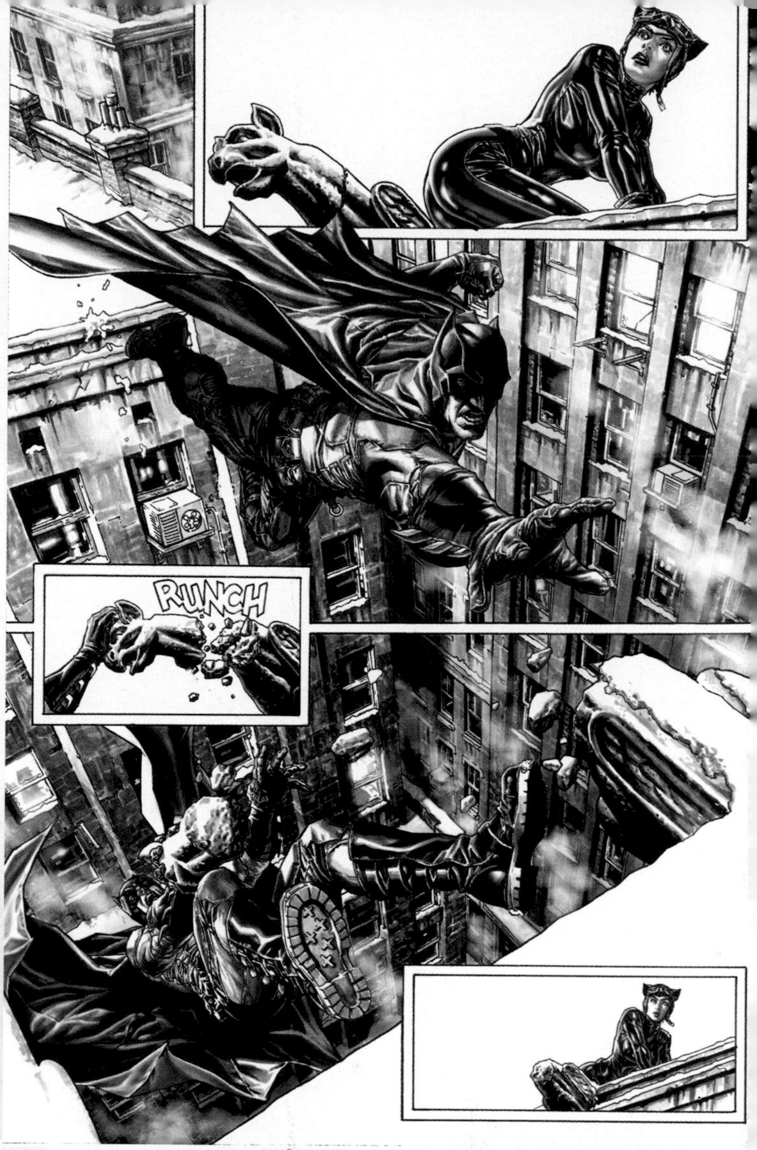
RUNCH

Layouts. As you can see, some finished pages change quite a bit when it comes down to actually drawing them. In fact, I usually use the layout phase to show me what NOT to do...

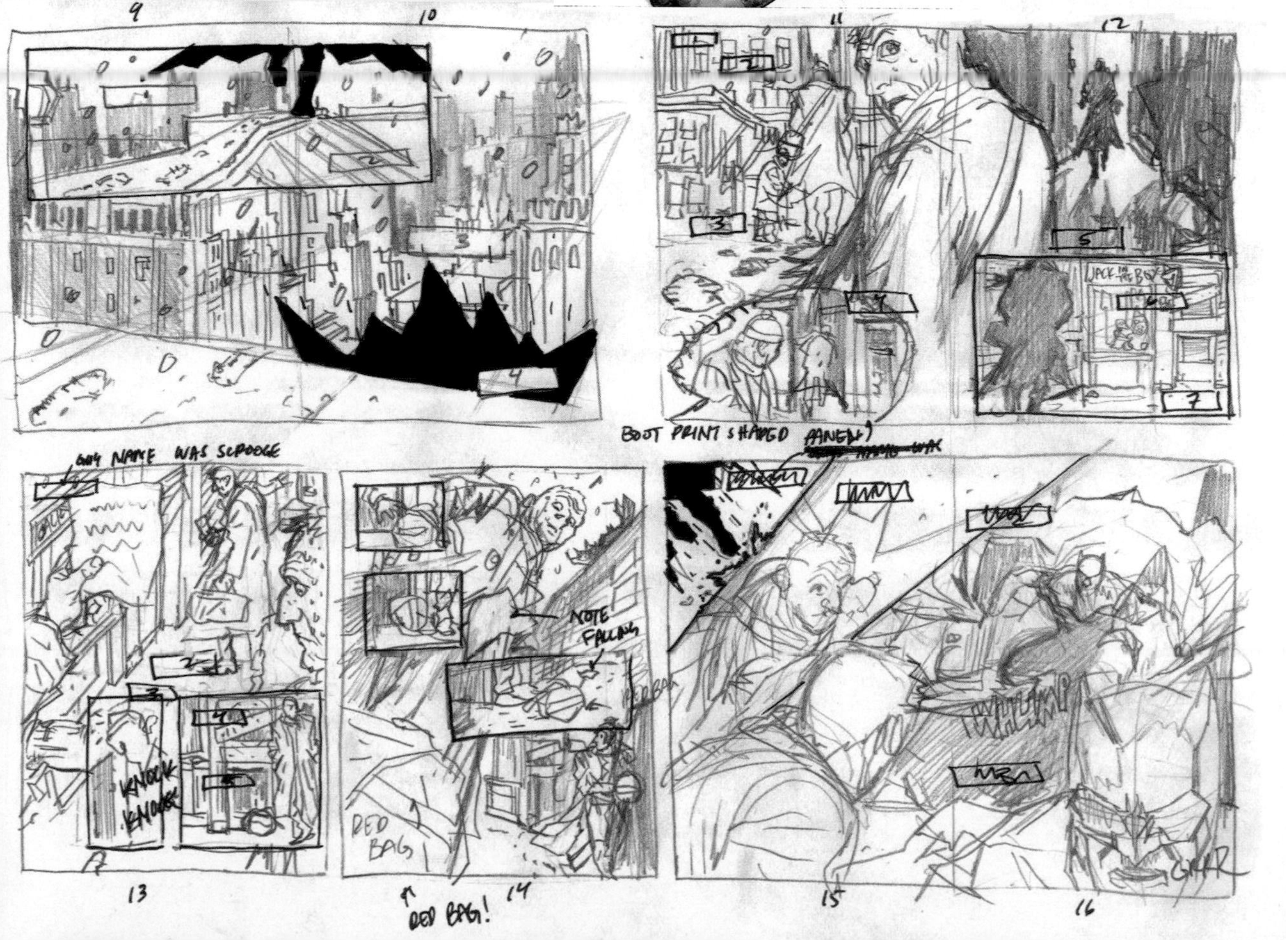
9
10
11
12
GUY NAME WAS SCROOGE
BOOT PRINT SHAPED PANEL
NOTE FALLING
KNOCK KNOCK
RED BAG
13
RED BAG!
14
15
16

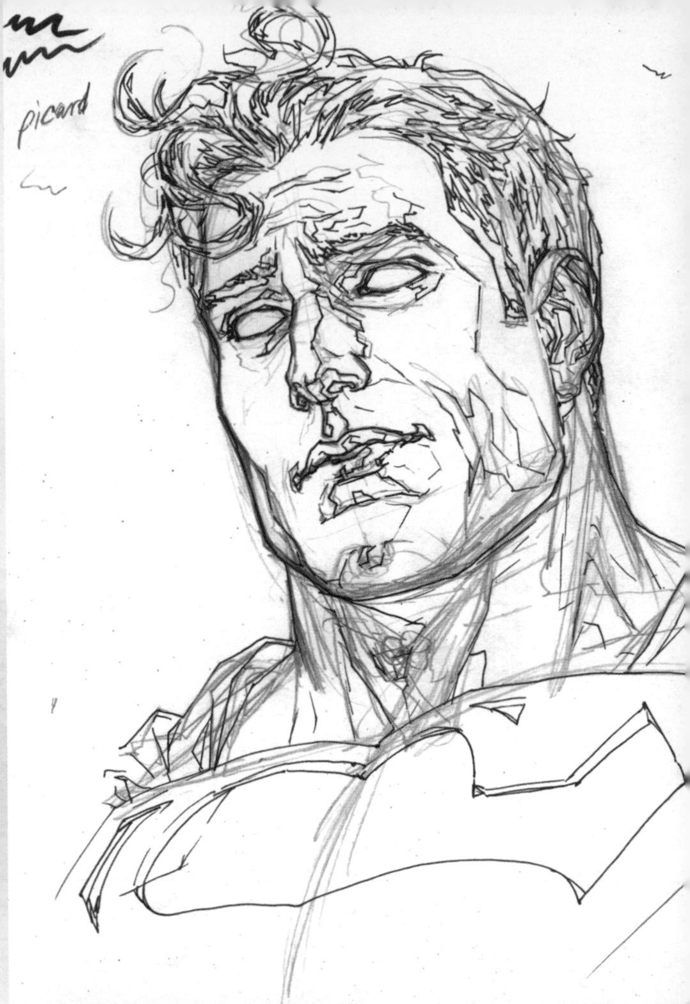
picard

This is a good example of how I work out facial expressions...a lot of scribbling. I still refer to Curt Swan's original character sheets for Superman, using a box shape as opposed to an oval to chisel his facial features.

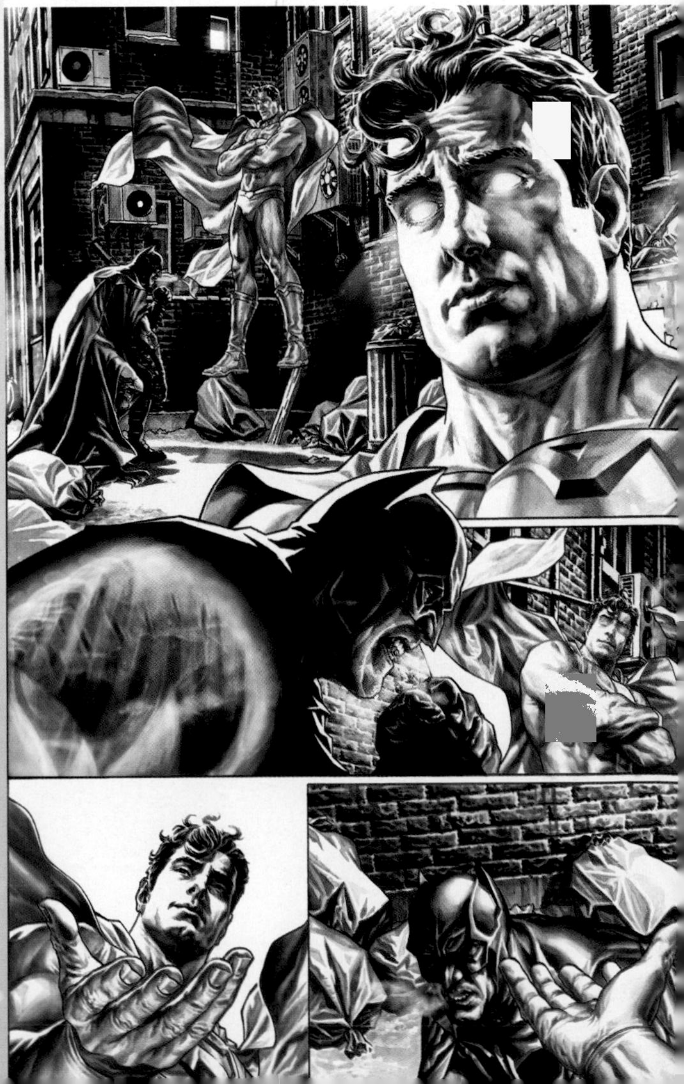

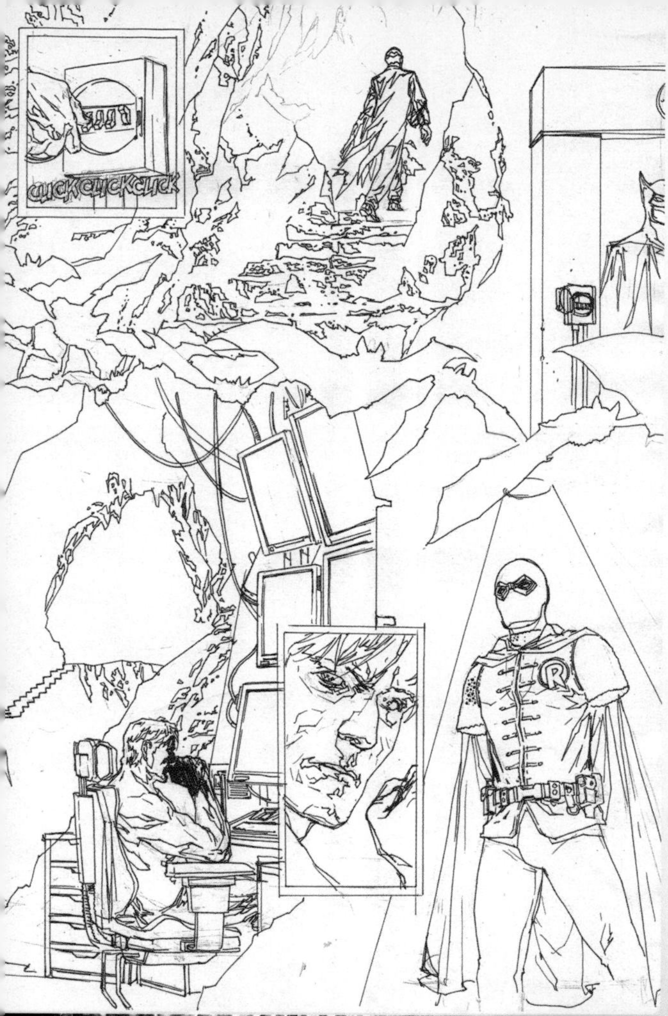
CLICKCLICKCLICK

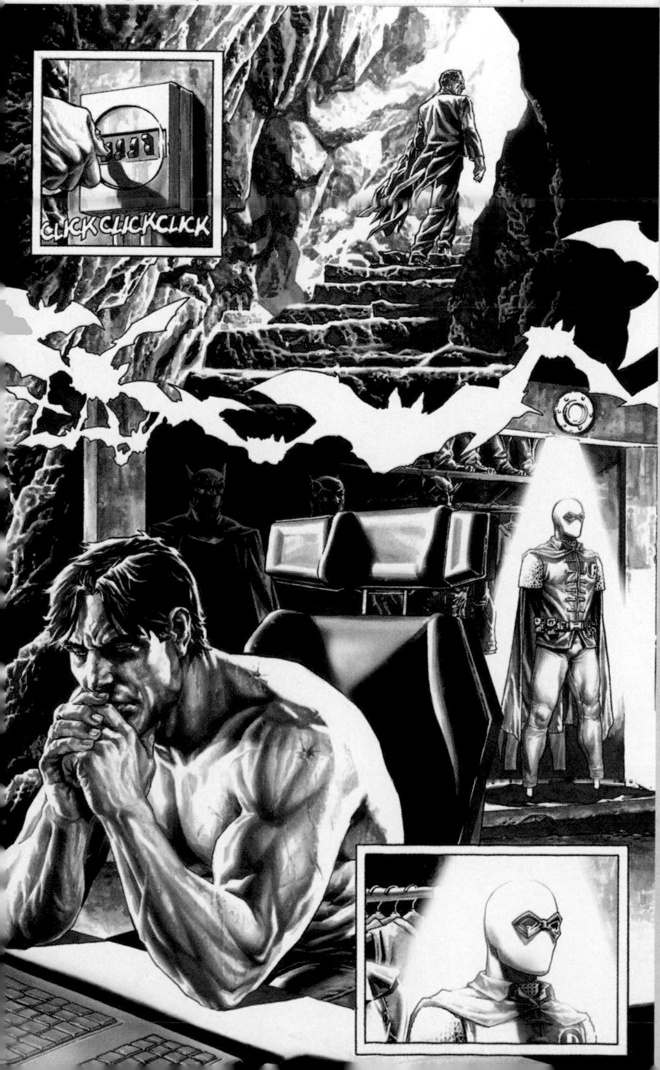
CLICK CLICKCLICK

An abandoned layout for page 34. While the top half of the page worked for me, the bottom seemed too cramped. Still, I was able to utilize some of it for page 37.

Lee Bermejo began drawing comics in 1997 for WildStorm Studios in San Diego at age 19. He collaborated with acclaimed writer Brian Azzarello on the graphic novels JOKER and LUTHOR, and worked with writer John Arcudi on the Superman feature in WEDNESDAY COMICS. He has also worked on HELLBLAZER with writer Mike Carey and GLOBAL FREQUENCY with writer Warren Ellis. Bermejo has illustrated covers for the line of Vertigo Crime graphic novels, beginning with FILTHY RICH, written by Brian Azzarello, and DARK ENTRIES, written by Ian Rankin. Bermejo has lived in Italy since 2003.

Barbara Ciardo is an Italian colorist, who operates primarily in the American comics industry. She started out with Italian publisher GG Studio before coloring for Marvel, Disney, and Top Cow. After a brief experience with the French market, she broke into American comics by working with Lee Bermejo on WildStorm covers. They collaborated on the Superman story in DC's WEDNESDAY COMICS. Barbara is now a DC exclusive colorist, and her work can be found in SUPERMAN: EARTH ONE, BRIGHTEST DAY AFTERMATH: THE SEARCH FOR SWAMP THING, and other popular DC and Vertigo titles.

Todd Klein has been lettering comics since 1977. He is perhaps best known for lettering THE SANDMAN written by Neil Gaiman, nearly all of the AMERICA'S BEST COMICS line written by Alan Moore, and all of FABLES written by Bill Willingham. Todd has won sixteen Eisner Awards, eight Harvey Awards, and numerous other honors for his work. Current projects include iZOMBIE and BATWOMAN. Todd lives in rural southern New Jersey with his wife Ellen and several cats.